Anonymous

A Collection of Sermons by the Most Eminent American Rabbis

Anonymous

A Collection of Sermons by the Most Eminent American Rabbis

ISBN/EAN: 9783337087265

Printed in Europe, USA, Canada, Australia, Japan

Cover: Foto ©Lupo / pixelio.de

More available books at **www.hansebooks.com**

THE AMERICAN JEWISH PULPIT,

A COLLECTION OF SERMONS

—— BY THE ——

MOST EMINENT AMERICAN RABBIS.

CINCINNATI:
BLOCH & CO., PUBLISHERS AND PRINTERS.
1881.

CONTENTS.

	PAGE.
Arise and Give Light; or, Judaism and the Jewish Pulpit, Rev. Dr. K. Kohler.	1
Passover .... Rev. S. Morais.	11
New Year .... Rev. George Jacobs.	17
Israel, a Missionary People ...... Rev. Dr. H. Vidaver.	25
Simchath Torah .... Rev. Dr. M. Jastrow.	31
A Few Thoughts About the Day of Rest, Rev. Dr. S. H. Sonneschein.	41
Thrice Holy is the Lord ...... Rev. Dr. Benjamin Szold.	51
Spirituality of God's Law ...... Rev. I. L. Leucht.	59
Jewish Ideas Conquer the World, a Shabuoth Sermon. Rev. Dr. B. Felsenthal.	67
The Offering of Isaac ...... Rev. Dr. Max Landsberg.	77
Moses Spake Truly ...... Rev. Prof. Abraham DeSola.	85
Spiritual Manhood ...... Rev. Dr. Max Samfield.	95
The Immortality of the Soul ...... Rev. Dr. James K. Gutheim.	105
Sermon at the Dedication of a New Sefer Thorah, Rev. Dr. M. Schlesinger.	115
Sermon at the Dedication of a New Burial Ground, Rev. Dr. M. Schlesinger.	121
Rosh Hashanah ...... Isaac M. Wise.	127
The Crossing of the Jordan ...... Rev. Dr. E. G. Hirsch.	139
Religion or no Religion, Yom Kippur Sermon. Rev. Dr. Max Lilienthal.	155
The Festival of the Spring ...... Rev. Isaac S. Moses.	173
Hanukah Sermon ...... Isaac M. Wise.	185
Israel's Influence on Civilization ...... Rev. Dr. Falk Vidaver.	191
Hebrew Monotheism, Rev. Dr. I. M. Wise.	199
The Main Lesson of Israel's Sanctuary, Rev. Dr. I. M. Wise.	209
The Fourth of July, Rev. Dr. I. M. Wise.	219
The Word of God, Rev. Dr. I. M. Wise.	227
Shebouth ...... Rev. Dr. D. Einhorn.	235

(Translated from Dr. David Einhorn's "Ausgewaehlte Predigten und Reden," by permission of Dr. K. Kohler.)

ARISE AND GIVE LIGHT,

OR,

"JUDAISM AND THE JEWISH PULPIT."

BY REV. DR. K. KOHLER,
(*Of Temple Beth-El, New York.*)

TEXT:—Isaiah ii. 5 and lx. 1.

Light is the emblem of Judaism. Among all the sacred pieces of the tabernacle the greatest prominence is given in the law to the golden seven-armed candlestick. To keep its lights in purest order and brightness is one of the chief duties of the priesthood, suggestive, no doubt, of the diffusion of knowledge of God incumbent on the guardian of the sanctuary. Indeed, Heathendom in general marked religion by the glare of fire, by the sacrificial blaze and smoke whirling up to heaven. To Christendom, too, religion is a hazy mysticism, a blind belief rather than an enlightening and convincing truth. And ask the modern pagan, the atheistic moralist, after the nature of that feeling which prompts man to kneel before a Supreme Being, and he will respond in similar strains: This is all emotion and pathos, a fire within, a steam engine to impel the soul to a right conduct, yet wrongly applied to our thinking faculty. The Jewish religion, on the contrary, presents itself as a light to brighten up the path of man and as a convincing truth to guide him. It desires him to walk in the clear daylight of reason, not in the dim twilight of a misty faith. What the sun is to the earth, God is to spiritual man, the central source of all light, life and progress. whether moral or intellectual. Of course, when first rising over a world wrapped in the night of idolatry and vice, the sun of Sinai beamed forth, all draped in crimson, like the fiery orb on the sky, to consume the host of darkness; but as it progressed on its triumphant march, it bathed the wide globe in its radiant splendor. Like light, truth wants to spread; so does Judaism. Far, however, from enforcing its world-redeeming doctrines on the surrounding world, it casts its seeds of heavenly blessing abroad, waiting for their gradual growth in the hearts of men. Following the divine call: "Arise and give light!" it yearns for the day when all nations shall say: "Oh, house of Jacob, come, let us walk in the light of God!" It holds forth its great truths, saying: "Let there be light!" Let the light of God be *on nature, on man and on human history*, that His majesty may fill heaven and earth! This is its glorious calling and particularly the privilege of the Jewish pulpit. Let me dwell on these three points to-day.

God in nature! This is the first stream of light emanating from Jewish revelation. The much-admired wisdom of to-day, that philosophy called *positive*, because it denies all that can not be grasped by the senses or measured and weighed by chemical analysis, wants to confine religion to the duty of man toward man, leaving God and soul as insoluble problems out of sight. But pray, can we, indeed, shut our eyes to all the beauties of light reflected in myriads of shades and colors on the bold rocks and the luxuriant meadows beneath, on the wings of the butterfly and on the nocturnal sky? Can we cease wondering at the peals of thunder and at the melodious notes of yon sweet warblers reaching our ear out of creation's grand chorus? Can we help asking who has vaulted this blue dome studded with so many silver and golden groups of stars? Who has dug these mighty water basins and set those huge rocks against them as dams? Shall we no longer with Job inquire after the wisdom of the raindrop and the treasures of the snow? Behold, the universe reveals us the King of Glory! Who does not crave after a glimpse of the hem of His garment? The melodious harmonies of endless worlds fall upon our ears. Who does not long to catch a tune of these wondrous symphonies? To perceive this majestic order of wisdom and beauty is to revere and to adore, not the blind cosmos, nor the primordial matter but the Sublime Mind who arranged all this with a spirit akin, though infinitely superior, to ours. Be not deceived by the idiotic assertion: This is all nature's action, the work of law. For what is law but divine wisdom's rule? Through Jewish monotheism alone the mighty empire of law has been established throughout the universe. Heathenism saw but force and chance everywhere. Even the God conceived of by its philosophers of India and Greece lacked self-consciousness and freedom, forming only the uppermost scale in the range of beings. Only a God, at whose bidding nature rushed into life, could set boundaries to the sea and the snow-flake, fixing for man and star their course according to one harmonious plan. Only the Jewish idea of God is compatible with reason and science, and, while it illuminates the majestic temple of nature, it also casts its rays on the holy of holies, where in darkness and awe faith alone spreads its Cherub wings to bear witness of God's presence.

There is no more than one truth in heaven and earth, for heart and brain. This conviction led the rabbis of the Talmud and the Jewish philosophers of Alexandria, Persia and Spain ever to blend reason and faith, to harmonize the biblical miracle stories with the unchangeable laws of creation. And we to-day dare break away from the holy ground of revelation, because our insight into the world's process of formation and order of beings has grown deeper and clearer ever since. Ought we not rather to sing the psalms of David tuned to more majestic organ-peals? Ought we not to read the grand poetry of Job and the sublime prose of Genesis with greater rapture, as, bewildered by the great spectacle of wheels within wheels and lives upon lives strewn along the infinities of time and space, the soul comes back with a cry for the Father whose footsteps it traced everywhere, but whose face it failed to see? Yes, we welcome the light cast on God's creation by modern research. Religion, being itself light, can as little be consumed by any light of knowledge as, to use a rabbinical metaphor, the fiery salamander can by fire. Let the shallow-pated be dazzled by the torch of science! Let the fool curse the sun, because the feeble-eyed can not stand its sight! Shall God withhold the light of day, because some worship it as their god? No. Reason, our armor and our lantern on our victorious campaign against old heathenism, will also force modern paganism to surrender at last. Superficiality of knowledge leads to atheism, says the English thinker; true enlightenment ushers man into the presence of God, the fountain-head of all light and wisdom. Now, it is, as it ever was, the privilege of the Jewish pulpit to let this sacred truth shine forth in all its captivating luster, not as buried in old venerable books, but as bright and fresh as the crystal water flowing forth from the rock. Forsooth, we can not live in air stored up deep down in the earth by ages past, nor by the sunshine closeted in coal beds thousands of years ago. We want the healthy air and cheering sunlight of the day. How can we expect that a religion made ours only by the chance of birth and education will offer us real comfort and hope, unless it be the very substance and marrow of our own feelings and thoughts and aspirations? If we are to take shelter under Israel's Rock of Ages, committing to Him all our cares and burdens, we must realize, that He who spoke to Moses and Elijah through the fire and fed and clothed our fathers in the wilderness is still with us today, revealing himself in the wonders of creation, providing all our wants, guiding us through all perplexities and responding from on high to all our cries from the deep. Doubt and error must flee before the presence of the benign Ruler, on whose bosom the soul may expect to find rest and peace. Religion must be, like nature, an actual revelation of God, ever true and fresh, striking and enrapturing. Hence it follows that, in order to inspire, the preacher of God's word must be inspired. He must keep within the full sweep of the ruling ideas of the age, and with eyes wide open to the views and achievements of the surrounding world, imbibe the invigorating mountain air of freedom and still feel within his breast the electric current of the past, the warm pulse of history running through all the centuries. He must, in order to offer religion as a living power, ever try to keep pace with the rapid progress of the time and yet burn with unabated zeal and reverence for the undying teachings of the Jewish seers and rabbis of yore, on which the souls of his hearers are to be fed, their hearts inflamed, their minds enlightened. A glorious task, indeed, yet how difficult, how much beset with obstacles and dangers! How impossible without sincere humility and prayer for God's gracious help!

II.

And the second flood of light streaming forth from Judaism to lighten up the dark recesses of the heart and the various avenues of the brain is the revelation of *God in man*. God is the Father, man the son; God the sun of truth and righteousness, man's soul a spark of His rays. God the fountain and ideal of all that is, man the image and outflow. This is the basis of all ethics, the master-key to all philosophy. Science may succeed in explaining some part or other; this explains the whole of man. Many a noble trait and faculty was, no doubt, roused and cultivated in man by this and that religion; Judaism alone accorded to him his full dignity by placing him in the center of creation and investing him with the scepter and mantle of royalty, with the nobility of heaven-born freedom and immortality. It beholds in the human soul a lamp, in which God's light shines, fed on earthly life, but radiating now His infinite wisdom and then glowing as a live coal from the divine empyrean of love. Language and art, religion and morals, philosophy and science, only reflect the bright central orb hidden to mortal eyes. And the contrast of truth and error, of right and wrong, of beauty and ugliness, of happiness and misery, shows merely the polarization of light, the prismatic shades of the divine, the battle within us between earth and heaven, between God and the brute. All the black spots and shortcomings we see are only in our own eyes; for we stand on a small island and still feel that ours is the shoreless ocean.

Our foot rests on earth and yet we feel drawn up toward the center of numberless worlds. And what is the most precious jewel in the diadem of our law, all men are children of light; none is doomed to everlasting darkness Of course, the heart ever mirrors the world above, as the lake does the sky overarching it. A world divided between good and evil powers rends the human soul in twain; a partial and local God rendered humanity also partial and local. Humanity as a unit was cradled only in the confines of Judea. The light which rose in Abraham reflected new glory on the whole human race. All the differences between a Noah and an Abraham, between a Balaam and a Moses, between a Buddha and an Isaiah, between Gentile and Jew, or between a Negro and a Caucasian, are merged in the name *Man*. To strive for the good and the right, to subdue the beast and let the spirit of God rise, is to win the prize of eternity; and each human struggle for independence and greatness, the life and property, the household, the honor and happiness of each member of society, is marked as holy unto God by the seal of religion.

Now, friends, is there any truth by which this Sinaitic doctrine about man can be superseded and obscured? As well may the bright sun some day be eclipsed by any new light of human invention. No, never will man be robbed of his crown of divine nobility; never will he allow himself to be ranked among baboons and chimpanzees. Darwinism, so far as it renders the world an interaction of mere mechanic forces, tends, like socialism, its twin brother, to glorify the struggle not for right, which is celestial, but for *might*, which is brutal. Amid the all-leveling tendencies of our age *self* has become the watchword. It means rebellion against God and the world. It drives the conceited thinker into pestiferous atheism, the reckless, discontented citizen into ruinous Nihilism, and the disappointed lover and money speculator into a suicide's grave. Is there any remedy in a system of morals which either drowns the individual in the State or an international laboratory, or launches him out into the foggy sea of an aimless, God-forsaken world? Only a religion which regards man not as a mere wheel in the mill, nor as a passing wave in the ocean, but as a child and co-laborer of God; only a theistic system of ethics which works with the frown and smile of the Eternal, with the threats and promises of a divine justice on the springs and motives of the human will; only the Sinaitic revelation will guide and save mankind from shipwreck and misery.

And of this the Jewish pulpit must be the shining reflector, a beacon to the storm-tossed, to rescue the one from the whirlpool of a deceptive science and the other from the dangerous cliff of exclusive church dogmatism. In order to prove a stanch defender of man's greatness, the modern Jewish preacher must, while comparing the spirit of past ages with that of our own, point out ever anew the matchless luster of Jewish morals, their constant progress with and their controlling influence on civilization. Above all, he must recognize and show, that נר מצוה ותורה אור the religious forms and statutes are but the frail lamp of the age, made to nourish the light of all ages in the human breast. And instead of yoking people to a ritualism and ceremonialism which have lost hold on their minds, he must, like the prophets of old, emphasize the eternal moral laws, the rules of conduct written with the divine finger on the tablets of the human heart as the kernel and essence of revelation. He must herald the true religion of humanity. And, indeed, it requires all the earnestness and unbending firmness of the holy seers of old, the boldness and uncompromising zeal of an Elijah and Isaiah, to be in these days a builder-up of characters, a teacher and monitor of virtue and holiness, a restorer of the old paths of integrity and righteousness, in an age addicted to greed and passion to become a repairer of breaks, a regainer of souls for God and His truth!

III.

And last, but not least, is the ray of light shed by Judaism on the path of *human history*. The idea of progress, though modern in its phrase, is of Jewish extraction. As the rabbis say, the Creator's word, "Let there be light!" pointed to the great Messianic aim and ideal. It suggested an ever-rising day of truth and justice. Of course, Heathendom, unaware of a great Designer and a harmonious plan of the world, could not well look for a great common end in the future. A world grown by chance must needs fall a prey again to chance. Without a God as its Ruler the beautiful cosmos necessarily ends in eternal night and chaos whence it came, in dismal Nirwana. Only the Jewish prophets, watching amid the downfall of nations the steady rise of Israel's glorious heritage, the knowledge of the one and holy God, detected the standard with which the world's moral and intellectual progress was to be measured. Before their eyes there loomed up the kingdom of the God of righteousness and love, to which all lands and ages were to contribute their share while toiling and working for the beautiful, the good and the true. In Mount Zion they beheld the lofty goal of humanity, on the altar of which all nations offered their manifold gifts as a token of homage to God, their common King and Father, while Israel, the first-born, was to serve as the temple's guardian, the bearer of the promise, as witness of God's covenant with the entire human family. True, this inspiring hope of a Messianic kingdom did in the garb of national expectations, under the disguise of personal and sectarian dreams and visions, bring many sad disappointments and sorrows upon mankind, and particularly on Israel, its heaven-sent apostle, its heroic priest and martyr. Nevertheless, in creating world-conquering religions, it scattered the seeds of truth abroad. It established great centers of light to unite the race. And when this light had in the hands of Christianity grown into a scorching hell-fire to consign the larger majority of the world to eternal doom, the Jewish people, at the price of their own precious blood, held aloft the light of divine salvation as a promise for undivided mankind, securing eternal salvation to all righteous and good of whatever race or religion. Nor have they worked and waited in vain. Behold, the church walls of intolerant fanaticism are tottering and sinking to-day. Insults offered to Jews or to any other sect or race are resented by the governments, the pulpit and the press of the whole civilized world. The common brotherhood of man is established. By bonds of iron and steel, by the interests of commerce and industry, by material and intellectual pursuits, the wide world is rendered one. Words of peace and concord are with lightning's speed flashed from one continent to another. But then has human civilization not reached its pinnacle? Has not the day of reason come? What is the use of still carrying the lantern about, needed only during the night which lies behind? Thus the short-sighted crowd shouts forth, taking the dawn of the new era for the midday. Brethren, the struggle is not ended yet; our mission as watchmen of human civilization is by far not fulfilled. Darkness still prevails round about us. Selfishness casts its large earthly shadow upon the sun of life, interfering between man and man, between nation and nation, between heart and brain, between time and eternity. God, the true bond of union, is not felt. Universal brotherhood, morality and humanity still lack the center and soul, the recognition of God's fatherhood.

Israelites, we stand for true cosmopolitan humanity today as we ever did! Are you ashamed of the name Jew? It means the guardianship of mankind's highest truths. Let prejudice never so fiercely scorn and blast it! Let apostasy and skepticism never so haughtily belittle it! Our storm-beaten but never-surrendered flag stands for further rise and progress. Our national priesthood, our Sabbath and historical festival days remain a pledge of that covenant of light and bliss which, including all sects and races, renders the whole earth a mountain of God shining in heaven's everlasting splendor. Oh, how holy, how grand and important is the task of the Jewish minister in this materialistic age of ours to hold this lofty mission of the Jewish people forth as a lamp unto their feet and as a light unto their path! But it requires pure and sacred oil to keep the golden luminary burning in the sanctuary. The oil is not wanting; it streams forth, as from a wondrous fountain, without ceasing, but the vessels are missing to receive it. The young fail to offer their heart to be filled with the divine blessing. Like Rachel of old, the Jewish religion to-day cries forth: "Give me children or else I die!" The Jewish pulpit must by all feasible ways and means be brought within the reach of the rising generation and rendered an attractive source of instruction and enlightenment, awakening thirst for Jewish knowledge in all, young or old, rich or poor, and kindling ardent love and zeal for our great history and mission. It must become a magnetic power of centralization and spiritual elevation to render all our sons and daughters enthusiastic defenders and upholders of our time-honored heritage, true teachers and sincere practicers of our religion, a people of priests and prophets. As the sun, in shining upon mount and vale, land and sea, renders tree and flower, stone and water-drop many-colored bearers and reflectors of its light, so the word of divine revelation says to each and every one: "Arise and give light, for thy light hath come and the glory of God shineth over thee!" Would to God that His help and grace be with my work in your midst, that I may succeed in following this ideal to become a bearer of light and truth, a true priest with lips overflowing with blessing for you each and all, for Israel and humanity. Amen.

AN ADDRESS DELIVERED ON PASSOVER.

BY REV. S. MORAIS.

CHILDREN OF THE PATRIARCHS:—Before we part on this anniversary day of Israel's nativity, let us infuse into each other the warmth of brotherly affection, and add to the religious fervor which our joint thanksgivings have aroused. * * * A short time ago I read a description that enchained my attention against my will. In the Church of the Vatican the late Pope, clothed in a robe which rivaled driven snow in whiteness, crowned with a triple mitre, on which gems resplendently shone, had mounted up the height of a window whence he might be seen by an anxious throng below. His arms were extended as if eager to hold in a single embrace the Catholic world. All knelt, with upraised countenances to drink in a blessing dealt out at Rome, to be carried to distant lands till it reached the torrid zones and the tropics, for pilgrims of every clime were there. They had come from Abyssinia and from Hayti. They had arrived from where the sun " goeth forth * * * rejoicing like a hero to run a race," and from the spot where it hides itself as in a pavillion. Missionaries and propagandists were there. They would catch a word, a look of "God's vicegerent," as a talisman to papal devotees. Chiming bells greeted the scene, organs discoursed intoxicating music, and nature, awakened from her winter sleep, smiled upon that gathering with the radiant smile which spring gives the serene sky of Italy. For it was on Easter Sunday that a stranger gazed upon that scene, conjuring up fancies of a universal faith supremely loved.

Not far from the Vatican, men who had not bent to receive the apostolic benediction, issued on that Easter Sunday from the dens into which ages of proscription had consigned them. Toward those inhabitants of Rome curses had been hurled; yet, they appeared joyful when, dressed in holiday garments, they entered a dingy hall. Had the traveler followed their steps and mingled in their assemblies he would have heard weird songs in an Oriental language, hymns that flowed from throbbing hearts which oppression can not crush. He would have seen none of the pageantry displayed amid a pantheon of heathen images chiseled in marble, or drawn on canvas and canonized as saints. He would have beheld but two unpretending tablets, the writing of which had served a hapless people as spiritual manna through a wilderness of misery. That morning those sons of Rome, still under Pontifical dominion, celebrated the birthday of their religious existence—an existence older than St. Peter, more ancient than the seven-hilled city. They solemnized the Passover instituted in Egypt on a night of a divinely-wrought redemption. Priesthood vested in the stock of Aaron had died, but Judaism lived. The Palestinian Vatican—Zion Hill and its turreted temple—had sunk beneath a heap of ruin; but the people of Judea stood erect in their manhood, to worship the same God who avenged their cause, to keep the same Law which had bid their fathers hold in sacred memory the feast of unleavened bread " at its season from year to year."

The traveler might then have flung aside the spell laid on his senses by the glitter of pomp and the parade of number. His eyes would have discovered a stirring, a restless vitality in the few who prayed in the gloomy ghetto, and decay in the church surrounded by colonnades of porphyry and colossal figures of gilded bronze; aye, he would have detected a skeleton attired in an attractive garb. The flesh and bones and sinews which had once covered the compact body had been worn away in the very fire lighted to burn the martyrs of independent thought.

You remember, my brethren, the story of that Babylonian King who set up a huge statue of massive gold in the plains of Dura. At the sound of a thousand instruments the glories of that idol were heralded. Woe unto them that did not then kiss the ground in humble adoration! Three men dared disobey. A furnace is made ready, but so fiercely hot that in approaching it the messengers of the royal will, charged to cast in the righteous, become themselves a prey to the devouring flames. In like manner it has happened with the representative of the Church of Rome. The blazing pyre, which reduced to ashes John Huss and Jerome of Prague, Fra Savonarola and Giordano Bruno, consumed the power that thrust them in. The head of that Church saw the power, whilom insuperably strong, wane into a shadow, and he imagined he could yet restore it to its former grandeur. He encircled his person with new charms, bewitching to the credulous masses. He proclaimed himself a divinity infallible as God, and from the earthly heaven to which he up lifted his deified-self, launched anathemas against liberty and social progress.

In vain: mankind mocked the impotent attempt to drive back the tidal waves which roll in the accumulated wealth of long and hard labors—unrestricted knowledge, freedom of speech and freedom of press. Micah's prophecy has been fulfilled: "As in the days of the deliverance from Egypt I will show them marvels."

How fares now Judaism? you ask it? Why, it lives and thrives under the new regime, because it has nothing to fear from the extension of the domains of thought. When the most searching minds shall have dived into all that is knowable in science and metaphysics, the result will only be a confirmation of what Moses taught. From the unity of design in the creation, whether effected in six successive periods or by evolutions, we learn to adore a Creator, the Prime Mover of all that exists, the Omnipotent and Eternal God. Astronomers with their improved telescopes, physiologists with their analyses, philosophers with their touch-stones, will never find that Israel's belief is an error, detracting from the honor due to the Supreme, or offensive to reason, and to an inborn sentiment of human dignity.

But will not the external agencies by which Judaism has preserved that ennobling belief suffer wreck on the sea of ever-changing opinions? No, if considered in the spirit of the great Legislator. Thus this festival which sees us gathered in solemn convocation is History rehearsing the past and exacting from the monotheistic race a promise of fealty to their one God. The bread we eat is a reminder not of a fiction, as the flesh in the eucharist, but of a wonderful episode in our annals. The wine we drink, while inviting our children's attention to that episode, is not the imaginary blood of transubstantiation, but the symbol of a flow of joy at the recollection of an unparalleled salvation. Not of a god that died we preach at this season; not of a god resuscitated we sing; our speeches and our psalmodies are dedicated to Him who abides everlastingly. Oh, that we would always shed a halo round Jewish practices! we would be nearer to truth; we would keep closer to the main point on which the future of Israel, as the acknowleged teacher of humanity, hinges.

And, indeed, when I contemplate such scenes as that presented here this morning, my nature, often desponding, grows buoyant with sustaining hopes. I picture to my mind America as the virgin soil in which the ritual system governing Judaism will be regenerated, when the quarter of a million of Hebrews, destined to increase twofold, shall join hands in brotherly affection to cast in that soil the seeds of union. Union in worship; union in training the young to prize the language of Holy Writ and give it preference in congregational services; union in maintaining the Sabbath and holidays, covenanted at Sinai, in sanctifying home by significant ceremonies, lopping off excrescences, but cultivating the choice branches of the Judaic tree of traditions. Let me tell it without any possible ambiguity. I long for a union which will wisely retain all which tends to strengthen our conviction in the immutability of God's essence; all which recalls the goodness and mercy of the world's Creator, the apostolate of Israel, as harbingers of soul-elevating verities; all that incites deeds of beneficence, that softens hardships and comforts us in distress; but a union which also rejects whatever is the offspring of prejudice and superstition, engendered by clanishness resulting from ages of social debasement. That is my aspiration, and you can transform it into a splendid reality. I am not indifferent to the struggle among contending parties in our religious camp. I rather favor the agitation which discloses activity—a determination to test the soundness of principles. It is by winnowing the grain that the chaff is separated. Perhaps opposite views will finally settle into a universal acceptance of what agrees with our mission and promotes the object of our selection. That which I dread is stagnation, a total stoppage of the current of thought on subjects which concern Judaism and the happiness of my people. But your crowded attendance dispels that apprehension. You feel your pulsations beat high for your fathers' faith; you still love the flock of God's pasture. With them you are content to be led into the path that Moses pointed out and the sages leveled and graded.

The eyes of your European brethren are upon you. If the franchises you can claim do not have the power to wean your hearts away from tenets which our ancestors preserved at all hazards; if, notwithstanding your free and friendly intercourse with persons of different creeds and denominations, you enter into no entangling alliances with the worshipers of a man-god, be he represented in gilded images or in the outward form of church architecture, then you will serve as the ideal which your fellow-believers, enjoying now in part the immunities you vastly possess, will eagerly follow in shaping their future course. But if you evince a wavering disposition or heedlessness, fatal will be the effect in generations yet unborn in this land and baneful in the extreme to our emancipated co-religionists abroad. * * * Oh, no, you will. not shame liberty by abjuring faith! Sinai, Judea, will be the signet by which all shall recognize your names, as men loyal to God, faithful to Israel, while glorying in being called citizens of the American Republic.

THE NEW YEAR.

A SERMON.

BY REV. GEORGE JACOBS,

(Minister of the Beth-El Emeth Congregation, Philadelphia, Pa.)

With the setting of yesterday's sun a new year was ushered into the House of Israel—a new year which is not of human making or establishment, but a new year which brings to our mind the creation of this vast universe and all that is therein contained—a new year which tells us of a Great Creator, who formed every object on which our eye can rest, and all other things in heaven and earth, "which are dreamt not in *our* philosophy."

This constant revolution—these perpetual evidences of close and beginning—destruction and renewal must remind us that nothing on earth is stationary or unchangeable. Each returning year sets plainly before us that the wheels of time never cease moving; they perform their allotted task day by day and year after year, while the transitions which pass before our eyes tell us plainly and unmistakably that there is a Supreme Being who holds in His hand the lines of our existence and measures out to each of us his allotted portion of that line.

But in celebrating the New Year we are struck with the peculiarity of this day of gathering in comparison with others. Each of the "Festivals of the Lord" has its defined mode of observance, but, apart from sounding the cornet, this is merely *Yom Hazikaron*, "A Day of Memorial;" and yet what a wide range is presented before us! We look backward and forward. Recollection will readily present to us, in the past, a busy period filled with an admixture of business and pleasures, anxieties and cares, joys and sorrows. We will note plans formed and pursuits entered upon with avidity, and yet how many of them have been really completed, how many of them have reached the culmination we have ardently desired? Let me ask, dear friends, if you review the past year aright, what proportion of the things that have happened, could have been foreseen or foretold by you,—how many have occurred of which you had not the least expectation? Some, perhaps, have succeeded beyond your anticipations, and a few of you have reaped a rich harvest of hopes fulfilled; while others, very many others, have met with nought but disappointment, realizing most bitter regrets, and are forced to make the acknowledgment, how tardy soever it may be, that while man was devising the way, Providence was directing the event.

Well, we may liken ourselves to a traveler proceeding on a long and tedious journey, who pauses, at times, to cast a glance upon the portion he has already accomplished, and seeing the long distance which lieth beyond, resumes his march with increased celerity and diligence. So, dear friends, in our passage through this world to the unknown beyond, it is the part of wisdom to look *back* at what it hath pleased God to dispense unto us, and to look *forward* to His unfailing mercy, so as to be material gainers in resuming the journey.

The scene of the past is now closed. The tale of *that* year has been told. We now look *forward* to that which has just dawned upon us, and what do we behold there? A perfect blank is in view, an unknown expanse presents itself before us. We are, as it were, entering on a new, untried, undiscovered country. As each week rolls around, new scenes may open, new objects may engage our attention, new ties may be contracted, new affections may ripen, of which we have *now* not the slightest idea,—yea, there may be changes at home and abroad, changes among those with whom we mix every day, or in our own domestic circle; changes which may alter the whole current of our lives and vary all our calculations. New connections, which we are about to form, may be close at hand, old ones may be gradually being loosened without our slightest knowledge, till the unwelcome truth comes before us in all its pain and anguish. Yes, friends, there is no denying the amount of uncertainty which a new year places before us. With all our experience of the past, life and death, prosperity and adversity, joy and sorrow,—all lie in one indistinguishable mass, where our eye can descry nothing through the obscurity that envelops it.

Now, contemplating this uncertainty in human affairs; this blindness, so far as the future is concerned, this want of knowledge as to what will be the result of our striving, the words of the wise Koheleth, מה יתרון לאדם בכל עמלו שיעמל תחת השמש come strikingly before us:

"What profit hath a man of all his labor, which he laboreth under the sun?" Eccl. i. 3.

Let this be our New Year's reflection, and full of profit will it be to us, if undertaken in the right spirit.

In secular affairs, the close of one year and the opening of another, generally finds us busy and active. The accounts of the past twelve months have to be carefully looked over; the various transactions inquired into, profits and losses estimated, and the balance struck. This is but a right procedure. It is just what a careful and prudent man should do, so as to know his exact position, and be guided in his future transactions. He who does otherwise, and takes no account of his affairs at periodical times, but merely goes on at haphazard, would be looked upon not merely as unwise, but as a very unsafe man with whom to have business relations; while he who looks carefully over his books and notices where he can safely expend and where he should retrench, commends himself to us, in a commercial point of view, as coming up to the proper standard. This is but an outline of the affairs between man and man. These profits and losses are the *worldly* ones, which are the result of man's earthly toil, "in all his labor which he laboreth under the sun."

Now, if we realize the fact that we are something *more* than mere flesh and blood, that we have been placed highest in the scale of creation, that we have within us an immortal soul, which evidences that we have been fashioned after the image and likeness of the Divine Artificer, then we must readily acknowledge that as we are accountable to each other for *some* of the various transactions of life, we are, to a greater extent, accountable to God for *all* the transactions of life.

Your very presence here this day is an admission, full and complete, that you recognize in Deity " the King of Justice;" that is to say, that although it has been asserted that according to the doctrines of our holy faith, *final* judgment will not be pronounced till the grave has closed over us and we have entered the gates of eternity: still, this day is one of strict accountability to God, who reviews our actions of the past year, and will either " blot out our iniquities " or inscribe them in the book of unfading record, to be finally sealed on the approaching Yom-Kippur. Have you come here, dear friends and fellow-believers, to observe the New Year as it should really be observed? Have you come to make up your accounts with God, to strike the *true* balance and to realize, in the words of the text, the actual profit of "the labor you have labored under the sun?"

You may be able to point to transactions in the past year in which you have been unsuccessful; speculations in which you embarked that turned out badly, while, with a glowing heart, you may be able to show your sharpness and acuteness in many others, whereby you have realized largely; indeed, no matter *who* has *lost, you* have *gained*. But has not experience taught you that such gains often have wings; that what is made in *one* year may be lost in the *next*, and that while it is necessary for a man to have his daily avocations and not to lag behind in the race of life, there are accounts and transactions which should have equally as high a place in his daily affairs? This, too, is a New Year—the old one has recently closed and another dawned. This Yom Hazikaron is no *time* set by man, but is from God, God who created *us* and *all* things around us. Will you do less in religious than in secular affairs? Will you not compute your accounts mentally, think of the result of your labors and strike the *true* balance? This is the real object of the day of memorial, and how painful soever may be the retrospect, how full of sorrow for our short-comings, yet must we enter faithfully upon the duties I have pointed out to you, if we desire to observe this day in the spirit of its institution.

The balance, I repeat, must be struck, and we will see plainly that too many of us, who have dealt fairly and squarely with our fellow-men, have been defaulters in our transactions with God. We have been intrusted by HIM ABOVE with a certain amount of "capital" in life, health, energy, intelligence and circumspection. We have been supplied with these means when we have been in sore need of them day after day, and have had an undying light to show us the way we must go. What return have we made for these things? Some can point with pride to their balance sheet and show the good they have done on earth, the bleeding wounds they have stanched, the tottering limbs they have sustained, the naked they have clothed, the hungry they have fed, the despondent they have cheered, the ignorant they have educated and *the religion they have upheld*,—all of which have been duly placed to their credit by the Great Accountant Above, "who glanceth not at externals," but "*looketh* into the innermost recesses of the heart" and understandeth its every emotion.

But there are many who make a fair show before the world and stand in good credit, who are far behindhand with Deity when this secret account is called up. How many have built up their earthly substantiability on the ruin of others' fortunes, good names and expectations? How many transactions that have been kept within the strict bounds of the law have been far from equitable? How many have thrown away dollars for trash who have begrudged cents for God and His worship, while there are hosts who are ready to fulfill the demands of their neighbor, but who will not in gratitude give anything or make any sacrifice on the altar of faith? Is year after year to roll around, and although we are advancing with rapid strides to "the place appointed for all living," are we to be as inconsistent in our actions and take no steps to place ourselves in better condition with our Maker? Shall Israel, the race intrusted with the promulgation of God's laws and ordinances, be the very people to disregard them? Shall we continue, week after week, to tell our children, "This is the Law which Moses set before the children of Israel," and "which man shall perform and thereby live," and yet give the lie to what we utter? Shall we come here year after year and acknowledge God as the Judge of mankind, that all our actions pass in review before Him, and that it is our bounden duty to make the three great principles, " Penitence. Prayer and Benevolence." the three pillars on which our moral and spiritual edifice is to be erected, while at the very moment we are uttering the words with apparent sincerity, we *know* we have no intention of heeding them?

There is a cry for a change on all sides. We do need a change—a most vital change in many respects, and no one admits it in more truth and sincerity than I do, but while we regard the shell, let us not forget the kernel; while endeavoring to beautify and adorn the casket, let us not underestimate the priceless jewel which lieth within.

Strike the balance of your heavenly accounts, my dear hearers, and see where you really stand. " If peace answereth thee," it is well, but if it does not, then, for God's sake, let this be truly a *new* year, one wherein you will honestly endeavor to lay by things to your credit, to pay the Almighty His just due, and permit the recording angel to inscribe much in your favor in the Book of Heavenly record.

While we are taught by our sages that " man is judged daily," yet it is an accepted truth that this day our Father in Heaven sits in judgment over those who do not daily commune with themselves and who turn a deaf ear to the warnings of conscience, while it is a *landmark* in the course of our earthly pilgrimage.

Shall we not take advantage of a day so benificently accorded to us, to wipe out all our shortcomings in the past by being at once prepared for the *Kippur*, which will, by the blessing of God, soon be with us? Shall we not endeavor to make the open book, whose pages are blank before us, be inscribed with acts and deeds to our credit, and gain for us a reward from On High which can *never* be lost, which can *never* perish?

Oh. let us strive to make this New Year different from past ones ; let us be animated with the spirit of *true* religion, which consists not in the length of our orisons, the vehemence of our tones nor the volubility of our utterance; let us vow to "do justly, to love mercy and to walk humbly before our God," to enter on a course of true penitence, heartfelt prayer and deeds of benevolence; *then*, when our last hour on earth has arrived, and the trump of recall to our true home has been sounded, we will truly realize " what is the actual profit of a man's labor, which he laboreth under the sun."

ISRAEL A MISSIONARY PEOPLE.

SABBATH "SACHOR" SERMON.

BY REV. DR. H. VIDAVER,
(Of San Francisco, Cal.)

Text:—Exodus, cap. 17. v. 11. "And it came to pass when Moses lifted up his hand, and Israel triumphed."

On the Sabbath preceding the Feast of Purim we read, according to time-honored custom, the narration of Amalek's brutal attack upon Israel, and Israel's triumph over Amalek. This is a very significant custom. It is not merely a meaningless calling into mind of an event that since thousands of years had been buried in the gulf of oblivion, but it is rather an indispensable keeping alive of an *idea* which underlies that very event and which penetrates the whole long and wonderful career of our people, from the time of their redemption from Egypt's thraldom to this very day; and which will pervade our life and constitute our main destiny on earth until that day will arrive when:

> "God's temple will be all space,
> His altars, earth, sea and skies;
> One chorus all mankind will raise,
> To *one* God, the All-loving and All-wise!"

It was and is the idea of Israel's struggles; implying the struggles against Amalek, that is against "Idolatry" in all shapes and manners; against inhumanity in all ways and forms. It was and is the idea of Israel's triumphs, implying the triumph of truth, the triumph of a pure faith in the "Unity" of God and the moral elevation of the human race.

An explanation given by the ancient sages of the Mishnah to our text presents to us in the brightest light the whole scope and nature of Israel's contests and Israel's victories. "What," ask the rabbis, "does it mean: that when Moses lifted up his hand Israel triumphed?" וכי ידיו של משה עושות או שוברות מלחמה Did the issues of the war depend upon the lifting up of the hands of the Prophet? Certainly not, is their answer, but it signifies the glorious fact that so long as Israel will be in an uplifting attitude, having his heart and mind directed heavenward, triumph will surely be his in all climes and all times. דבר גדול דבר הנב הנביא This is a glorious word spoken by the ancient rabbi; it is fully verified by the divine testimony of history.

My friends, a glance through the wide vista of our checkered annals will satisfy every unbiased mind that Israel was appointed by an All-wise Providence to be for *all* times "a kingdom of priests," that is a *missionary people* among the children of man. It was and is the will of God that through Israel His divine light of pure faith should be dispensed among the human kind; that through Israel the blessings of truth should be ministered to the human family at large; in brief, it was and is the will of God that, through the agency of the Jewish people, mankind should gradually abandon their idolatries and become *converted* to the true faith. But no one, knowing the spirit of Judaism, could for a moment suppose that Israel's destiny to convert mankind was ever to be carried out by dint of aggressive and warlike means; by acts of coercion or persecution, by the use of burning racks or hissing stakes. Nor will any one, knowing the true aim of Judaism, suppose that Israel's duty was or is to obtrude his *Thora* upon any one belonging to another race: to go on highways and byways and *preach* his faith "to every creature." No, No! Israel's mission was *never* to convert mankind into *Judaism*, *i. e.*, to bring over non-Israelites to the folds of the synagogue, to cause non-Jews to share the *peculiar* duties and obligations devolved upon Israel as such; as the people of the "*distinct* covenant:" no, but it was and is Israel's task *to convert mankind to the* IDEA *of Judaism*. It was and is Israel's duty to help in the uplifting of the human mind to the Pisgahheights of the purest conception of the Deity as *One* absolute Godhead, and the uplifting of the human heart to the blessed conception of humanity as the broadest, most comprehensive principle of love.

Oh, friends, only such as aspire to convert others to their sectarian churches, the offspring of their narrow minds; only those that are striving to see others embrace their *dogmatic* creeds, the outcome of their own beclouded brains, will overstep the boundaries of reason, and their zeal will soon deepen into the blackest bigotry and fanaticism, and will soon have recourse to weapons deadly and persecutions infernal, and deal damnation to each they deem their opponent. The tyrant of all times has but one motto: אני ואפסיעוד "I am, and no one shall be besides me," hence the tyrant's furious zeal for absolute power and aggrandizement; hence his restless suspiciousness, his impatience of opposition or contradiction, and hence his inhumanity and barbarity. "I and none else" has been the motto likewise of church tyranny. The priestly tyrant, like the imperial despot, must needs become impatient, suspicious, oppressive and barbarous. "Outside of the Islam there is no hope," was the tyrannical cry of Mohammedanism, hence the sword became its means of conversion. "*Extra ecclesiam nulla salus*":—outside of the Church there is no salvation, was the motto of the Christian Church, hence its infernal instruments of conversion; hence its bloody inquisitions and hellish tribunals of conscience; hence all the curses of the Middle Ages—the legitimate offspring of Church tyranny, which was nothing but the natural outcome of mean-spirited sectarianism; a monster that knows no rest, no peace; it must, Amalek-like, pounce upon helpless innocence and seek its destruction.

But, לא כאלה חלק יעקב "such was never nor can ever be, the portion of Jacob." Israel was and is a *missionary people* in the holiest sense of the word. Israel's mission was not to propagate dogmatisms, or the *peculiar* laws of the synagogue; his mission was not to gain votaries to the distinctive covenant of his race, and thus to *increase numerically* the adherents to this or that *form* of worship; but his manifest destiny was and is to gain adherents to the glowing *idea* of the purest faith in the absolute *unity of God* and votaries to a progressive and an all-embracing humanity. The blood flowing in the heart of the Jew needs no admixture of that of any other race in order to *increase* its *current*. Numerically we are forever to be מעט מכל העמים " the smallest of all people," but spiritually we are always to be עליון על כל הגוים " superior to all nations."

The Jew was and is to be a missionary among mankind, not to disseminate the dogmatic doctrines of a religious sect, but to teach an all-embracing faith; the Jew is to be the missionary, not of a peculiar church, but of a common humanity. Hence, while the followers of fanaticism used means of destruction to encompass their despotic ends, Israel was told אל בחיל וכי׳ that through the "spirit" he was to triumph—through the spirit of *truth*, *justice* and *love* which he was to represent and which alone he was to teach and propagate. Never did the prophets of ancient Israel promise in the name of God that the ultimate triumph of Israel would consist in converting all nations into the covenant of the flesh and bringing them over to the synagogue, and adopt the Hebrew as their language, but those inspired seers foretold Israel's triumph in seeing the day approach when all mankind will conjointly with Israel acknowledge Adonai as *God One*.

Now the question arises, did Israel act up to his *missionary* calling, and did he help to convert mankind gradually to the *pure idea* of faith, and the ennobling *conception* of humanity? Verily, Israel did at all times past live up to his sacred calling. True, he never sent out salaried preachers; he never spread tracts on highways and byways; he never marred the peace of families by alienating from their fireside some weak-minded members. The Jew never believed in the efficacy of pious cant and sanctimonious and empty words. The Jew as a missionary was *silent* but *active*. Not his *tongue* but his *life* ; not his *lips* but his whole *being*, spoke of God and his law, of love and justice.

It was, as our rabbi explains our text, Israel's incessant uplifting of his heart heavenward which performed so well his missionary work. It was the Jew's heroic patience in his unequaled sufferings; it was his wonderful perseverance in his fiery trials, which could not be considered as anything else but the result of his firm belief in the Holy One, and thus the Jew truly testified in the face of the sun to a pure faith in a Supreme Being.

Very often did Amalek attack Israel, but whenever Israel lifted up his heart heavenward, being fully convinced that his destiny was like that of the Heavens above, to silently and emphatically relate the glory of God, his triumph and that of his faith was sure. By the rivers of Babylon the poor Hebrew captives were taunted by their idolatrous conquerors, "Where is your God?" Silently the poor Hebrew lifted up his heart heavenward, and triumph was his. When after years of repose in Palestine, the spirit of Hellas rose in fury against the spirit of Judaism, it was not the strength of matter, but that of the spirit of truth, that made Israel triumph. It was the uplifting of the heart heavenward of but a few firm believers in the Holy One that subdued the idolatrous spirit of Hellas and made Israel's truth radiant in triumphant glory. But even more than this. After the crushing hand of Rome destroyed Israel's nationality and flung Israel down to the ground, and fully believing Israel vanquished forever, and Israel's faith blotted out entirely; all this time Israel was silently lifting up his heart heavenward and his faith was triumphing. Well might the proud Roman sneer at the audacity of the downtrodden Jew pointing to his banner with the inscription: Hear, O Israel, Adonai is our God—Adonai is *One!* Little did the haughty Roman think that this broken-down Jew was silently lifting his heart heavenward and thus destroying Rome's temples and altars, and gradually converting the pagan world to Israel's invisible God, the Holy *One*.

During the Middle Ages Amalek was relentless in his attack against the Jew, the worshiper of "Adonai Echod." The Amaleks of the Middle Ages appeared in diverse forms. You behold them in the garb of kings, in the holy robes of priests; you see them as feudal barons, knights and brutish mobs.

At times you behold them all leagued together against the helpless Jew. To revile, to plunder and torture the Jew, was praised as a Christian duty. But to all the attacks of Amalek, for more than seventeen hundred years, the Jew opposed only his *unflinching patience*, his *unconquerable perseverance* and his pure faith. Through the long, dreary night of mediæval ages Israel silently lifted up his heart heavenward, to his God and his father's God, the Holy One for whose truth he suffered, fully convinced that so sure as the earth turns upon its axis and sees again the sun, so would the sun of peace smile upon him again. And, thanks to God, Israel triumphed over the Amaleks of the Middle Ages. In the very nature of his struggles, namely, in the constancy and patience with which he passed through all those bitter contests and terrible ordeals, lay his missionary labors and his glorious triumphs.

Tortured and reviled, the Jew was still distinguished from his relentless persecutors by the *regularity* of his habits, by the *purity* of his morals, by the *chastity* of his domestic hearth, by his diligent industry, by his scholarship and loftiness of faith. His *industry* triumphed over feudal *indolence;* his constant and pure faith triumphed over the hellish inquisition and barbarous fanatacism; and his intelligence and intellectual pursuits triumphed against the demons of ignorance, Church superstition and moral darkness, that spread their sable folds over king, priest and peasant.

Thus the Jew was the only true missionary on earth; his life, his being, his sufferings, his patience, his moral and intellectual labors and active virtues preached *God, law, order, love, truth, justice, charity* and *good will* more eloquently than all preachers and missionaries of Christendom ever did, or will ever be able to do.

My friends, we of the present generation have to continue the missionary labors of our fathers. Let our pure family lives, our honesty and integrity, our purity of faith, be our active missionaries and teach "love and peace" now and forevermore.

שמחת תורה

(*Simchath Torah.*)

BY REV. DR. M. JASTROW.

Dies ist die Thora, dies das Wort,
Das Gott uns hat gegeben,
Daß wir's bewahren fort und fort
Und tragen durch das Leben!

Weis' auf, Volk Juda, hoch sie auf,
Du darfst mit Stolz sie zeigen,
Sie ist gekauft um hohen Kauf,
Um hohen Preis dein eigen.

Du gabst ja hin für dieses Gut,
Was nur der Mensch besitzet;
Glück, Habe, Freiheit, Ehre,—Blut
Hast du darum verspritzet.

Dies ist das himmlische Panier,
Um das wir muthig stritten,
Und tausend Tode haben wir
Um dies Panier gelitten.

Gott, unser König, Gott der Macht,
Du gabst es unsern Ahnen;
Sie sind gefall'n in mancher Schlacht,
Doch hier sind uns're Fahnen.

Die Kämpfer sanken um sie her
An Menge nicht zu zählen;
Doch ließ der Rest sich nimmermehr
Zu feigem Abfall quälen.

Es quoll Verderben rings hervor,
Wir schwammen durch die Fluthen;
Hoch hielten wir die Fahn' empor
Aus Lavastromes Gluthen.

Wohl Mancher ward, in sie gehüllt,
Den Flammen übergeben,
Wohl Mancher ließ auf diesem Schild
Durchbohrt sein tapfres Leben.

Der Feind schoß Pfeile, Feuer, Gift
Im nie gestillten Streite;
Wir retteten die Gottesschrift,
Sonst Alles ward zur Beute!

Drum heben wir sie freudig auf;
Wir dürfen kühn sie zeigen,
Sie ist gekauft um hohen Kauf,
Um hohen Preis uns eigen.

Die Kämpfe ruh'n; doch würden sie
Je wieder uns erreichen,
Sie sollen's finden, daß wir nie
Von uns'rer Fahne weichen.

The poem just read is a feeble rendition of a German composition, called "Hagbahah," and refers to the minister's lifting up the unfolded scrolls of the Law and calling out זאת התורה "This is the Torah which Moses placed before the children of Israel by the command of the Lord." It directly introduces us into the special celebration of this day, which custom has attached to the Festival of Conclusion, under the appellation of Simchath Torah, or the "Rejoicing of the Law." As you are aware, it is an ancient custom preserved to this day, on every Sabbath to read a portion of the Pentateuch successively, and when the book is gone through, its last portion is read on this festival and at the same time it is commenced anew, as if to indicate that the duty of preserving and studying the Law is a thing of infinity, which ends where it commences and commences where it ends.

For the sake of shortening the service and giving more time to lectures which of late have become an integral part of our devotion, some congregations, reviving an ancient, nearly forgotten custom, reintroduced the so-called Triennial Cycle by dividing the Book of the Law into about one hundred and fifty successive sections, so that three years are required to finish the book and celebrate the Simchath Torah, which, consequently, can not take place but every three years. We, in our congregation—and another one in this city has followed our example—have adopted a somewhat different course, inasmuch as we read on every Sabbath one-third part of the Weekly Lesson of the old arrangement, by doing which we proceed in concert with all our brethren all over the world and avoid the confusion of which innovations frequently are the cause, and finally have the benefit of celebrating the Simchath Torah every year with the rest of our brethren.

The festival is called The Rejoicing of the Law, and indeed the older generation among us, from sight or hearing, recollects with what demonstrations of sincere joy that day was celebrated in our devotional communions. It seemed as if the oppressed, tortured, derided, wretched Jew on this day was determined to challenge the hostile world around and give vent to a defying hilarity, as if exclaiming, "Ye outside of this, our dark, melancholy, isolated and hidden, place of worship, with all your persecution and hatred and contempt and vexation, you can not rob us of that joy which has its seat in the soul of him who lives in peace with his God; with all your tortures and pyres and deaths you could not make us desert this our banner of freedom; you could not dispossess us of this treasure." תורה צוה לנו משה מורשה קהלת יעקב "The Law which Moses commanded us is and will remain the inheritance of the congregation of Jacob." All the blithe humor which, it seems, is one of the peculiarities of our race, would break forth on that day of rejoicing, and old and young conspired in making the place of worship which but a few days back, had been the witness of tears and contritions, a scene of unsurpassed though sacred mirth on the day when the words were read תורה צוה לנו משה "The Law which Moses commanded us is the inherited possession of the congregation of Jacob."

Now, my friends, what caused them so to rejoice in the possession of a book that had brought on them nothing but misery and wretchedness?

They rejoiced in the mission that God had laid upon their shoulders, that they should carry it over the world for the benefit of the human race. They rejoiced in the possession of a treasure which made them nobler than the princes and nobles that persecuted them, which made them superior to their superiors and the teachers of their enemies. Whenever we cast a glance at the sufferings which our ancestors endured, with almost superhuman strength, the question forces itself on our mind: Will the Jew of our day, whom we see so busily engaged in his worldly pursuits and to all appearances so carelessly given up to the enjoyment of his present happiness, stand by his faith as firm and unshaken, his holy banner overhead, should persecutions visit him similar to those his forefathers had to encounter? Will not the spoiled child of the bright present cast away the scroll which he may now uplift with pride and frankly show to all the world, should it again bring disgrace over him, instead of honor?

Some may say it is an idle question, since "the combats now rest," and, let us hope, will rest forever. But I say it is a question well worth asking, for it invites self-examination, and self-examination is never an idle dream, but always productive of reform and strength. It is a question which is apt to enhance in our age the value of what we possess, just as a mother will press her child with joy and affection to her heart, when thinking that somebody might attempt to snatch it from her lap.

And shall I give a conscientious answer? It is my deep-felt conviction that, notwithstanding the apparent indifference to the teachings of our creed prevailing especially among many of our younger generation, who having hitherto tasted but the amenities of youth, have not yet descended into the depths of their own hearts to which life's earnest experiences and visitations invite; notwithstanding their frequent sneers at religion and anything that lifts us up to its golden heights: persecution, which may God keep aloof from us,—persecution would find those very indifferent ones, those very sneerers and unbelievers among the ready combatants around the banner of the Torah, and they would exclaim with the fervor of our ancestors, תורה צוה לנו "The law which Moses commanded us, is and shall forever remain the inheritance of the congregation of Jacob."

From the beginning, Israel, lax as he periodically might have been, was ever conscious that he had a mission for all mankind, intrusted to him by Divine Providence, watching over which mission he may sometimes fall into drowsiness, but is sure to be aroused to his duty when the slightest noise of approaching footsteps reminds him of the possibility of being robbed. The Law that Moses commanded us, as regards its universal principles, carries with itself the tendency to spread among all the human family, not by means of conversion, not by calling upon Israel to go forth with the rough sword of force, or the bland word of persuasion, but by the power which a truth once placed on earth and sternly adhered to by its original owners possesses, and which advances in proportion with the general culture of nations.

The Law that Moses commanded us, is the inheritance of Jacob's congregation, and yet tending to become the property of all nations and races of the earth. Is this not a contradiction in itself? No; just as little as there is an inconsistency in a father appointing his oldest son the administrator of a fortune, the improvement and increase of which should benefit all his minor brothers and sisters. It is a trust placed in him, and why should not the father hope that his son will prove equal to it? Besides, our sages remark, "Come and see the difference between worldly goods and mental possessions. As to the former, he that giveth away is the loser and the recipient the gainer; not so he who dispenses intellectual goods; the more he giveth away the richer he groweth himself." Or will you believe that a Law founded on the Ten Commandments, which begin with the unity and spirituality of the Lord of the Universe, and in the name of this Lord secures truth, property, family, honor, in short all that makes life worth living; will you believe that such a law is destined only for one nation and for such a small one as Israel at all times was, when numbered and not weighed? Will you believe that the Lord of all would impart the foundations of existence only to one people, mindless whether the others lived and grew or decayed and died? Or can you believe that the mere existence of a people with a law so peculiar, so antagonistic to the views of all around it, as soon as it came in contact with others, could work otherwise but beneficially?

Ask history and it will tell you that not in vain did Israel lift up his banner, saying: "And this is the Law which Moses set before the children of Israel." Passing over periods of remote antiquity, which history has as yet failed clearly to illustrate—I mean the period of the Babylonian captivity and the influence our people must undoubtedly have exercised on the rise of a creed in Persia, upsetting idolatrous statues and proclaiming the reign of spirit over matter—let us commence with an epoch distinguished and universally known for its great achievements.

When the great Alexander opened the portals separating nation from nation, and the wise and enlightened Greeks formed the acquaintance of a people wise and enlightened in quite a different way: oh, how great was their astonishment at the sternness of Israelitish laws and the vigor of Israelitish life! One of the most learned men of those days wrote a book on the Jews, full of admiration for their consistency, their holy and sublime views, and their enlightenment.

Soon after, the sacred books of our Bible, at the request, it is said, of an Egyptian king, were rendered into Greek, and the stream of Jewish ideas was directed into a foreign channel. For a moment, a feeling of regret prevailed among the Israelites at seeing what was most sacred to them given into the ruthless hands of strangers. They must have felt as parents feel that see their darling child, on whom all possible care was bestowed, start forth to live among strangers, when the anxious question arises: "What fate will our darling meet with?" Such must have been the feelings of the Israelitish people when sending forth their cherished books, to be scrutinized by profane eyes. But afterwards seeing a new range of ideas grow up in Egypt where Jewish philosophers ranked among the foremost thinkers, they said that there was no foreign language flexible enough to render the Biblical ideas except the Greek.

Their Law was respected, their views honored, and yet, wonderfully enough, their own share was persecution from those very races that learning sat at their feet. Remember the Maccabean period, and hear its heroes, lifting up the Scroll, exclaim: "The Law which Moses has commanded us, is and shall ever be the inheritance of the congregation of Jacob." The light was appreciated by the thoughtful, but the torch-bearers were trampled upon. Remember the hatred of the Egyptian Greeks toward the most enlightened and influential Egyptian Jews! Remember the Roman persecutions, cruel as none before them! But Israel's wisest men gave the example of endurance.

The way once paved through the amalgamation of Jewish ideas with Greek culture, the Law went forth from Zion and the word of the Lord from Jerusalem, or, to use another figure of the prophet, the living waters went forth from Jerusalem, part toward the Eastern Sea and part toward the Western Sea of nations, establishing the religion that was destined to spread westward, and the other that took hold of the Eastern nations, thus giving a part of Jacob's inheritance to two different races, civilizing barbarians and tempering the savage conquerors that stormed the decayed Roman world, that brass colossus with the legs of clay.

It was but a *part* of the living waters that was given to each of these races. I may say, it was the accumulated interests that the first-born suffered to be divided among his brothers, the principle still remaining in his possession for further improvement. And again the brother's gift was honored and admired, but the giver was hated and persecuted.

Who describes the sufferings through which our ancestors passed since they had given forth the two daughter-religions? Exile, slaughter, mobs, dungeons, funeral pyres, vexatious laws, contempt, spite; say what infernal invention for excruciating soul and body and crushing life and its zest, was not turned against our people, from the remotest days of barbarism up to our enlightened age, until the contemned finally looked contemptible, and those shunned by men finally became repulsive in manners and exterior, as we may still see them in the countries of their persecutors, though even there always nobler than their foes and more intelligent than the persecuting mobs.

But up to our days, under all circumstances, they lifted up the Scroll and rejoicing, said: "The Torah which Moses has bequeathed to us, is our everlasting inheritance."

Indeed, were it only this one idea of religious liberty, constantly agitated through Israel's existence and resistance, it alone would have been sufficient to give our people among the nations the seat of honor as a benefactor of mankind. Imagine, my friends, for one moment, what would be the aspect of our civilized countries in the present age, had Israel yielded to force, abandoned his own standard and station, and merged

into that world-commanding creed which said: אני ואפסי עוד
"I am and none besides me." One religion would, so far as we in our short-sightedness can conjecture, prevail all over Europe and her daughter-colonies, opposition to the doctrines of which would mean sure death. Uniformity of creed would reign, for no sects could ever arise but for the liberty of conscience constantly professed and combatted for and kept alive by our ancestors; uniformity of creed would reign, such as even in our country the bigoted and blind wish for as an imagined blessing, but it would be the uniformity of death that holds its sway in the graveyard,—all silent, all motionless, no life, no exertion, no progress, no science, no research.

It was Israel that set the example of resistance to power whenever conscience was interfered with, and instinctively felt that in fighting for his own liberty of religious profession, he was bestowing an unappreciable benefit on all the human race. In the consciousness of this, his mission, he rejoiced at the Law whenever he had finished its pages to commence them anew, and whatever hatred and calumny did to destroy him, it was of no avail so long as Israel did not abandon himself, so long as he lifted up his sacred Scroll, exclaiming: "And yet this is the Law that Moses placed before the children of Israel, as their perpetual inheritance."

I have finished unrolling before you an historical picture worth looking at. I shall not ask what lesson it teaches us, for I am of the opinion that every mental occupation has its object and reason in itself, inasmuch as it elevates the mind above the material world constantly claiming our attendance and attention, and ennobles the heart by enriching it. I am no believer in the distinction between practical and theoretical studies. Every study has its practical results, provided we look on culture, refinement, and enlargement of the mind's view as practical benefits. Nor did our ancestors, when enduring persecution, ask of what *practical* value was to them their Law, so as to make it worth clinging to a creed with such pertinacity. They said: "The Law that Moses gave unto us, is our inheritance," and we will do likewise:

"To God be thanks, the combats rest,
O, may they rest forever,
But we will watch our sires' bequest,
And leave our standard never."

יהי יי אלהינו עמנו And may the Lord our God be with us as he has been with our fathers; may He never forsake us or abandon us, so that we may incline our hearts to Him, walk in all his ways, and observe all his commands and statutes and ordinances which he commanded our fathers. Amen.

A FEW THOUGHTS ABOUT THE DAY OF REST.

A SABBATH EVE DISCOURSE.

BY S. H. SONNESCHEIN,

(Temple "Shaare Emeth," St. Louis.)

"Keep the Sabbath day to sanctify it, as the Eternal thy God has commanded thee. Six days shalt thou labor and do all thy work, but the seventh day is the Sabbath belonging to the Eternal thy God. Thou shalt not do any work, thou, nor thy son, nor thy daughter, nor thy man-servant, nor thy maid-servant, nor any of thy cattle, nor the stranger that is within thy gates, in order that thy man-servant and thy maid-servant may rest as well as thou. And remember, that thou wast a slave in the land of Egypt and that the Eternal thy God has brought thee out thence through a mighty hand and by a stretched-out arm; therefore, the Eternal thy God commanded thee to make the Sabbath-day.—[DEUTERONOMY, v. 13-15.

Once, on a bright Sabbath morning many a year ago, in the old country, when I was just settled as a minister of a small but progressive congregation, and full of fervor like a young soldier burning for his first battle, I met on the street an elderly gentleman, one of my parishioners, with a cigar in his mouth. In that good old country, even at that recent time, smoking a cigar was considered by many a profanation of the Sabbath, and believing it my duty to admonish my parishioner, I approached him seriously and asked him why he was doing thus on the Sabbath day. He answered coolly and with a good deal of humor: "Why, I thought you knew better, I supposed that you, a young rabbi, educated according to the standard of modern views, would not consider this a sin at all. In fact," he continued, "what is Sabbath-breaking? Is the Sabbath a divine institution? Then it can not be broken. Anything which is divine can not be broken. And since I can break the Sabbath it is not worth while to keep it. It is worthy only to be broken.

I trembled with passion, but, composing myself, said: "My friend, do you believe that the heart of a mother is a divine institution?" "Oh, yes," said he, "Every pulse in my being teaches me that." I asked him: "Do you not believe that a great many break that divine institution, the mother's heart?" That was the end of our conversation. But this apt little story of that which happened between me and my friend— because we afterwards became true friends—reminds me vividly of the indifferent aspect in which the progressive and busy men in modern times view the Sabbath. "The Sabbath," they say, "is not a divine institution, for it can be easily broken, without any serious and harmful consequences. A thing which is thus easily broken is not worth keeping." This is the sum and substance of all the argument brought forward even by the thoughtful Sabbath-breaker. At the same time these thoughtful Sabbath-breakers—I call them by that name in the customary sense—forget entirely that Nature, which is their mother, is broken into a thousand pieces when the Sabbath is broken. Nature, not only the nature around us, but our inmost soul, or soul-life, demands peremptorily that the Sabbath day be kept. He who profanes the Sabbath desecrates nature, stultifies his better self and extinguishes that glowing spark which distinguishes him from the soulless and inanimate world around him.

What is the Sabbath? A day of rest. In fact, every moment that we keep aloof from our labor and daily task—any little breathing spell in our work—is a Sabbath in miniature. If you go on a Wednesday evening, after three or four days' work, to listen to a lecturer of deserved prominence, or to attend a concert of some celebrated singer, that is a Sabbath in miniature, an hour or three of rest. If you go to the art gallery, and, looking upon the beautiful works of masterhands, forget yourself—the din of labor beneath, the rattle of wheels and the shrill sound of steam whistles being alike unheeded and unheard—you are in a higher sphere, you enjoy and edify yourself, that is a Sabbath in miniature. Not exactly *the day of rest*, but an hour of sublime recreation, for you feel stronger, better, purer and nobler when you go back to your daily toil. And as Nature herself has given to the woods, gardens and fields the nights and the winter months in which to rest and recreate themselves, so has she given to the human race a rational division of time in which to rest and gain new thoughts and powers for soul-work. Four times seven days make a lunar month. We observe in heaven four aspects of the moon, and, since we could watch these different phases, the human race universally adopted that division of time called a week, a term of seven days, *six for labor and the last for rest and recreation*. That is the origin of the Sabbath. You are not to rest on the Sabbath day as Nature seemingly does—outwardly calm, serene, motionless, powerless. Your rest must be recreation. And, in fact, if you look behind the outward appearance of Nature's rest, you will find that she does not sleep at all. What we call winter is only a co-operation of hidden forces working beneath the surface, still and slow and sure. And such, too, is the Sabbath recreation of man in the highest sense of the word. He rests, but not in sleepy sloth, for his heart, his soul is awake.

And now, lest we go too far into psychological and doctrinal questions, let us return to the theme before us. *The Sabbath is a divine institution*. Breaking the Sabbath is breaking a divine law. We are, many of us, entirely mistaken in our conceptions of the mutual relations between toil and rest, trouble and pleasure, labor and enjoyment, these cardinal alternations of human life. For a great many who do not work at all, who only live for pleasure, this, their very pleasure seems labor. Only behold and watch them! How restless they are, as if they had a thousand different things to do, with hardly a single moment of time in which to take breath. You ask them what they do and they answer, "Oh, I am enjoying myself; I have so much amusement; I am so delightfully situated; I am living for my own pleasure." A creature living for his own pleasure is the most unhappy and hapless thing in the world. Others again we hear complain: "Work is the burden of that curse which drove us out of Eden, that beautiful spot which was colonized by God Almighty himself. That was a nice place to live in, indeed. There, everywhere, grew the sweetest fruits. There were a great many shady nooks in which to take a nap and to promote digestion, and there were so many nice, innocent games and plays and no trouble, no work at all!" It seems, according to the real significance of that sacred myth, as though Adam and Eve never worked at all, because if they had done so and attended to their duty in that Garden Eden, they would never have been driven out. It was because they were lazy and slothful that temptation worked their ruin. Work is not a burden. It is a curse only to him who is a slave working for others and not for himself, who has no will of his own, who in the sweat of his brow only toils and struggles for the benefit and pleasure of others. To him work is a burden and a heavy one indeed. But it is not so with the small farmer who industriously tills his own soil, or with the tradesman who owns a little shop in some obscure by-way in town. Take the latter. He does not owe anybody a cent. Everything in the shop, the shop itself, is his own, and he works with a ready will. How he grows! How his face beams with satisfaction! How he prospers! He would not exchange even with Jay Gould himself. He enjoys the fruit of his labor. Work to such a man is not a burden but a blessing; and rest to such a man means not mere sleep and oblivion, but active joy and recreation. He good-naturedly contemplates: "What I earn, I earn for the benefit of myself, for the benefit of my wife, of my children, and yet I have something to spare for those who can not work, who are sick and destitute." Work and rest, week days and Sabbath day are both God-given to him, and both contribute to his happiness and enlarge his soul-life.

"Keep the Sabbath day—and remember that thou wast a slave in the land of Egypt." The Sabbath is a great liberator, a real redeemer of the human race. If we only think of rest for ourselves; if our recreation has the same selfish motives as our daily toil, then, of course, the Sabbath loses its real object and significance. Then we are proud to declare: "I work as long as I can. I work as opportunities are good and to my advantage. I will cease to work as soon as I have no occasion so to do, as soon as I shall have earned enough to seek without restraint my pleasures and enjoyments. And what do I care for the Sabbath? What does God care for the Sabbath? What is it to him whether I keep my day of rest on Tuesday or on Friday, or not at all? What is the difference to him? I must make money, money. They tell me money is the soul of our existence, the standard of our value. What am I without money?" Of course you are not much if you have no money, but, my dear friend, I tell you, you are still more worthless if you have no soul. If a man has no money but has a fresh, vigorous human soul, sympathetic to everything noble and brave, ready to undertake, if necessary, the most self-sacrificing act, such a man, though he be not permitted to enter the Stock Exchange of New York or London, may yet be entitled to the most noble human society that God's earth has ever sustained. The keeping of the day of rest liberates you from the bonds of selfishness, softens your harsh impulses and sanctifies your life. If you desecrate the Sabbath you profane yourself by proving that you are the slave of your daily task and not the master of your will; you degrade your independence, this greatest privilege of your nature, you separate yourself from everything which is heavenly and only stick to the mud and slum of this lower life. That is why the Sabbath is a divine institution.

Scoffing will not do. There are a great many who sneer at any well-established law in human nature. There are, for instance, some who, knowing that by excessive indulgence in heavy liquor they are destroying themselves, still go on in their habit till they have no power to resist its call, and scoffingly say: "It won't do me any good or any harm; I mean to enjoy myself as long as I live. What care I whether I die to-morrow or prolong my life for a few years more. Human life is but a dream, a dreamy nothingness." But that scoffer burns within himself. His conscience smites him at every syllable he thus utters. The greater the scoffer the more unhappy he is. So it is with those who sneer at the idea of keeping the Sabbath day holy. They are the very ones who need it most, who are constantly at work in the treadmill of money-making and the slaves of that most oppressive of all task-masters, called "business." How much happier would they be heeding the divine institution of the Sabbath: *Six days for money-making and the seventh for soul-making.* This is emancipation and a blessing indeed.

"Six days shalt thou labor and do all thy work." This is as much your sacred duty as the keeping of the day of rest. He who has nothing to do during the week days can not keep any Sabbath. The man without work or occupation is undoubtedly out of place in this world. Only he who labors during the six days of the week can enjoy the blessings of the Sabbath. And right here you must mark the distinct words, "*all thy work,*" words applicable but to that work which is entirely under your own control, the work which is your own in fee simple, allotted to your sole care and management. Such is the occupation of the farmer, of the mechanic, of the tradesman, the artist and the like. Their work is of a kind which by a well-spent activity during the week days, yet allows the amplest room for the day of rest, the most comfortable ease for recreation. They can do "*all their work*" during the week for the given time or purpose. But there is another class of men whose occupation is beyond their own control, who can not do "*all their work*" at a given time and then rest on the Sabbath day with perfect ease. Take the fireman. He can not keep the Sabbath. Conflagrations and the havoc the firefiend plays, are beyond calculation. Take the physician. Just as much as he has to attend to his work at the midnight hour when called upon, while all the world is at rest, just the same he will have to administer his help to the patient on the Sabbath day whenever wanted. So the soldier, so the statesman, in fact everybody whose occupation is inseparably connected with public affairs and the incessant, peremptory demands of public concern. Anyone listening to me to-night might say: "You preachers have it nice. Six days in the week you do nothing and follow your occupation only on the seventh day. And while *you* make your living on the Sabbath, you tell *me* to stay idle." But in making such a cutting remark my friend forgets that paying close attention to a good sermon once or twice on a Sabbath is vivid recreation and no leaden drowsiness; and that a preacher, whose words are not idle talk, but spiritual food and cure, has plenty to do to observe and to study during the week, in order to make his preaching a living success and bringing forth good fruits. In short, the Sabbath is the day of rest for those who, during the week are deeply concerned with interests of their own, and just because they work for the selfish motives of mere gain and greed, are prone to become the slaves of their trade and occupation.

Free yourself! Be once in the week free for twenty-four hours! Leave money-making for that one day and spend it in soul-making, in good cheer, in recreation, in spiritual edification! For one day in the week leave all the drudgery and burdensome toil behind you and be free!

The Sabbath is a divine institution and can be broken, but the Sabbath-breaker is doing more harm to himself than to the Sabbath. The Sabbath will remain but the Sabbath-breaker may go very soon. The Sabbath is the soul-making institution of our Religion, of the Religion of Humanity. *From the faithful and intelligent observance of this day of rest our religious nature draws nearly all the virtues and energies which contribute so largely to the perfection of men and to the glory of God.* Our rabbis of old, in their allegorizing way of teaching, have given the following beautifully poetic description of the Sabbath institution:

"Every Friday evening," they say, "when the Sabbath is ushered in amidst the dusk and stillness of the approaching night, two angels, the dark accuser and the bright defender, are watching every household, to see whether they are prepared for the reception of the Sabbath-bride, or not. If they meet the unmistakable signs of the holiday cheer and peace, joy and devotion, then the bright angel exclaims: 'May peace and happiness forever find their home here!' And the dark angel, the accuser, is compelled to say: 'So mote it be. Amen!' Even Satan must admit the blessedness of the pious, devoted Sabbath-keeper. On the other hand, when the man goes on forgetting the Sabbath, does not care for it at all, his household showing no sweet tokens of satisfaction, his wife, children and servants enjoying no periods of calm and quiet repose, then the dark angel says: 'Condemned be he who so far forgets himself and all the interests of domestic tenderness, as to neglect the Sabbath.' And the good angel —the pure and innocent one, who wishes no harm to any, who is the messenger of God's grace and loving kindness—is obliged to respond, though with tears, to the words of the dark angel: 'So mote it be. Amen!'"

This, you will say, is but poetry. There is nothing real and tangible in it. Granted; but poetry of this kind produces an effect, even on the most prosaic mind, which is not easily effaced or obliterated. It is the celestial bearer of the eternal truth that the Sabbath is a divine institution.

On the Sabbath day we should subdue and govern passion. Our passions rule us through all the other days of the week: ambition, pleasure, avarice, we give them scope and leave to dominate our daily lives. On the Sabbath we should escape from their dominion and dwell in the serene atmosphere of rest, peace and liberty.

You will remember that the Sabbath commandment says something of the ox and other kinds of cattle. This may serve well to symbolize our lower passions. On the Sabbath these ought to have no exercise or sway. Let them lie chained and still in the dark and sullen stall of forced repose.

So, the man-servant and the maid-servant of the sacred text may typify Will and Love. These have been subordinate throughout the week to lower and baser passions. The twilight of the Sabbath eve is the signal for their enfranchisement. Remember, that their rest is liberty and action. Loosen them! let them go free! Let soul conquer sense and will subjugate passion. Let the spirit aspire to the high and the holy and wing its strong flight to the bosom of the Infinite. This is the Sabbath of the soul. Let us keep it for our dear souls' sake.

So, too, of Love. All the week days she is thrust aside, condemned, chained, beaten. Our stern self-seeking gives her no room nor place. On the Sabbath she, too, is free. Then comes the sweet and placid reunion of hearts. Then husband and wife, parent and child, friend and friend, neighbor and neighbor join hands and kiss hearts with one another. The Sabbath is the divine fountain wherein Love renews her youth and reinforces her strength, and so becomes immortal even on the earth. Sabbath-desecration is her death, as Sabbath-keeping is her life. This, if you will receive it, is the meaning of the Sabbath. This divine institution changes not. It is for all time and all eternity. Whoso keepeth it, keepeth himself from evil. Amen.

THRICE HOLY IS THE LORD.

BY REV. DR. BENJAMIN SZOLD,
(Of Baltimore, Md.)

Religion, like every other system of truths and principles, has its foundations, bearing and supporting the whole superstructure, and it is of the greatest importance to know which they are, and by what characteristic signs they can be recognized as such. Our guiding standard, in our search of them, must be one that is generally admitted. It would not suffice merely to point out a certain set of truths and declare them to be cardinal. Upon whatever ground this were done, room would still be left for dispute and variety of opinions. Some would claim pre-eminence for one order of principles and some for another; and, indeed, some would even maintain (and the number of these theologians is not small) that every detail in religion, every observance, every custom, is fundamental. There is no such thing, they say, as a primary principle in religion; all its teachings, laws, tenets and behests are alike vital. We must, therefore, in order to place the result at which we wish to arrive beyond dispute, start from a point conceded by every thinking man. Whatever will be reached then, in our inquiries, as the elements of religion, will bear the evidence of its own truth in itself, and thus enforce the recognition of all.

Let us then proceed from Revelation. All have to admit that those truths are essential—and only those—which are revealed to us; that is, the knowledge of which comes to us most directly from within and without: truths innate in our inner life, latent and organic in the life of nature; truths dominant in all the affairs and relations of man's world, through all the stages and phases of its development; these must be acknowledged by all to be the basis, to which everything else that religion teaches must be referred in order to claim our recognition.

Measured by this infallible standard, we may reduce our whole system of religion to three primary principles: *The existence of God; the divine origin of Law, and the belief in future reward and punishment.** These teachings are the fundamentals. Their full exposition will show that they did not ascend upon the horizon of our knowledge at any stated epoch; neither were they discovered by human research. They are revelations, as old as nature, as original as the world of man; though it is true that they were more clearly perceived and more lucidly taught by some geniuses, especially by our prophets, who were men with eyes, ears and hearts widely opened for all the wonders and teachings of creation. To them refers the exclamation heard from out of the mouth of the seraphim, by the great prophet Isaiah, whom the Haftarah of this Sabbath introduces to us at the most solemn moment of his life, when he first received his prophetic mission. He then had a wonderful vision, which he describes in fiery language. He saw the Lord seated on an exalted throne, the temple was filled with the splendor and glory of His majesty. The seraphim stood round about him, and, from mouth to mouth, swelling into a powerful chorus, ran the words:

קדוש קדוש קדוש יי צבאות.

"Holy, holy, holy is the Lord of Hosts!" (Isaiah vi. 1-3). This sentence is thus beautifully paraphrased by an ancient expounder of the Scriptures:

קדיש בשמי מרומא עלאה בית שכנתיה
קדיש על ארעה עובד גבורתיה
קדיש לעלם ולעלמי עלמיא

"Holy in the exalted skies, the temple of His glory: holy on earth, the scene of His governing strength; holy forever and in all eternity."

---

* These three doctrines are declared the fundamentals of our religion by Joseph Albo in his book Judaism, and are in Judaism generally accepted as such.

I. Holy is the Lord in the exalted skies, the temple of His glory! All in nature points to Him above as the Most Supreme and the Source of all existence. The wonderful harmony with which the myriads of creatures work together, their wise arrangement, their usefulness, their beauty and their grandeur, strongly and irresistibly impress upon the human mind the idea of an Infinite Intellect, from whom they all emanated. Wherever we look and whatever we observe around us, we find revealed and reflected the endless Spirit enthroned on High. Chance can not bring forth works of wisdom; chance can not produce harmony, beauty and goodness. You ask, looking around you, overpowered by the vastness of the universe, with its countless wonders and splendors: Where is God? And with a thousand voices, echo answers: Where is God not? Intuitively, you see Him seated on an exalted throne and you hear the seraphim, standing around Him, exclaim: Holy is the Lord on high in the temple of His glory!

So visibly is the idea of God stamped upon every work and being of nature that its conception entered, or might have entered, upon the consciousness of the very first man, who had no other tutor, no other source of knowledge than the surrounding world and his inner powers. When Adam—let us take him as the type of the entire human family—first opened his eyes upon the outer world, when, looking above, the vast arches of the blue vault, illumined either by the wondrous light of the sun, or by the milder radiance of the stars, met his astonished gaze, and when, casting his eyes to the ground in confused reflection, his attention was riveted by the gay sward which clothed the earth with freshness, when he heard the symphonic tones of the birds' morning song, when he first tasted the luscious fruits which hung in all their tempting ripeness just above his head, while he was held in the embrace of gentle zephyrs and the genial warmth of the sun; what could have been his thoughts, if they did not turn upon the Unseen Power which conjured all these scenes and sights and sounds and tastes before his senses? He must have asked himself: How came I on this stage, and who is the author of all these numberless things? In one grand chorus, they all replied: Our Author resides בישמי מרומא עלאה in yon high skies. He created thee and all thou seest in the vast universe which is בית שכנתיה the temple of His glory.

II. But not only is the world God's residence, He is also its Governor. "Holy is God on earth, the scene of His governing strength." There is a law for every creature, there is a design and a plan underlying the whole of creation. Or, do you think it possible that the spheres would move in their orbits so regularly, and complete their circuits in the heavens with unchanging uniformity, that day and night, summer and winter, warmth and cold, birth and death, growth and decay, would alternate so accurately, were there no law and no statute?

חוק וזמן נתן להם שלא ישנו את תפקידם

"The Creator instituted statute and time for every being not to change its course and destination." Nature thus is to man a book of revelation, in which he reads God's eternal laws and regulations which urge him to inquire into the laws and regulations the Lawgiver has set to him. If every other being is subservient to some immutable law, why should he, the masterpiece of all God's creatures, be lawless, and destined to move on unrestrained and ungoverned? Nothing could be more absurd than to harbor such a thought. There must be some decree for his action, too, some method for his spiritual growth and development. And where is this decree given and this method laid down? They are not in heaven, not beyond the sea; they are near to him, within his own heart. The higher law for man's guidance is not the product of science, not the result of any laborious research, it is an element of his mental constitution, an ingredient of his higher nature. Even Adam felt, or might have felt, the promptings of his moral sense of right and wrong; he already recognized a higher authority whose voice man has to obey. When he gazed upon the scene where he had been placed, he must have asked himself: Am I perhaps charged by the Power that has placed me here, to perform some task, or have I no duty whatever to fulfill, and can I roam wildly in this beautiful garden and do as pleases my wanton fancy? If so, what then can be the meaning of this whispering within my breast, this commanding and warning voice? I am certainly a moral being and have to conform my doings to the commands which my Creator has engraven upon the tablets of my heart.

History also certifies to the truth of the doctrine of God's government. We perceive clearly purpose and plan in the annals of the past. We observe one grand design, one dominant thought and will throughout all the convulsions and revolutions of mankind. We notice, on the long march of time, a steady progress toward the better. Every event brought man forward, every incident furthered the process of civilization. This steady, onward march of humanity evidences the existence of a Supreme Lawgiver, an Endless Intellect, scheming and premeditating upon mankind's spiritual growth, and thus history re-echoes what so loudly resounds through the universe: "Holy is the Lord on earth, the scene of His governing strength."

III. Still one more stay is necessary to prop the edifice of religion. It is the conviction that there is a Hereafter, where man reaps the fruit of his deeds. Without this assurance, law, duty, virtue and morality would be mere empty, meaningless sounds. What is to sustain man in the midst of a life of trials and struggles; what shall encourage him to foster virtue and practice self-abnegation, if he has not the belief in a world of retribution? Here, in this short span of existence, he experiences, no matter whether he be just or vicious, only sorrows and troubles; frequently, he even sees the wicked thrive, the rogue enjoying all the goods of this world, while the righteous bend under insupportable burdens. If, in spite of the adverse circumstances which surround him, he is to remain faithful to the higher standard that law sets to him, he must be sustained by the hope of a life beyond. This hope is thus closely allied with the idea of law and a supreme Lawgiver; He who directs man to do the right and to shun the wrong, rewards him according to his ways, for "Holy is He forever and in all eternity."

This also is a thought which Adam fully perceived, or might have perceived, as is illustrated by the following legend in the Talmud:

When God said to Adam: "Thorns and thistles shall the ground bring forth to thee," tears coursed down his cheeks and he cried out: אני וחמורי נאכל באבוס אחד Shall I and my ass feed from out of the same crib? But when God completed the sentence: "In the sweat of thy face shalt thou eat thy bread," his grief subsided. נתקררה דעתו

The Talmud means thereby that this last, apparently more rigid sentence of judgment, implies the pledge of man's higher destiny. It foretold the abundance God has in store for man, whom he charged to eat bread in the sweat of his face. Must I work, Adam said, for the meager food, which the ground brings forth spontaneously for the animal, must I toil and labor; am I placed here to till the ground, to cultivate it and change all into a beautiful garden, and thus leave behind me footprints in the sand of time, then the grave can not be my goal, and my destiny can not, like that of the ass, be fulfilled here on earth. All that I see testifies to the existence of a God of love, mercy and justice; how then can He charge me with so heavy a task and yet have no reward in store for me? He commands me to work—this is a privilege, and entitles me to claim as my due share, eternal felicities. Here below there is no reward; there must come a life when the beads of perspiration will be wiped off from my brows, where imperishable glories will crown my head. There must be a world in which God's justice will be fully manifested, where the faithful laborer is amply rewarded for the good he has accomplished here on earth, for "Holy is the Lord forever and in all eternities."

Thrice holy is the Lord! God is the Source of existence, the Author of Law and the Dispenser of retribution. These three truths are fundamental. Upon them the edifice of religion firmly rests. They are the criterions of all truth, the standards of all religion. With these three primary truths the Book of books opens. The first chapter describes the creative process of God, the Author of all being. The second represents Him as the Educator and Governor of man, to whom He gives His decree, to mould his conduct thereby. The third shows that God lets man find according to his ways. These three elementary principles stamp the Book of books to the Book of Revelation. It teaches what is revealed to man, and what comes to his knowledge in the most direct way. And, like revelation, so is this Book an everlasting source of knowledge. It is permanent and can never be dried up. It can not be superseded by any other creed, nor can it be removed by any other civilizing factor. In other creeds, whatever is true is not new, and whatever is new is not true. It also has no need to dread the ascendancy of science. The sphere of this great factor in civilization is quite a different one. Science deals with details, with simple facts and laws. Religion teaches the universal, the constituent, intellectual and moral elements of all existence, of all that is latent in the universe, innate in man, and organic to the history of his spiritual growth and development. Science is the aggregate of all the results of invention, human research and the labor of mind, it is the sum total of all the knowledge to which man has attained by means of discursive thought. Religion, however, teaches what man perceives intuitively, what man knows, or can know, from ever and forever.

We, the seed of Abraham, the disciples of the Prophets, are the bearers, teachers, priests and expounders of these truths, the permanent foundations of all truth. The Scriptures, in our hands, are the credentials for our appointment, for our prophetic mission. We are the messengers of God to mankind. We have to tell humanity the vision we see, the sounds we hear. We see God seated on an exalted throne, filling the great temple of nature with the splendor and glory of His presence. And the Seraphim, standing around Him, we hear exclaiming: " Holy is the Lord on high, holy on earth, the scene of His government, holy forever and in all eternity." Amen.

SPIRITUALITY OF GOD'S LAW.

BY REV. I. L. LEUCHT.

TEXT:—Exodus xxxii. 19-20.

Free at length from the Egyptian yoke, the children of Israel rapidly grew into a nation, for they acknowledged God to be the Lord and accepted His laws. Awestruck, they had listened to the ten words of Sinai, and with trembling voices sent up to Heaven the watchword of Judaism, נעשה ונשמע "We will hearken and we will obey."

But alas, for human stability! How long did the Israelites remain loyal to their vows? The 32d chapter of the book of Exodus but too graphically portrays the fickle and ungrateful character of the national heart.

Moses, the great hero, deeply impressed with the solemn issues of his days, believed also, no doubt, that his people were equally imbued with devotion to the heavenly Deliverer. He seems to have acted on this persuasion if not conviction; for in order to get engraven on tablets of stone the perfect laws which had been transmitted to us, he withdrew himself, as we learn, to mount Sinai for a season.

This absence tried the faith of the nation, and unhappily the best proved their weakness. The judgment of God had not taken root in the Jewish breast. The lofty and world-embracing teachings of Jehovah had not yet penetrated the soul of Israel. To the *growing* nation the Lawgiver is the incarnation of Deity. To the ignorant, demoralized slave, the cardinal truth, that a spiritual God created the heavens and the earth, is altogether inconceivable. With the person of Moses, therefore, departed also the spirit of Moses.

Wild and horror-stricken, the people imagined that his absence was an awful intimation to them that they were forsaken of God Himself. They therefore clamored for gods to go before, gods that would not leave, gods who would not forsake them. Aaron, the peace-loving and meek brother of Moses, whose life no doubt in this trying emergency was in imminent peril, demanded gold and silver, ostensibly to mould the idol. This yielding to the popular will, however, was only an apparent concession. He would throw oil on the troubled waters, and as our sages narrate, he did not believe that the daughters of Israel would part with their jewels. This persuasion was verified by the event. The infuriated men, however, took by force what was denied to entreaty and command. They stripped their wives of all their ornaments and gave them to Aaron, who, in a moment of despair, cast the golden calf.

Now, returning from the mountain with the ל׳ הברית Moses as he drew near the camp heard strange sounds of festivity and rejoicing. The shouts of the people, who were dancing around their newly-made Deity, reached him, afar off.

And here let us pause to contemplate that reverend sage, whose face reflected the sheen of the Divine presence, when his eye and ear fully took in the frenzy and intoxication of his people, who, before their idol-god, continued loudly to exclaim: אלה אלהיך ישראל "This is the God of Israel."

Anger of the noblest kind characterizes his every feature, amazement and indignation take possession of his soul, and in his righteous displeasure, commanding the faithless offenders to destroy their sin, he casts down and breaks into pieces that Law divine which was engraven on the tablets in his hands, and at the same time causes the idol to be ground to powder and be mingled with the sands of the desert.

Now, in carefully perusing this historical incident, the question arises: Why did Moses annihilate the golden calf and at the same time break to pieces the law of God? We could readily supply a motive for his actions had he ground the idol to dust and in its place erected God's divine teachings.

Why destroy a work which Moses himself declared to be written ב׳ אצבע אלהים with the finger of God?

Now I desire and propose in this discourse to prove that the destruction of the idol and the tablets of the covenant had one and the same end in view, to teach the fundamental doctrine of all revealed religion, *that God's law is altogether spiritual.* To show this from the historical incident above narrated, is the task for this evening's hour.

I.

By destroying the golden calf, Moses inculcated the doctrine that God's law is spiritual. It must be clear to any candid mind, though no high-sounding name or authority can be quoted in favor of this opinion, that Moses, when returning from Mt. Sinai was not overcome by sinful anger on discovering the Egyptian idol in the midst of his excited people. From no wrathful impulse or disappointed hopes did he with a mighty hand destroy the golden image. The Bible says: The Lord spoke to Moses: "Get thee down, for thy people, which thou hast brought up out of the land of Egypt, have become corrupt. And now let me alone and my wrath shall wax hot against them and I will make an end of them." But Moses, dreading nothing so much as the execution of this Divine menace, fell on his knees before the Lord, covered his head and with trembling voice exclaimed: "Oh, Lord, forgive their sin, but if not, blot me out, I pray thee, from the book which thou hast written."

Here then is evidence that this great Moses must have found the sin of the people at least pardonable. And why? The records of antecedent ages will furnish the answer to this inquiry. See in their tents encircling Mt. Sinai, the children of Israel, with careworn faces and stupified looks. Whence come these mighty hordes? From the land of Egypt, the house of bondage, where they had been in slavery during four hundred years. They had borne the iron fetters of despotism for centuries, forsaken by that glorious God of their fathers, whom they had also forgotten. Now in the land of their captivity, in Egypt, they had with their own eyes seen gods, which to their minds blessed and protected the nation. Israel, the servant of Jehovah, was the slave, while the worshiper of false gods of idols, was the master. And this persuasion remained until Moses appeared and liberated them in the name of that God who seemed to have departed from them. As long as the Israelites beheld Moses, as long as he was in presence before them, he was to them the very incarnation of God Himself. We learn, however, that Moses stayed away during forty days and forty nights, and then Israel no doubt reasoned: "Our God has forsaken us again. He has left us without a master and without a guide." They gathered about the hut of Aaron. Terror-stricken, they exclaimed: "Up, make us gods that shall go before us, for as far as this man Moses, who brought us up here, we know not what has become of him. We desire gods to go before us, we must perceive them with our senses and have them always in our midst."

At one glance, as it seems, Moses took in all the circumstances of the actual situation. His surprise, indignation and grief were, doubtless, great; but, did he lose his self-possession? The meekest man on the face of the earth did not give away to unbounded wrath even at the thanklessness of those whom he had rescued from bondage, whom through mighty wonders, he had safely conducted to life, freedom and peace. As we have already observed, foreseeing God's righteous displeasure, he could even pray for the daring offenders. The golden calf, however, was doomed. It was ground into dust and strewn upon the waters, to teach the misguided people that Adonai alone is God—that no image, no idol, no likeness, can be made of him who has said: "I am the Lord and thou shall have no other gods before my face."

II.

The divine nature is spiritual. The incomprehensible Godhead can not be bound or conceived by the senses. And thus far our position has not been very difficult to sustain, for the destruction of an idol can only be construed as an argument in favor of the God of Moses, for the honor of God and the vindication of His law. "Thou shall have no other gods before me." But to proceed, we further maintain that the annihilation of the two tables of the covenant was intended to promulgate within the camp of Israel the same doctrine, the doctrine of the spirituality of God's nature, on which we now insist.

It is well known that Moses was a man of quick sensibilities. Whenever the principles of truth and justice were attacked he hesitated not to apply the proper remedy, without fear or favor. The Egyptian who had beaten an Israelite atoned for his offense by death. The Sabbath-breaker was immediately executed, and thousands dyed with their blood the burning sand of the desert, because they obstinately refused to obey the laws of God. The maxim of Moses was יקוב הדין את ההר "Right pierces even through mountains." Now the sin of the Israelites was the occasion for manifesting this leading feature of the temper of Moses. His anger was awakened by their rebellion against God, and as we have seen, it was justifiable. His spirit was stirred within him because the Israelites had forsaken the path of duty and safety, and following the imagination of their own hearts, they were eagerly pursuing the highway back to slavery and to death.

Moses did not, however, conclude from this revolt that no beneficial result could be attained, when a nation thus willfully forget their God, even in the short space of forty days. Did he break the tables of the Covenant into fragments as a sign that he has now lost all hopes in the future of Israel? God forbid! I would incline to this view indeed, perhaps, had he not in the very moment of his displeasure, prayed to God, saying: "Forgive thy people, or blot me out of existence." Surely Moses must have had a firm belief in the sublime mission of Israel, otherwise his prayer was but a solemn mockery, an act void of any purpose. And here, perhaps, some one will object, and say: "If Moses did indeed hope in the regeneration of Israel, how came it that he destroyed the two tables of the Law, which according to his own word, had been written by God himself, which, therefore, belonged not to Moses, but were the property of the whole nation?" This objection may thus be met: By reducing the golden idol to dust, Moses had but shown that the gods of Egypt were nothing but vanity, nothing but the handiwork of man, and therefore unfit for adoration. Again, in his hands he held two tables of stone, engraven, as he said, with the finger of God. And yet the people being strongly inclined toward idolatry, may have so reasoned: "We were indeed at fault in worshiping the golden calf, but here Moses, our leader and guide, brings us an idol of stone; surely, this is the God of Israel come back again to us." The Israelites, we repeat, were but newly emancipated, they were accustomed to see gods with their bodily eyes. The gods with which they were familiar had been within reach of their senses, and so they were ready, from a holy terror, to fall down and worship the tables of stone as they had done the golden calf. It offered an example, therefore, worthy of him of whom it is said: לא קם כמשה עוד "No man like him will adore the world again." Moses, in their very presence, broke into fragments that work which they certainly considered to be an essential part of their religion. And this act spoke with a living tongue: "O Israel, I have destroyed your Egyptian idol, but perchance in your vain imagination you deem the God of Israel to be in need of stone or gold to establish this kingdom in this world. Sons of Jacob, behold torn into fragments the material forms of the divine Law. Look to the heart only, whereon all the divine commandments must be inscribed. God and God's will, His only image, must be sought for in the integrity and purity of man's soul. The divine rule is not treasured up in books, it is not confined to tables of stone or of gold, neither is it enshrined in a holy ark. God and the laws of God are all of them spiritual." And once more. If we accept this interpretation of the course of Moses, we shall find it to be as a golden key to open that mysterious phrase of the Talmud, (שבת 87): "When Moses had broken the tables of the covenant, God said to him, יישר כחך ששברת

Thou hast done well this act of destruction." It does not require now to take refuge in cabbalistic mysticism to understand this phrase of the Talmud, we comprehend fully what our sages desire to convey. The spirit of God, the genius of our religion, extolled Moses for his courageous act, for by this zeal he showed that our faith could not be endangered even should every emblem, the very book of the Law itself, be destroyed, and thus removed from our sight. Moses won the praise of our Lord. He has left for our edification a vivid and brilliant declaration, a prophetic declaration, that forms must yield whenever they are in the way of God's truth. The Rock of Israel can only be conceived by the spirit as a spirit. The tables of the covenant were hewn a second time. Where are they? What has become of them? They also were destroyed as the golden calf. The laws of the decalogue, they still exist and are destined to govern this universe until the last soul shall enter its last resting place. Thus let our religion be a faith not depending on outward forms, they are only essential when the living spirit of our God is found within its fold, and must be shattered to fragments when the רוח הקדש the holy spirit does not dwell there any more. Let our faith forever be an עץ חיים a living tree, whose branches rise heavenward, and whose time-beaten stem points to the One Father, the God of all mankind. Amen.

JEWISH IDEAS CONQUER THE WORLD.

A SHABUOTH SERMON.

BY REV. DR. B. FELSENTHAL,
(Of Chicago.)

Text:—"Ye are my witnesses, says the Lord * * I, I am the Lord, and besides me there is no savior."—[Isaiah xliii. 10-11.

The festival which we celebrate to-day bears the biblical name, '*Hag ha-Shabuoth*, "Feast of Weeks," and this name has been given to it because on this day concluded the seven weeks which, according to the old Mosaic law, had been devoted to the work of garnering in the grain. As long as the Jews had been a nation in the political sense of the word, and had as such dwelt in Palestine, all the grain of the land was gathered in during these seven weeks. Full were the barns of barley, of rye, and of wheat. And now a proper time for a festive day had come—the time for '*Hag ha-Shabuoth*.

Besides the name "Feast of Weeks," we meet in the Bible with another name for this festival. It is also called *Yom ha-Biccurim*, "Day of the First Fruits." And the reason for calling it so, was because of the various kinds of fruits the first ripe ones were, in this time of the year, brought as a thank-offering into the temple of the Lord.

From the two names quoted it is easily to be inferred, and hardly do we need any other witness to prove the fact, that this day was originally intended to be an agricultural festival. In the course of historical development, however, it lost its original signification, and, in post-biblical times, other ideas, even higher and nobler than those that in the first caused the institution of *'Hag ha-Shabuoth*, became connected with this day. Since times immemorial, Israel celebrates the day as *Zeman Mattan Torah*, as a day on which the fact is to be commemorated that God blessed Israel with the Torah, and especially do we on this day gratefully remember the proclaiming of the ten Sinaitic words.

Truly, dear friends, the Lord's Torah and the Lord's commandments, they are fruits of an infinitely higher value than barley and wheat. For not of bread alone does man live. He yearns after another nourishment, after a nourishment for the spirit that is within him. With all our hearts do we praise our good Father in heaven for the corn and the wheat, the bread and the wine He blesses us with. Still more do we praise Him for the gift of religion, the true bread of life, wherewith He stills the hunger of our hearts, and for the wine of our Torah, wherewith he quenches the thirst of our souls.

Truly, this was a great time of harvesting, when the eternal doctrines and laws of Judaism were gathered in first by a few select ones in Israel, by our patriarchs and prophets, by our singers and sages, afterwards by all Israel, and still later by other nations. This harvest-time will be at an end when finally all mankind will participate in the full possession and enjoyment of the treasure of Judah, in the truth and moral law of Judaism, and when the whole human race, in common with the house of Jacob, will walk in the light of God, the Eternal.

In the golden age of mankind, which was not in the remote past, as we are told by Grecian myths, but which, rather, will be in the future, or, to use Biblical language, in the Messianic time coming, Jewish ideas will have conquered the world and will rule it.

Thus far Jewish ideas have already progressed wonderfully. They are already acknowledged, willingly or unwillingly, by the nations standing highest on the ladder of civilization—by those nations that profess Christianity or Mohammedanism, while and because they profess the same. For both these religions are nothing more nor less than direct offsprings from

Judaism, and whatever is good and true in them they have directly appropriated from the treasures of Judah. We, from our Jewish standpoint, only regret the fact that the Jewish doctrines, when borrowed by others, were not carefully guarded against adulteration by and intermixture with foreign elements, with elements un-Jewish and anti-Jewish. Time, however, slowly but surely will effect a thorough purification, and pure and unadulterated Jewish ideas, we repeat it, will finally rule the world.

These are great hopes, and you might gainsay, will they, indeed, be realized? Are these hopes not based upon self-deception and illusions? Are these expectations not brought forth by our prejudices naturally entertained in favor of the religion in which we have been reared?

In order to show you, my friends, that we may truly expect the fulfillment of our hopes, let us examine the teachings of Judaism, and let us furthermore see in how far the present state of the religious world justifies our hopes.

I invite you, first, to a thorough examination of Judaism. Whosoever studies Judaism earnestly, be he Jew or non-Jew; whosoever frees himself of his erroneous notions concerning the same, and becomes familiar with its tenets, will surely, and must surely, admit that Judaism justly claims the possession of absolute truth, and that, therefore, its doctrines and teachings *deserve* to become the property of mankind. And as truth in the end will always be victorious, so will Judaism certainly be victorious.

We will not deny that true and good doctrines are also maintained and are also taught in other religious systems. Gladly do we admit that eternal truths and moral precepts are taught even by those heathenish religious systems whose origin and growth we can not trace back to the religion of Israel, and whose holy books have not the least connection with the Bible of the Jews. Justly we may assert that the so-called New Testament of the Christians and the Koran of the Mohammedans would not and could not exist if our Jewish Bible had not existed before them. But neither the Brahmans with their Vedas, nor the Parsees with their Zendavesta, neither the Buddhists with their Tripitaka, nor the Chinese with their, to them, holy books of Confucius and Laotse, are in the least connected with Israel and its Torah. Still we joyfully concede that by them many true doctrines are taught and many good laws are prescribed, which deserve all acknowledgment. Even more, even those religious systems which have not produced any holy books at all—holy in the sense as used in reference to the writings already named—as, for instance, the religions of Hellas and Rome, of the Teutons and the Celts, of the Africans and Indians, etc., even they were the vehicles to spread, in some degree, truth and morality, and, therefore, our appreciation is due to them also. How could it be otherwise? The Creator has bestowed on all nations and all individuals thereof a conscience, and has blessed them with mental faculties more or less exalted. These faculties of the mind and this inborn consciousness of what is right and what is wrong, although they are more or less liable to err, are the common root whence have grown the manifold truths found everywhere, and it is a theory quite unnecessary and quite false to suppose that one nation must have borrowed the same from another nation. Different nations have discovered them independently of one another. But what we claim is this, that besides these grains of truth, which are to be found in the non-Jewish systems, there are also to be found there great masses of errors, intellectual ones and moral ones, of which Judaism, and only Judaism is free.

There is none entitled to pronounce judgment in this all-important issue except the God-enlightened human reason. To this judge do we appeal. Before his bench we plead our cause.

It is not often, my dear friends, that we make such comparisons. We do not undervalue the blessings which the powerful daughters of Judaism have brought to the nations in the East and in the West. We like, rather, to dwell upon the great merits and historic importance of these forerunners of the Messianic times, and we render unto them praise and thanks for their deserts. But when we so often perceive that partly malice, partly ignorance and prejudice, and partly an ill-directed zeal for un-Jewish doctrines, lead to belittleings and attacks of our own Judaism, then we are certainly justified when we point to our creed shining in brilliancy and in glory.

What does Judaism teach? Does it, indeed, teach that God is merely the national God of Israel? Does it not, on the contrary, say and repeat, the Lord alone is God, and besides Him there is none other? Brethren, I can not stop, in this short hour, to furnish the proofs for all this. Hints must suffice for to-day. And so I say, in a few words, Judaism teaches since its very earliest days one God—one God for all mankind! This does not exclude the fact that, in times long gone by, the Monotheistic idea was more or less imperfectly understood by the unlearned and unthinking part of the people. Does our religion really teach that our God is a God of anger and revenge? Does it not, on the contrary, say by the mouths of all its inspired prophets and all its teachers, that God is a God of mercy and of love? Does it not, in a categorical imperative, demand of its confessor: Love thy neighbor, even the poor and forsaken stranger, as thyself, and grant to him equal rights with thee? Does it not unrelentingly insist that we have to sanctify even our desires, even the very thoughts of our hearts, by enjoining us not to covet what belongs to our neighbor? Does it, furthermore, not require of us, in several laws that have been laid down in the Pentateuch, to be merciful toward the mute animal creation?

Brethren, we might go on with similar questions for quite a length of time, we could challenge the opposite world to answer them, and in the greatest composure of mind we could await the answers.

But it might be said that similar doctrines and similar laws are taught by others as well, and particularly by that powerful daughter of Judaism to whom, at present, nearly all the occidental world, nearly all Europe and America pay homage. If this is so, we see therein the progress of *Jewish* ideas. For Christianity, in its main parts, and its best parts, is nothing else than Judaism, and we do not hesitate to admit that it also effected, for the benefit of mankind, a great progress in so far that it abolished petrified laws and hollow formalities, when that party in early Christianity, whose leader and mouthpiece was the apostle Paul, gained the upper-hand over an opposite party, and in so far we ought to profit by the example. But Christianity branched off from the mother Church and went astray, when, especially by the same Paulinian party, foreign elements were intermixed, when the fanciful reveries of the Neoplatonic school of philosophers and the bottomless speculations of the Gnostics were ingrafted upon our rational, pure and noble Judaism, and when, in order to make it more palatable to the heathens of Europe, it did not shrink from admitting ito its body such doctrines, which we, from our Monothestic standpoint, must necessarily call idolatrous.

Do we Jews teach a god incarnate? a god who ate, and drank, and slept, and suffered, and died? a god by whose blood the sins of mankind were atoned for? Do we teach that our God is so cruel as to give over to eternal perdition those that do not believe as we do? Do we not, on the contrary, explicitly teach that every good man, of whatever creed or nationality he may be, will participate in salvation? Does Judaism curse, or damn, or persecute any non-Jew on account of his religious views? Do we state, or claim, that any man is, or was, infallible? Is Judaism in conflict with science? Does it not grant to the scientific inquirer the fullest and most unlimited freedom? A Galileo and Copernicus, a Darwin and a Huxley, a Haeckel and a Virchow, can follow their researches unmolested by Judaism, and the astronomer and the geologist, the speculator on the age of the human race and on the age of the world, on the origin of species and on the origin of languages can proceed with his studies without meeting any interference or any protest from our side. There is nothing like a *credo* in Judaism that might stand as an obstacle in the way of the searcher after truth. There is only one doctrine which is regarded in Judaism as firm and unshakable—*the doctrine of the one supernatural and preternatural God.* And there is only one kind of laws for which unchangeability is claimed—*the moral laws.* And these laws we might sum up in one sentence: Sanctify your thoughts and actions. Or, as the Bible has it: "Ye shall be holy, for holy am I, the Lord, your God." This being the state of facts, we again ask: Is Judaism in anywise on any point, inimical to science?

And again we might go on with our questions; again we might ask of the thinking and unprejudiced world to answer these questions, and confidently we might await the answers. We will not deny, my friends, that there are many individual Jews illiberal in their views, queer in their notions, narrow-minded and narrow-hearted. We will not deny that some of our fellow-Israelites entertain ideas and lead a life not at all becoming an Israelite, who, as a member of the "chosen people," ought to feel doubly obliged to shun darkness and to walk in the light. We will not deny even, that, in days past and days present, untenable ideas found expression by some Jewish authors of high repute. But the fact is not to be lost sight of that all these things are totally unessential in Judaism. Cast them off, ye my fellow-Israelites, and you still remain Jews. Cast off whatever is irrational, whatever is in conflict with the demands of sound modern culture and civilization, whatever is obsolete and antiquated, and Judaism remains; it remains as long as it maintains its opposition to every kind of heathenism, as long as it holds fast to the sole, living God, and as long as it acknowledges the obligatory character of the moral laws.

Where else do you find such a power to eternally rejuvenate itself? Ask any earnest and sincere Christian theologian, and if you do not know it, you will then learn it, that as soon as the doctrine of the trinity, of the atoning power of the death of Christ, of the deification of the same, of the original sin, etc., are done away with, Christianity ceases to be. You might—so this knowing Christian will inform you—*call* what remains Christianity, by politeness, or by thoughtlessness; people who do not adhere any more to these peculiar articles of creed may, perhaps, honestly delude themselves into still *claiming* to be Christians; but they are such only in name and not in reality.

Now look how the world stands on these questions. Of nominal Christians there are thousands who in reality are not Christians. Jewish ideas, liberal ideas prevail among them. Those un-Jewish ideas are daily losing ground in the midst of the educated classes, while the rational and Jewish elements in our great sister-Church make rapid and triumphant progress.

But now comes our liberal friend, and says: "Why do you designate the liberal views we entertain as Jewish? You assume too much."

My friends—so we answer—in arts and sciences the Occidental world has its teachers and models, not among the Israelites, but among the so-called classical nations of antiquity In religion proper, however, Judaism is the ground whence the truth came to the Western nations. You can not trace your religious views to the Hindoos or to the Chinese. Even if you find among them sublime doctrines similar to those you and I believe in, you must confess that the teachings of the Hindoos and the Chinese did not have the least influence upon the formation and development of the Western mind. Judaism did. And as well as we can, on the hand of history, follow the stream of our mental philosophy back to Aristotle and Plato, and the stream of our jurisprudence back to Rome and Byzanz, so we are led back to Sinai and Judea if we start from the present state of the ruling religious ideas, and follow the thread of their historical development back to their origin.

The spiritual world is not yet fully conquered. Not yet is heathenism fully overthrown. Nations are not born in one day, and such gigantic labors are not accomplished in one short period of time. But much *is* already accomplished, great victories *are* already won. We have no childish pride in names. We do not complain when the people hesitate in accepting the *name* of Jews, and we are fully satisfied with the fact, and glory in it, that Judaism in its essence—one God, one mankind—is daily, more and more, acknowledged and accepted. May we not hope, however, that honest people will ere long honor the truth, and will, individually and collectively, declare: We are no Christians—we even disclaim the name of such? And who knows whether the reformator is not born already, who, like Luther in the sixteenth century, will stand up boldly, fearlessly, and true to his innermost convictions, and to the dictates of his conscience, and who, full of zeal and enthusiasm, will call up the people and say: "As three hundred years ago it was time to renounce popery and Roman Catholicism, so it is now the time to renounce the deification of a man and all the ideas connected therewith—to renounce Christianity. And as Luther and his contemporaries returned, or intended to return, to the Christianity of the first century, so it is time for us to return to the spirit of the prophets of Israel." Who knows whether some of us may not live to see the great religious revolution? When the same will take place—and many signs of the times point to the event coming that casts its shadows beforehand—then it will be obvious, even for dim eyes, that Judaism *is* a power in the world.

Dear brethren, to our patriarchs already it has been promised, By you and your seed all the nations of the earth shall be blessed. This promise the God in history fulfills. He caused Israel to be dispersed all over the world, in order, as the Talmud says, to bring over proselytes to Judaism. Happy in the consciousness of their high mission, Israelites dwell now in all parts of the inhabited globe, living witnesses of Him, the Holy One of Israel, who said, through the mouth of His prophet: "I, even I, am the Lord, and besides me there is no savior." Let us thank our Heavenly Father that he has chosen Israel from among the nations and has entrusted it with such an exalted mission. Let us thank Him for our dispersion. Let us remain faithful and true to our mission. Let us never forget to be a witness of Him, the Holy One, the God of the Universe, by walking in His ways. His name be praised forever and ever. Amen.

THE OFFERING OF ISAAC.

BY REV. DR. MAX LANDSBERG,
(Of Rochester, N. Y.)

Text:—Gen. xxii. 1-13.

If I should be asked to give a short and concise explanation of the time of the Messiah or the so-called kingdom of God, of the most blessed aim and end of the human race toward which we are striving, I would answer thus: At that time all men will unanimously recognize as the word of God the supremacy of the moral law, which forms the foundation of all social progress, and of all institutions that constitute the stronghold of society, and there will be no discord, no dissension regarding the means by which that noble aim is to be reached. I do not pretend to believe that there will ever be a time when all men will give expression to their religious sensations by the same forms and ceremonies; I do not pretend to hope that all men will profess the same doctrines of belief and belong to the same religious denomination, but it is my firm and unshaken conviction that a period will come when the final aim will alone be considered as essential; when all men will consciously and conscientiously strive toward righteousness, while acknowledging that numerous different roads may lead to the same goal, and, therefore, not presuming that theirs must of necessity be the shortest and easiest path, but merely the one which seems preferable to themselves.

To teach this truth, to make mankind aware of this dispensation is the loftiest end and aim of the spiritual labor of man, the most fragrant blossom, the sweetest fruit on the tree of Judaism, of all true religion.

Oh, that we were able to see ourselves with the same eyes as others see us; oh, that man could gain that fairness of judgment, that clearness of thinking, which induced him to put his own doctrines, his own ideas, his own peculiarities into the same crucible, to submit them to the same test of logical evidence, wherewith he is at all times ready to approach the religious belief, the superstition, the distinctive characteristics of his fellow-men!

How many centuries, yea, thousands of years, has it taken to teach mankind in the most civilized countries of our globe, to teach those nations who are boasting of their high culture, the lesson of toleration! How difficult has it been to break the soil of the hearts and prepare it for the truth that no State or government has a right to force its citizens to belong to any established church and support the same, but that every man is allowed his own religious opinion and worship, when contrary to or different from those of the established belief! And how crude and unsatisfactory seems such privilege to every one who has an understanding of the full scope of freedom and liberality! For what is toleration, but the allowance of what is by no means wholly approved? If the necessary power would exist, differing opinions would be suppressed, their utterance prohibited, their promulgation checked, their professors persecuted. Thus toleration is simply the consequence of a lack of power, while true liberality toward which we strive, which we consider to be the final aim of religion, does not only tolerate, but gives the benefit of the doubt, openly avows that others, though differing with us, may be right so long as they remain within the boundaries of morality and respect the fundamental laws of society on which all well-meaning men agree, and by which a protecting wall is erected around life and property, the safety of the State and the individual, the purity of the family and the virtue of the community.

But in order to contribute toward reaching such a

desirable aim, we must not be fearful, we must not shrink from looking the truth straight in the face, we must without winking accept it with all its consequences, and have the moral courage of investigating our own belief with the same impartiality and freedom of prejudice with which we adjudicate upon that of others. How seldom is such clear judgment used by us; how rarely do we abide by the old rule אל תהי דן את חברך עד שתגיע למקומו "You have no right to judge over your neighbor except you have put yourselves in his place!" How often do we laugh at the credulity, at the folly of our fellow-men? How often do we look down with sadness, yea, with horror, upon what we call their narrow-mindedness and their superstitions—altogether forgetful that in their eyes we may appear as foolish and senseless as they do to us, that the doctrines and practices which arouse our indignation and horror, which make our hair stand on end, may be nothing but the extreme logical consequences of what we ourselves consider as truth, proclaim as a doctrine of faith, worship as the word, as the very utterance from the mouth of God!

We are horrified when we read how the most various nations of antiquity practiced the dastardly rite of sacrificing human beings, and especially children, in honor of the deities. We are ready to join with our old prophets in the most ringing denunciations of abominations practiced at the statue of the Phœnician god, Moloch. We can hardly believe that among the Greeks, King Agamemnon could be persuaded to sacrifice his virgin daughter, Iphigenia, to the goddess Diana, and that up to a very late time men were sacrificed by the most prominent and highly-educated individuals, as by Julius Cæsar at a sedition of his soldiers, by Augustus, after the victory over Mark Antony, and by other Roman emperors as late as to the fourth century of the present era; and when in our own days, in one of the most enlightened States of our Union, a father* and mother deliberately take their sweet little

---

* Freeman, at Pocasset, Massachusetts, in April, 1879.

four-year-old girl, slaughter her with a large carving knife, as "an odor of sweet smell, a sacrifice acceptable to God," and far from regretting the bloody deed, claim that they would do it over again and meet with the approval of their co-religionists—we are very ready to attribute the horrible action to religious madness without looking for any further explanation—while most assuredly it is nothing but the logical consequence of the manner in which Bible stories are considered by the overwhelming majority of people in our country.

Freeman was sure, he says, that in the decisive moment God would stay his arm, and by a visible or audible token, show that, as in the case of Abraham, he was satisfied with the will instead of the deed. But since such a sign was not given to him, he was convinced that he had done nothing but execute the will of God. But, my friends, where is the difference between the intended deed of Abraham and that of the child-murderer? True, it is said, seemingly the cases are equal, but in reality the story of Abraham's intended sacrifice of his son, is misunderstood (of course, we say the same, and shall explain our view further on), but how misunderstood, so long as the words of the Bible are claimed to be inspired by supernatural revelation, as long as the word "God spoke to so and so," is taken literally! Many try to explain away the difficulty thus: "God never commanded Abraham to literally slay his son. That Abraham so understood him is true, but he misunderstood him, and we have in the opening verses of chapter xxii. of Genesis not what God really required, but Abraham's misunderstanding of God's requirement, according to the standpoint of his heathenish notions of sacrifice." But is this a satisfactory explanation, does it alter one iota of the similarity between Abraham and any one who would to-day attempt to imitate him? The only difference is that Abraham was fortunate enough to hear the voice of God: "Do not kill your son, I am satisfied with your good will." Is it not at least a very dangerous thing about the voice of God, if it is capable of so being misconstrued? And would such an error be punishable? Would you punish your child if from a plain misunderstanding of your words, which have been framed in such a shape as to allow the child's interpretation, it had done wrong, even committed what otherwise would be branded as a crime? Where is the culpability of a man who misunderstood the command of God in the same manner as Abraham? And why should he not misunderstand it in spite of the most ingenious interpretations? Does not the story end: "And the angel of God called to Abraham a second time and said, By myself I swear, says the Lord, indeed because thou hast done this thing, and hast not withheld thy son, thy only one. Indeed I shall bless thee abundantly and shall multiply thy seed exceedingly, as the stars of heaven, and as the sand which is upon the sea shore, since thou hast obeyed my voice!" And is not Abraham praised rather for his willingness to give up his son than for his obedience to the second call, that he should spare him? And has not the readiness of Abraham to sacrifice his son, always been considered as the greatest deed of faith committed by man, the most striking proof of his piety? And did it not become the basis on which the Israelites founded their claims of election among the nations, and in later times the hopes of atonement of their sins? Read the traditional prayers for the New Year's day and the Day of Atonement still in use among the overwhelming majority of the Jews and you find them crowded to overflowing with reminiscences of the "Akeda," the sacrifice of Isaac. God is urged not to forget it, but let all the descendants of Abraham and Isaac reap the fruit of this highest זכות אבות of the merit of Abraham, which consisted in his readiness to offer his son on the altar?

Can we, therefore, be satisfied with the explanation that Abraham was commanded by God, but misunderstood his words? Is not then every man, are not we ourselves, exposed to such frightful misunderstanding? No, my friends, there is only one cure for such evil, and a radical cure. It is not sufficient, as it used to be the custom, to interpret into the words of the Bible that which happens to be convenient, but it is a necessity, an irrepressible duty, over against all opposition, without any consideration of those who are afraid religion will be lost if the Bible is not regarded as a supernatural book—to be firm in our conviction, to declare openly over and over again and to implant the knowledge into the hearts of our children—that there is only one manner in which God speaks to man—through his own spirit—that there is only *one* revelation, that the voice of God can not be misunderstood, for it makes itself manifest to us in the revelations of science and nature; it is subject to the laws of morality and controlled by the rules of logical thinking, and it is growing, like everything else, a natural growth, it is undergoing a constitutional evolution, a never-ceasing development.

We know that human sacrifices were practiced among the Jews up to the Babylonian captivity, we are told in the Bible itself that David offered them, that Solomon built a temple to Moloch and that this worship was most of the time the established State religion in Judah, and that not more than sixty years before Jerusalem's first destruction, King Manasseh offered his son to Moloch. These circumstances alone would prove that the story of Isaac's sacrifice must have been written at a very late time, and indeed all indications point toward the conclusion that—in its present form—it was not written before the eighth century by prophets who, like Micah, have proclaimed such words as: " Shall I give you my first-born for my sin, my own child to obtain forgiveness? No! He has shown you, oh man, what is good, and what God requires of you. It is to do right, to hold mercy dear, and to walk humbly with thy God." Then the biblical author, not minding the anachronism committed, placed at the beginning of Israel's history an event which expresses the spirit of his own time. The prophets of that age were fighting single-handed the great struggle against the idolatry of the court and the nation; they branded with their fiery eloquence as the worst crime what was then considered as worship of the Deity; they dared to give utterance to their opinions before a populace who were assured that their good fortune had left them since they had ceased praying and sacrificing to Moloch and the Queen of the Heavens. It was by men of such stamp that the old tradition of Isaac's sacrifice was used and transformed in the sense of their own advanced religious ideas, to teach the people that Abraham had allowed his sound reason to interfere with the voice of his heart, which was that of heathen superstition, and to make their contemporaries understand that not even the most devoted allegiance to God and the deepest piety require or justify human sacrifices, that God is satisfied with the heart of those who worship him and that he crowns with a splendid reward those who by their shining example crush superstition and dare to have the courage of an independent opinion.

Such ideas would be expressed to-day and made accessible to the people by writing a book on ethics and morals; but in the childhood of the literature of all nations nothing was written and appreciated but poetry. The history related in the Bible is clothed in a poetical garment, it is to a great extent resting upon a historical basis, while a great deal of it is mere fiction, elaborated to convey certain moral ideas. God has never spoken to men in any other manner than he does to-day; God's revelation was not a whit more supernatural two or four thousand years ago than it is at our own time; God's voice is heard in thunder and lightning to-day as it was on Sinai and was then not otherwise than it is now. The laws of nature have never been disturbed nor perverted; they have changed as little as God has himself. All that has changed is man; from a state of childhood, when he was pleased with fables and stories of supernatural miracles, he has developed into an adult man, who wants facts, knows or commences to be aware of his mental capacities, looks forward for ever greater development and improvement, and turns backward only to regard with the highest interest the evolution of the religious idea and of civilization, from the crudest beginnings of antiquity to our own time. This development of a thousand years in the life and history of our forefathers is preserved to us in the number of fragments and remnants from their ancient literature, which constitute "The Book" or "Bible." It is holy to us as an old inheritance from our ancestors; it is sacred to us as the fountain from which our religious truth and civilization have grown, as the ancient records of the history of our fathers; it is dear to us because it is stained with the lifeblood of millions of our people, who have clung to it amidst terrible persecutions when exposed to the most cruel fanaticism, and have by its inspiration become the bannerbearers of freedom and liberality; but our eyes are not blind to prevent us from recognizing its true value, to make us over-estimate it and consider all its contents, without discrimination, as a rule of life and a guide of our conduct.

Let us fearlessly proclaim this truth, let us make our voice heard wherever it will penetrate, and we shall fulfill Israel's mission, to bless mankind with enlightenment and teach all the families of the earth the true and pure word of God Amen.

MOSES SPAKE TRULY.

A SERMON.

BY REV. PROF. ABRAHAM DE SOLA, LL. D.,

(Minister of the Portuguese Congregation, Montreal.)

BRETHREN:—In the 6th chapter of Exodus, at the 9th verse, we read these words:

וידבר משה כן אל בני ישראל ולא שמעו אל משה מקצר רוח ומעבדה קשה:

"Moses spake so unto the children of Israel, but they hearkened not unto Moses, from shortness of spirit and from hard bondage."

I have translated the text according to its plain, literal meaning. Doubtless the words "Moses spake so unto the children of Israel," refer to the all-gracious and all-assuring message which God had directed him to deliver to them, and which is contained in the seven verses immediately preceding the text just read. This message, in the first place, consisted of a revelation by God to Israel of the ineffable name "*Adonai*," GOD-ETERNAL, in addition to the name "*El Shaddai*," GOD-ALL-SUFFICIENT, by which he had been known to Abraham, to Isaac, to Jacob, and to themselves, until now. The all-important message further contained God's blessed assurance that he remembered the covenant which he had made with the patriarchs, that he had heard the groaning of their enslaved and oppressed children, and that he would now miraculously deliver them from the galling yoke of their heartless taskmasters and lead them from Egypt to Canaan, and there become their God. The actual delivery of this message is, therefore, evidently referred to when the text tells us, "Moses spake so to the children of Israel." But notwithstanding this, and notwithstanding the safe principle laid down by our ancient teachers* to prefer a literal to a figurative exposition when possible, let us now, by a slight alteration of the generally received rendering of the text, endeavor to show that from words which certainly present nothing more than a mere historical statement, important ethical truths and valuable religious doctrines may be elicited. Let us see how the words of the text may be, and are, as applicable to the state of the children of Israel to-day, as of yore; let us see that we may even now obtain from them spiritual edification and profit. To this end let us proceed to consider two main questions which the text seems, evidently, to suggest:

I. How has Moses spoken to the children of Israel? and
II. Why have not the children of Israel hearkened unto Moses?

And may the Source of all wisdom and truth be with us and guide us in this hour of meditation and devotion. Amen.

I.

How has Moses spoken to the children of Israel? The text says that "he spoke *so*," in the original, כן "*ken;*" but this Hebrew word has other meanings. Primarily, it signifies a stand, or base, something standing upright and straight; but it has a secondary or figurative sense, conveying the abstract ideas of truth, faithfulness, honesty, uprightness and other kindred virtues, and then it becomes synonymous with נכון "*Nachon,*" proper, and is used as a neuter noun, an adjective, or an adverb. In Genesis xlii. 11, Joseph's brethren assure him they are "*Kaynim,*" true men. Joseph uses the word in the same sense at the 19th verse, and so it is employed in the 31st, 33d and 34th verses. In Exodus x. 29, Moses

---

* אין מקרא יוצא מידי פשוטו.

says to Pharoah: "Thou has spoken '*ken*,' well, truly." In Numbers xxvii. 7, we read: "The daughters of Zelophehad speak '*ken*,' rightly," and at the 35th chapter, 5th verse, we find, "The tribe of the sons of Joseph hath said '*ken*,' well." The word has the same meaning in post-pentateuchal writings. In Joshua ii. 4, are the words, "The men '*ken*' truly, or really, did come unto me;" and in II. Kings, vii. 7, it is written "We act not '*ken*,' rightly or honestly." And now, brethren, without departing entirely from a grammatical or literal rendering of the text, we have a reply to the first question which it suggests to us, and that reply is, "Moses spake TRULY unto the children of Israel." Yes, he spake truly, as became him who is described in the Yigdal-Hymn as נאמן ביתו "the faithful one of his house." Yes, he spake truly, for if the voice and writing were his, the inspiration, the words, were not his, but God's. And thus it is, O children of Israel! that when you entered on the blessed and blessing heritage which is yours, תורה צוה לנו משה "the Law which Moses commanded us," you became possessors of truths unspeakably valuable, of privileges great above all estimate. Yes, Moses has spoken truly to us, because he has imparted to us the greatest of fundamental truths, the only true knowledge we can possess of man's origin and of his vocation here—aye, and of the origin of all creatures and all things also. But, methinks, you would ask, is this indeed so? Do not the teachings of modern science conflict with those of Moses when he refers to physical facts, and is not this conflict more especially apparent in his statements respecting such subjects as the origin of the world and of man? Unhesitatingly, but not without having long considered the question, I answer, No! most emphatically, No! Certainly there has been a seeming conflict between the teachings of Moses and those of scientists in the past, but as the science of the earlier times to which I refer, has developed and advanced, its seeming contradiction with the biblical record has ceased to exist. In our own day, as new utterances and theories of scientists are put forth, new contradictions seem to exist between the teachings of

Moses and of science in the minds of some men, worthy and able men even—but only to exist until the Holy Book, in accordance with the requirements of the Talmudic sages* be subjected to a more strict and scientific exegesis than is generally given to it; only until the language and archæology of the Bible be better studied; only until science, modifying, altering and discarding its present teachings, according to its wont, shall become yet more fully advanced and developed. This must be so from the very nature of things, from the experience of the past, from the testimony of history which has clearly taught us the irrefragable truth that while human science has been constantly changing its utterances and shifting its ground, "the word of the Lord abideth alway," ועד דר ודר אמונתו " and his truth throughout all generations."

Now, if this be the experience we have already had of the character of the biblical and scientific records, of the divine word and the human word, the speaking of Moses and the teachings of those who proved themselves false prophets and teachers of error, it is all important to our present inquiry that we should lay down certain principles which will always enable us to judge whether Moses has spoken truly to us, should our minds become disturbed by the constantly recurring novelties and skepticisms of modern scientists. My friends, I have always objected to discuss in this holy place the platitudes of human wisdom, when we could so much more profitably occupy ourselves with the precious teachings of the divine word, or to ask your attention to the commonplaces of secular literature, when we have the sublimities of revelation before us. But, to-day, brethren, with the object of exhibiting the principles just referred to, I will depart from my usual course, to notice, in exemplification, one of the most recent creations of modern thought, known as the doctrine of Evolution or development. I do this, also, because I happen to know that the confidence with which it has

---

* הפוך בה והפוך בה דכולא בה.

been urged by some, has caused perplexity and pain to many pious persons around us, though, thank God, not among us.

First, then, my hearers, it is an admitted principle in *mental* science, it is a law in logic, that if either or both the premises of a syllogism, or an argument put in its regular logical form, be insufficient, or invalid, the conclusion drawn from such premises will also be insufficient and invalid, and must, then, be regarded as a mere fallacy; also, that a fallacious argument—that is, an apparent argument—is, in reality, none. Next, it is an admitted principle in *physical* science that only that is pure science or science proper which deals with facts and the deductions made from them by the strict laws of reasoning just mentioned. Now, judged by these standards, the evolution doctrine has no claim to the title of science; it can not, logically, ascend to the dignity of scientific truth, but must needs remain at the low level occupied by theory, aye, by exploded theories, too. It is not I who tell you this; it is not the mere theologian who declares this to you; but it is the true scientists themselves. It is the *practical* men of science, men famed for their original investigations in geology and physical science, who show you that those who maintain there is no need for an Almighty Creator of the Universe, of whom Moses speaks, but that inanimate matter could in the process of time be developed out of nothing, and, afterward, that living creatures could be developed out of dead matter, can not point to a single fact from which to draw their deductions; hence, they are merely theorists, speculators, not scientists. Their premises are insufficient and false, and their deductions are, therefore, also insufficient and false. And while it is not wonderful that men should be found speculating about things that are past their comprehension, as science always leads back to the things we can not comprehend, it is criminal to confound mere speculation with the deductions of science; and this is what the supporters of the development theory are doing, as they can not point to a single fact that goes to prove the truth of their pet theory. And although it has been a question with the learned in all ages whether a living thing can be produced out of those that are dead, there has not been found a single instance where a living thing has been produced without a previous living thing, nor have we any knowledge of separate species of animals being produced from other species; and to state that such may be done, is mere speculation, which must not be mixed up with the ascertained results of science.* We may be satisfied, then, that Moses spake truly to us when he taught us that "in the beginning God created the heavens and the earth," that great truth that forms the basis of Judaism, the existence of a personal God, who produced matter from nothing, who is, therefore, prior to matter, and was never dependent upon matter for his existence. These truths, taught us in the very first paragraph of the writings of Moses, are not accidentally or unintentionally told us, but with the design of confuting the errors of the existing cosmogonies taught by his contemporaries and predecessors. Therefore speaks Moses truly, also, when he teaches that God is "*El Shaddai*," THE ALL-SUFFICIENT AND ALMIGHTY GOD, the only power able to produce something from nothing המצא היש מאין Therefore speaks Moses truly, also, when he teaches us that this being, "*El Shaddai*," is also *Adonai*, THE ETERNAL,— eternal in his power; eternal in all his attributes; and that he must be, therefore, the sole object of man's worship forever. Therefore speaks Moses truly, also, when he teaches us

---

* Israelites who believe or who doubt that Moses has spoken truly on these important points, should alike refer to the able and convincing discussion of them by that distinguished scientist, Dr. J. W. Dawson, in his "Origin of the World," published in 1877, especially on pages 226 and 227, which exhibit five fatal objections to evolution as at present held. They should attentively read this book and his "Lectures on the Bible and Science." These, with his other most valuable works, to which I am only too happy to declare my indebtedness for most highly-prized instruction and edification, I would earnestly wish to see, side by side with the Bible, in every Jewish home, school and college. The style of the eminent investigator of the Laurentians and Devonians is such that his works may be perused even by the non-scientific reader with both profit and pleasure.

that this Eternal God is One, יי אחד as the unity of design and connection of plan in creation shows, even to the conviction of the most skeptical scientist.*

And, my hearers, truly speaks Moses to us when he imparts to us the knowledge of the divine attributes proclaimed when the Eternal passed before him. Brethren, bow down your heads in reverence while I repeat to you these solemn truths, as Moses spake them to the children of Israel, יי יי אל רחום וחנון ארך אפים ורב הסד ואמת נצר חסד לאלפים נשא עון ופשע וחטאה ונקה "Adonai is the immutable, eternal Being! the omnipotent God! merciful and gracious, long-suffering and abundant in beneficence and truth; showing mercy even unto the thousandth generation, forgiving iniquity, transgression and sin, and acquitting."† God is merciful and gracious, declares Moses, and therefore, as says David: "As a loving Father hath compassion on his children, so God hath compassion on those who fear him."‡ The God of whom Moses speaks does not disdain our love, our reverence, our supplications, our service; he does not spurn us from him as something too vile, too insignificant, too contemptible for notice. He delights not in the agonies of his creatures; therefore he desires not to be served with the rites of cruelty and impurity which have been used by those who have not known Moses; therefore he has not required at our hands the sacrifices of human beings. He knoweth man's frailty,§ כי הוא ידע יצרנו, as the potter knoweth the material of the vessel which he forms זכור כי עפר אנחנו therefore, as Moses speaks, he is "long-suf-

---

* Even John Stuart Mill, "who seems at one time to have taken ground against design," subsequently admitted its force, more especially as an argument of inductive value. See Dawson's "Lectures on the Bible and Science," and his recent refutation of Haeckel, in the *Princeton Review*, May, 1880.

† Exodus xxxiv. 5.

‡ Psalm ciii. 13.

§ Psalm ciii. 14.

fering, abundant in beneficence and truth," and, as Moses also shows us, only requires that we should sincerely "repent and listen to his voice," ושבת עד יי אלהיך ושמעת בקלו * Moses teaches that a sincere repentance of past transgressions and an equally sincere determination to listen and to amend in the future, are all sufficient conditions for restoration to God's favor, and that when these conditions are fulfilled, he will fully restore us to his love. And this in a direct manner, and not through the merits or mediatorship of another. No, teaches Moses, ונכרתה הנפש החוא "the sinning one shall himself be cut off,"† and again, ונשא עונו "he himself shall bear his sin."‡ Moses, therefore, speaks to us other truths of the highest importance when he teaches us that *we are responsible beings;* that our eternal destiny is consequently in our own hands; that we are placed here, merely to earn our reward in another sphere of intellectual and spiritual existence, that *the now* is when we are to labor to earn the wages paid us by a just and benevolent Master in *the hereafter.* God thus "passes by transgression" of his mere mercy and grace, so that if we be to-day impure in his sight, we may be to-morrow cleansed and purified before the Eternal; לפני ה׳ תטהרו § so that if our sins be at this moment "red as scarlet" before God, in the next they may appear to him "white as snow."‖ And this is not because there has been any change in him whom Moses teaches us is immutable, but because the change has been in ourselves; and hence, according to the consoling teaching of the synagogue, "the sincerely repentant sinner is loved and esteemed before the Creator, as if he had never sinned."¶

Thus has Moses spoken to us with reference to the being and attributes of God; and now, brethren, let me ask you,

---

* Deut. iv. 30.
† Ex. xii. 15-19, etc.
‡ Lev. v. 1.
§ Lev. xvi. 30.
‖ Isaiah i. 18.
¶ אהוב ונחמד הוא לפני הבורא כאלו לא חטא מעולם, Maimonides, "Hilchoth Teshubah, vii. 4.

is it not true that the human mind, which has sought during thousands of years to form correct ideas of the nature and attributes of deity, unaided by what Moses hath spoken, has never been able to ascend like him who spake ברוח הקדש "under the divine afflatus," to such grandeur of conception, to such sublimity of ideal? Who is he and where is he that has spoken to us on this, the highest of all themes, so truly as Moses hath spoken to us, words and teachings so true that they completely fill the soul, and thoroughly satisfy its longings for such light as it may obtain in this stage of its existence? Is it not true that the god begotten of human thought, of human science, whether it be of the philosophers, the mythologists, the pantheists of the past, or of the philosophers and pantheists of the present, is but an embodiment of weakness and insufficiency, insufficiency of intellectual as well as of physical power; the very reverse idea of EL SHADDAI; is it not an apotheosis of darkness and limitation of mind, the very reverse idea of ADONAI? And in the total absence of spirituality in such conceptions, do we not plainly perceive positive grossness? And in the fierce and senseless attacks of rampant materialism on what it can not and never will displace, do we not recognize the active and scarcely concealed desire of men to be freed from all that will check the fullest gratification of their lowest passions, from all that teaches them that they have heaven-born duties, obligations and responsibilities? to be freed from the ken and supervision of that omniscient and omnipresent Being of whom Moses speaks, from that all seeing-eye that can penetrate the innermost recesses of both matter and mind? My hearers, I leave you now to ponder these questions, but not without the fullest conviction that you will have but one all-comprehensive reply to all of them, and that this reply will be in the words of the text, וידבר משה כן אל בני ישראל "Moses has spoken TRULY to the children of Israel."

Under the divine favor, we will continue this subject at our next meeting, inquiring then whether Moses has spoken truly with reference to man's duties to man, and examining, even if briefly, the character of his ethical teachings. Till then, brethren, may God have you in his keeping; and may his spirit rest on you, so that your eyes may become opened to the wonders of his Law which Moses has so truly spoken to you. And may what has been said to-day be blessed to you all; so that it may be affirmed of you as it is written of your fathers, וייראו העם את יי ויאמינו ביי ובמשה עבדו "The people feared the Lord, and they believed in the Lord and Moses, his servant." Amen.

SPIRITUAL MANHOOD.

A SERMON.

BY REV. MAX SAMFIELD.
(Rabbi of the "Children of Israel" Congregation, Memphis, Tenn.)

במקום שאין אנשים השתדל להיות איש
"Where true men are wanting, strive thou to be a man."—PIRKE ABOTH, ii. 6.

The age in which Rabbi Hillel lived was one of agitation and commotion. The Jewish commonwealth had been broken into factions, each of which proclaimed religious and political doctrines of a different character. The royalistic party, attached to the house of Herod, stood on one side, demanding the subjection of religion to temporal policy and sensual enjoyment: the Sadducees on the other, insisting upon the absolute authority of the law, and on a literal compliance with the same. On either side were ranged thousands, representing as many shades of opinion, and often breaking out into open hostilities against each other. Between these, in all the beauty of manliness and firmness of character, stands Hillel, the noble Pharisee, the liberal-minded rabbi, like a rock in the midst of the tempest; and, unmoved by passion, untouched by partisan influence, there fall from his lips the golden words of wisdom, proclaiming the precious maxim of ethical discipline: "Where true men are wanting, strive thou to be a man."

He looks back of all those sectional doctrines, of all those transient phases of Judaism, to search for a fulcrum whereupon he could stand, to judge impartially, to be free from external influences, and yet to guard successfully the treasure of Judaism against loss and decay. And Hillel finds that fulcrum in a pure and undefiled manhood, in the manliness and dignity of a human character, which alone can attain that discipline of the human mind, to see things as they are and not what they seem to be. He places the reasoning mind above individual opinions, local and temporal conditions; he recognizes no authority but that which is based upon the demands of the human heart and human mind. Thus he comes in conflict with the school of Shammai; thus he allows practices which had previously been prohibited; thus he annuls ordinances which had heretofore been rigidly enforced. His wisdom shed new glory upon the house of Israel, and evolving from the manhood of religion which he taught his disciples and colleagues, we behold a new life springing up in Judaism, penetrating the homes and hearts of the Jewish people. Hillel's originality and independence of mind are the best proofs of his manliness.

His mental and moral faculties ripen under the influence of self-discipline and self-control, and convert the elements of human *nature* into a perfect organization of human *character*. Shammai is stubborn, Hillel is firm; Shammai is a negative religious zealot, Hillel a liberal teacher of a positive religion. And as Hillel's character was the best exemplification of his ethical proverb, so is the character of any man who acts upon it and abides by its moral standard. He who understands how to be a man among those who are unsettled in their opinions and vague in their ideas, who loses not the equilibrium of his mind amidst the diversity and variety of individual volition, is truly the masterpiece of God's creation, and worthy of the patent of nobility which the Deity has betsowed upon the mortal in the glorious title—*Man.* Neither sentimentality nor skepticism, neither materialism nor mysticism, can rule his emotions and govern his will. He takes counsel with his own soul; he reads, hears and investigates; but no other test than that of truth is applied to knowledge thus acquired.

Mind and heart sit together in judgment, and to their joint verdict he submits the important questions of the times. In matters of religion and religious reform this great quality of human character is a most important element. Leaving this element out in the evolution of the religious sentiment and in the development of any positive religion, progress and reform would be almost impossible. Whoever kindled the fire of holiness upon the altar of religion had first to strive to be a man; that is, to learn self-government and self-denial, to obtain all those virtues which give him a right to bear this most honorary title. Whoever undertook the solemn task of proclaiming freedom to the oppressed, light to those in darkness and redemption to those in bondage, had first of all to be a man in all the nobility of character and sentiment; he had to stand upon that elevation to which he intended to lift his unfortunate fellow-men. Behold our immortal teacher, the standard-bearer of moral ethics! What is the basis of his illustrious fame? What is the fundamental principle of his character? Why does he stand so far above the legislators of the ancient and modern world, to conceive ideas so grand and noble, written with letters of gold upon the magna charta of humanity? Ah, my friends, במקום שאין אנשים השתדל להיות איש. When his brethren were yet under the ban of oppression—when they were not freemen to think for themselves—he strove to be a *man*.

Scripture relates that Moses, when he went out to his brethren, witnessed the scene of an Egyptian beating an Israelite, which occurrence is recorded in the following language: ויפן כה וכה וירא כי אין איש "He turned in every direction, and he saw there was no man." An ancient Midrash, commenting upon this passage, says: Moses turned around to see whether men could be found in Israel who, like him, would have the manhood to stand up for a persecuted race, to defend the weak and maintain the principles of freedom and justice. But there was none to cheer him in the heroic task of redemption; none to unite with him in the solemn protest against tyranny and despotism. But in *his* soul the religion of manhood had already taken deep root, and *because* others were wanting to feel and comprehend the duties of the hour, he imposed the gigantic work upon himself. Turning a deaf ear to the soul-degrading teachings of the priests, he listened to the voice of reason and humanity, teaching him a better conception of godliness and virtue, of God and man, and he hesitated not to obey this great call. Renouncing all the sensual pleasures which Pharaoh's court offered him, resigning the royal honors and privileges which he enjoyed as a prince, he became rather a wanderer in the desert than a deserter from duty; and there, in solemn communion with his God, he decided to go forth as a man, as the leader of his people, to demand of the tyrannical Pharaoh, in the name of God, in the name of all that is right and true. that the slavery and oppression of his people should cease, that the native manhood of their souls should not be destroyed beneath the excessive burden of labor and sorrow. It was this manliness, fidelity and firmness of Moses which made him a fit instrument in the hands of Divine Providence to build the grand structure of Judaism and frame its laws and statutes. Because of the manhood of the religious sentiment in him, he could give to the Israelites a code of ethics which endowed them with such moral strength, and which richly deserves the title, Religion of Manhood. The highest encomium of praise which, therefore, the Bible bestows upon Moses is expressed in the significant words: והאיש משה "The MAN Moses." No high-sounding and pompous titles, as they are found in the religious books of ancient Egypt, or exhibited so conspicuously by our modern religious teachers, are bestowed upon Moses; the title of true manhood is nobler and greater than any title human invention could suggest.

And this spirit of manliness impressed itself upon ancient Israel and upon Judaism; its traces are visible in the character and practices of the Jewish people. There is no doubt that the religious precepts and ordinances of Judaism were mostly intrusted and recommended to the care and activity of men in order that the religious sentiment may partake of the vigor and energy of masculine discipline, and thus resist and survive the most adverse conditions. Objectively considered, these measures were not to serve as a disfranchisement of the women of Israel, but as means to endow Judaism with manly fortitude and lasting vitality; and history testifies to the efficacy of this educational principle. The fidelity of Israel to his God and his holy mission, the tenacity and perseverance which our people manifested in the midst of the dark and gloomy days of religious persecution, testify to the magnitude of that divine energy, begotten by manliness. The nations of the earth, however, never called this prominent virtue by the right name; they never called it the great principle of human dignity, " the constancy and firmness of the religious sentiment." They never accorded to Judaism the noble title, " Religion of Manhood." The contemporaries of Israel of the past called it obstinacy, stubborness and infidelity. The age in which they lived hurled curses upon them, denounced them as heretics, persecuted them and burned them because they would not bow down to the gods of the multitude, because they would not embrace the theology of the masses. Even to this very day the Israelite is frequently charged with obstinacy and infatuation, because he has the manhood to cling to the religion of reason and love, and thinks he serves God best by having the highest conception of him, and by discharging his duty toward his fellow-men in the spirit of integrity, manliness and fidelity. And yet that very religion of manhood which Israel so firmly maintained, and which they infused into every fibre of their being, was the great omnipotent power that upheld them in their fidelity to their God and their conscience; it was the strong armor of self-reliance and faithfulness, these principles of religious manhood, which ripened them into thinking men, which made them useful men, with minds full of intelligence and hearts full of charity and love. When other men hardly dared to think for themselves, when priestcraft and ignorance had smothered the noblest impulses and feelings of the human heart במקום שאין אנשים in places, where true men were wanting, the Israelite put forth his mental activity, his moral discipline, and tried to be a man in the highest sense of the word.

Even so, brethren, should the ethical precept of Hillel be embraced in our line of conduct at the present time. To-day the religious life in Israel is in a transitory state, and the religious sentiment in general is subjected to great changes; the intensity of the old spirit is broken before the spirit of the age. There is a confusion of ideas, a shifting of opinions on religion which bewilders the mind, especially that of the young. There is conflict of opinion and conviction, producing conflict of action, and every hour brings forth a new revelation of philosophy, around which new disciples gather. Some expound the principles of availability and utility, and argue that all religious questions in Israel should be settled by that standard. Others advocate that the binding force of authority should yet be recognized in the religious life of Israel. And then steps forth the sensualist, and, like the Epicuros of Hillel's time, desires religion and religious duty to be stricken out of the book of life as impediments to sensual indulgence; without a blush he proclaims as his doctrine: אכול ושתו כי מחר נמות "Let us eat and drink, for to-morrow we must die" (Isaiah xxii. 13). And the materialists, worshiping matter and denying God, with terrible indifference endeavors to make propaganda for his cheerless philosophy that there is no conscience, no moral responsibility, no higher law and no higher duty, that all is matter, and that the best thing man can do is to die and go down into the Nirwana of entire annihilation. Many superficial minds have lost the exercise of their mental faculties, and are swayed to and fro by this tempest of modern belief and unbelief, renouncing to-morrow what they believed to-day, and finally choosing the indolence of negative thinking and negative living. But we Israelites should not follow their example; *we* must not shirk the solemn duty of a deeper reasoning and of a more deliberate judgment, במקום שאין אנשים *because* true men are wanting, who will patiently and conscientiously judge the merits and efficacy of religion, who would solemnly deliberate before they abandon the higher spheres of a spiritual life. It is our duty, as sons of the Most High, to be men, men who are faithful to their conscience and mindful of the higher destiny of human life. It is true, in an age like ours, it requires much of self-denial, much of independence of mind, to rise above the multitudes, and to resist the strong current of popular philosophy; but the very language of our text indicates the strength that is required for the struggle in behalf of the good, noble and true.

השתדל, a word of Aramaic origin, means to make the most earnest and most strenuous efforts to put forth all energies and to unite them for one solemn purpose—to conquer at last. Thus, only he has reached the height of a spiritual manhood who dedicated every faculty of his heart and brain to the higher objects of life, and who never suffered one particle of religious sentiment to be lost on account of the materialistic and utilitarian tendencies of the age. Give me *men*, true men, who are willing to test the efficacy of our heaven-born faith, and I fear not to meet any issue of our time, any religious question of the present day.

As long as there are Israelites who, endowed with the spirit of manhood, are willing to exercise the faculties of heart and mind in behalf of their religion—as long as they believe in the dignity of human character and the exaltation of virtue—Judaism will live, no matter what outward changes it is compelled to undergo. It is Pessimism only, the surrender of the good and noble, the negation of beauty and happiness, which kills the spirit in man and frustrates the divine purpose of a rational religion. The religious teacher in Israel especially should remember this, and not give up his faith in human nature and in the efficacy of the religious sentiment. No system of speculative philosophy must tempt him; no literature must be absorbed by his mind, to hold exclusive sway over his judgment, or else he will be shifting to and fro like a ship without a compass. He must not be a Pessimist to-day because he read Schoppenhauer's works or the "Bechinath Olom" of Bechayah yesterday; he must not preach utilitarianism on the Sabbath because he read John Stuart Mill's "Essays" on Friday eve. The demands of the human heart and soul must be his compass to guide him upon the ocean of thought. These will always remain the same in men; books, however, are fallible, and philosophers err. No matter how many go astray in the bewildering paths of negative speculations, the religious teacher in Israel should stand firm and immovable upon the positive principle of Judaism: במקום שאין אנשים השתדל להיות איש Because men are losing their independence of thought in matters pertaining to religion, because congregations are sometimes made up of indifferent and negative people, it is his duty to maintain his manliness, his fidelity and constancy, to appeal to the mind and heart with equal force, so as to call out the whole divine energy of the people.

To you, my sisters, the maxim of Hillel also recommends itself for consideration. You must not think that, because I spoke of manhood, manliness and manly energy, this is a sermon to men exclusively. By no means; whenever the religious culture of Israel is under discussion, it is of deep concern to the WOMEN of Israel. Aye, they are even more active, more co-operative in the cause of religion; they are more susceptible to the benign influences of religious education than men. The overwise sages of our time desire to ascribe this to the weakness of feminine character, but they fail in their effort. On the contrary, it gives evidence of the wealth of sentiment, of the depth of feeling, and of moral strength as it is in woman. A religious woman is by far stronger than an irreligious man. To be truly religious requires, above all, self-denial, moral discipline and unselfish love, and who is stronger in these than a mother, a wife? Truly there is spiritual *manhood* in *woman*, and it often built up religion where the faithlessness and indifference of men had laid it waste. Therefore, my sister, if father, husband, son and brother lack the true spirit to lift on high the standard of religion, do thou plead in behalf of the noble and the good; hesitate not to put forth all the energies of heart and mind and to dedicate them to the highest ideal of moral perfection.

Where *men* are wanting to devote themselves to the culture and elevation of human character, where they cast off the higher conception of human life for lower propensities, strive thou to manifest manliness of conviction and the moral strength of character, and men will appear as weak and frail when compared with the inspired and devoted women of Israel. It will demonstrate that religious discipline and moral culture give life and strength to the mind and heart, and not the brutal force of physical power. Such a religious manhood once recognized, will dispel all Pessimistic views about the use of religion and the future of Judaism. This once acknowledged, every Israelite would be ashamed to shirk his duty or to be classed with the negative know-nothing and do-nothing party in Judaism. Every Jewish heart would be filled with the glorious promise of a better future, for, in the effort to learn how to become true men, we have already learned how to become faithful and enlightened Israelites; the spirit of confidence would inspire us to trust in the development and progress of our religion as the mariner trusts in the ship that carries him beyond the ocean. If we are true men, we will rest secure that Judaism will fulfill the mission assigned to it here on earth; if we are true men, we will not despair in the efficacy of our religion nor give up our faith in human nature. Judaism possesses a divine energy; with that, it will stand; without it, it would cease to exist, be it linked to the earth with a thousand chains. Therefore, brethren, be men who stand firm amidst all conflicting opinions, ideas and theories of our time—men who would, at least, not sacrifice eternal principles to temporal policy, to availability and convenience, but who, clothed in the radiant glory of a spiritual manhood, cling to Judaism, to their God, and all that is noble and good in fidelity and truth. Amen.

THE IMMORTALITY OF THE SOUL.

BY REV. JAMES K. GUTHEIM.

The immortality of the soul, the belief in the continued spiritual existence of man after death, is one of the cardinal doctrines, a dogma of Judaism. The belief in immortality is inseparable from the belief in God, and hence we find that throughout our religious records, from the very chapter on the creation of man, this doctrine is either implied or distinctly expressed. It is a product grown and nurtured in the soil of Judaism, and as such has been transplanted to those religious creeds which have sprung from Judaism. In proposing the immortality of the soul as the theme of our meditation, I do not intend to trace the historical development of this most important doctrine, nor to enter the field of speculation regarding the precise nature of the future state, but simply to illustrate this grand truth by such arguments as are directly furnished by human nature itself—arguments which common sense must acknowledge to be self-evident, and to which even the materialist and skeptic must give reluctant consent. I have selected for my text the eighth verse of the thirty-second chapter of Job:
אכן רוח היא באנוש ונשמת שדי תבינם "Surely there is a spirit in man, and the breath of the Almighty gives them understanding."

Man is created in the image of God, and consequently, in his spiritual nature and faculties, presents unmistakable marks of immortality.

First, then, we have a bright indication of the reality of a future existence in the inexhaustible love of knowledge which animates the human understanding. God has given to man a spirit which is evidently designed to expand through the universe, which disdains the confinement of space, and which, although for ages it has been making progress in the knowledge of nature, still thirsts for more extended information. There is a restlessness in the human mind which no acquisition can allay. Thought is forever enlarging its horizon.

Were man destined to live only in this world, his desires and powers would have been fitted wholly for this world, and his capacities would have been limited to the means of present enjoyment. But now his faculties are continually overleaping the bounds of earth; he delights in discoveries which have no relation to his existence on this planet; he calls science and art to his aid, not merely to render life comfortable, but to assist him in the most remote researches; invents instruments which extend his sight beyond these visible heavens, and reveal hidden stars and sidereal systems; and presses on and on to fathom the profoundest secrets of the universe. The human mind has an intense delight in what is vast and unexplored. Does such a mind carry with it no proof that it is destined to wider spheres of experience than earth affords—that it is designed to improve forever in the knowledge of God's wonderful works?

In man's power of looking forward with hope to distant and everlasting ages we have a second clear mark of a being destined to another existence. Were this world everything to man, his longings would not stray beyond its brief span. His anticipations would be proportioned to his being. Of what use, except to torment him, would be the idea of *eternity* to a creature of *time?* Why kindle in man the sublime sentiment of immortality if the grave is to be his doom? "Truly there is a spirit in man," ממעל אלוה חלק " a portion of God from on high," which from him came and to him will return.

Our capacity of knowing God is another indication that we are appointed to future modes of being. The human mind is not limited to objects of sense. It has a relish for the abstract, the unseen. It forever tends to rise from the effect to the cause, from creation to its author. This tendency may be pronounced one of the essential, instinctive principles of our nature.

Nor is this desire of acquaintance with God slight and transient. The human mind, by cultivation of pious sentiments, may be and has often been raised to an intimate union with the Divine Being, to a vivid feeling of His presence, to an habitual discernment of Him in His works and providence. It has attained to sentiments of rapture, to more than earthly joy, in praising, adoring, thanking Him; and just in proportion as the heart is the abode of these generous emotions, it desires a nearer approach to the Divinity, and longs for an improved condition in which God may be worshiped with pure and perfect love. When a mind has thus become alive to God, it clings to existence with increasing earnestness. It can not endure the thought of being blotted out from among God's works, of being deprived of the consciousness of his perfections, of losing forever his protection and favor. Piety necessarily takes this form of desire for near communion with the infinite Being in a future, better, endless existence; and what else do all these aspirations indicate but the reality of a future state?

It is for the cultivation of this sentiment that Moses enjoined the followers of the Eternal, וידעתם את ה׳ "You shall know the Lord," ולדבקה בו "You shall cling to the Lord." The Psalmist gives utterance to this sentiment in the pathetic words, קרבת אלהים לי טוב "The striving for God is my happiness."

We have another indication of man's future life in the moral sensibility which God has imparted to his soul.

The human mind, notwithstanding its frequent aberrations, has something in it congenial with excellence. It delights to hear and read of angelic worth and greatness of character. It loves to conceive of more perfect forms of human nature than real life exhibits. To this propensity poetry and fiction are indebted for their origin. Especially when the mind has

been refined by the practice of goodness does it naturally
represent to itself a beauty of virtue, such as has never been
attained on earth. It is dissatisfied with all that it has
gained, and pants for greater purity. Its very improvements
prompt it to desire a better existence, where present stains
and imperfections will be done away, where it will fill a wider
sphere of usefulness, where it may be united with the excel-
lent, whom it admires and loves, and become worthy of their
friendship. This delight in goodness, this thirst for perfection with which the human mind is instinct, is full of promise. Were this life everything to us, would God have formed
us thus capable of conceiving and desiring heights of excellence, which in this life are unattainable? Will he crush the
hope of moral progress, to which our very virtues give
intenseness? We are reassured by the Psalmist:

תודיעני ארח חיים שובע שמחות את פניך נעימת בימינך נצח:

"God has made known to us the path of life: fullness of joy
is in his presence, at his right hand happiness forever more."
(Ps. xvi.)

The man of piety, refinement and sensibility finds himself,
as it were, in accord with universal nature. Every scene,
every season, touches some spring in his heart. The stream,
the mountain, the ocean, the clouds, the distant constella-
tions, all speak to him in a language that he understands.
There is something in him akin to all this beauty and sublimity that gives him a claim to property in the whole creation. There is especially in the soul a sensibility to the
grand, awful scenes of nature. Whatever bears the impress
of infinite majesty, whatever is too vast to be grasped by the
senses, brings to the heart a mysterious delight. The storm,
the thunder, the raging ocean, fearful as they are, still awaken
a solemn pleasure, for they speak to us of Almighty power,
and accord with our love of greatness. Now, this sensibility
to whatever is great and fair in universal nature seems to at-
test the glory of the human soul and to point to it a sublime
destiny. Why has God placed man within this boundless
theater, revealed around him this endless creation, touched

his heart with the love of beauty, and given him this delightful and awful interest in all that meets his eye, if he is merely a creature of the earth, soon to shut his eyes on these majestic scenes and to be buried forever in a narrow grave? Does this love of the infinite, this attachment to the universe, seem suitable to so frail a nature? Do they not suggest the idea of a being who belongs to the universe and who is to fill an ever-widening sphere?

But there is another and more decisive indication of future life, which is furnished us by human nature. I refer to the capacity which man actually possesses of attaining to greatness of character. While man, in general, falls far below the perfection he desires, yet he is sometimes seen to ascend to a sublimity of virtue which does honor to our nature and proves that it was framed for heaven. We discover in history and real life persons not merely faithful in their regard to the prescribed duties of life, but who are filled with a grand disinterestedness of character, a sublime goodness, which outstrips what is positively demanded, which is prodigal of service to God and man, and overflows with sacrifices and sufferings in the cause of duty.

These great examples show us what man may become and what he is destined to be. These are lineaments of a noble nature, marks of a sublime capacity, a sublime destiny. We all have sometimes seen human nature manifested in these honorable forms, have seen great temptations and calamities calling forth great virtues, have seen the human countenance bright with the expression of magnanimous affections, and have felt how lovely and how glorious may be humanity. And can we believe that the soul of man, gifted with such capacities, is created for a day? Can we think that the great men, who have thrown such light on the past that it yet illumines the present, were but meteors, extinguished as soon as kindled, in the midst of their glory? Why were such sublime capacities given to a being of so humble a destiny? Does the All-wise Creator thus waste his noblest gifts, and is so unconcerned for those on whom these gifts have been bestowed?

It is a natural sentiment, entitled to respect, that exalted goodness can not perish. It is fitted for a better world than this, and the Creator would be dishonored were his noblest work to be lost. Nature may pass away, but can goodness, sublime goodness, that image of God, be destroyed! And if human nature be capable of this goodness, is it not destined to immortality?

Another indication of a future state suggested by our nature is to be found in the triumph which man often obtains over death, in the manner in which he passes through the last change.

To the sensible appearances of death, so sad and appalling, we should do well to oppose the energy of soul with which it is often encountered. Then death itself will furnish us with a proof of immortality. Sometimes the hour of death is an hour of peculiar glory for human nature. Instead of being conquered, man is seen to conquer the last foe; and he seems to suffer only that the greatness of humanity may be developed. In instances like these the last act of the soul is an assertion of its immortality. Can we believe that this moment of sublime virtue is the moment of annihilation, that the soul is extinguished when its beauty is most resplendent? If God intended that death should be an eternal extinction, would it be adorned, as it often is, with a radiance of the noblest, loveliest sentiments and affections of our nature? Would the greatest triumph of man be a harbinger of his ruin?

There is another view yet more sublime. I refer to the death of the martyr to his religion, to his country, to the cause of truth and human improvement. You have read of men who preferred death to desertion of duty. They encountered the menaces of power, they endured the gloom of prisons, and at length, in the fulness of their powers, were led to the place of execution. Their steps never faltered, their purpose never wavered, their looks were firm, yet mild and forgiving; and, with an unshaken trust in God, they counted it an honor to suffer in his cause.

As a striking example of heroic martyrdom, the death of R. Akiba, a renowned sage and patriot in the days of Hadrian, may be cited in illustration. The hour of his execution had arrived. T. Annius Rufus, a pliant tool of Hadrian's vengeance, intensified the agonies of death by fiendish torments, in ordering him to be flayed with iron pincers. While suffering this horrible torture the great martyr pronounced the "Hear, O Israel," etc. (the Shema), with a smile of satisfaction. Astounded at such extraordinary fortitude, Rufus asked him if he was a sorcerer to remain thus unaffected by the pain; whereupon R. Akiba answered: "I am no sorcerer; I only rejoice at having the opportunity of serving God with my life, having thus far only been able to love him with all my heart and all my might."

And what now shall we say of death? That it triumphed over these men of unsubdued virtue—that it quenched these bright spirits? Or shall we rather say that it was designed to illustrate the immortal energy of piety and virtue, and to show that the faithful soul is more than conqueror over the last foe? Can we think that God impels those who love him by the best principle in their nature, to encounter death in its most dreadful forms, and then abandons them to final extinction, at the very moment when they must be to him most worthy of his love? No, no! פודה ה" נפש עבדיו ולא יאשמו כל החתים בו "The Lord redeemeth the soul of his servants, and none shall be desolate who trust in him." (Ps. xxxiv.)

We find another indication of immortality in our nature, when we consider the principal source of human enjoyment. I ask, then, what is this principal source of human enjoyment? A slight observation will teach us that happiness is derived chiefly from activity, from conscious growth, from the successful effort to improve our powers, from rising by our own energy to an improved condition. It is not what we have already gained, be it knowledge, property, reputation or virtue, which constitutes our happiness, so much as the exertion of our faculties in further acquisitions. The idea of advancement is, of all others, most congenial with the human mind. We delight not so much in possession as in pursuit, not so much in holding the prize as in pressing forward to seize it with the eyes of hope. The feeling of progress is the great spring of happiness; and it is this which gives cheerfulness and animation under the severest lot.

Now, what does such a nature indicate? Is it true that man's chief happiness consists in animated pursuit, in consciousness of improvement—that, where his advancement is most swift and sure, this principle most prompts him to press forward—is not perfection, then, the end of his being? Is he not made to advance, to ascend forever? And does not this soaring nature discover a being designed for a forever brightening career? Would this insatiable thirst for progress have been given to a creature of a day, whose powers are to perish just when beginning to unfold, and whose attainments are to be buried with him in eternal oblivion? If this world were our home and our only portion, should we have sentiments implanted by our Creator which teach us to live above it, and impel us to feel that it is noble to renounce it? Were this our only sphere of enjoyment, could we ever deem it beneath us, unworthy of our nature? A sage of the Mishnah has embodied this idea in one concise sentence:

"יפה שעה אחת של קורת רוח בעולם הבא מכל חיי העולם הזה" "One hour's spiritual happiness in the future world is preferable to all the pleasures of this."

But this is not all; we not only honor men when they rise above the world, its pleasures and gains; we particularly revere them when they hold life itself with a degree of indifference, when they disdain it in comparison with principle and virtue, and advance to meet seeming destruction by a resolute and unshaken adherence to principle and duty. On the other hand we feel a contempt for those who cling to life as the best of blessings. We can not endure the coward, while we are lenient even toward the excess of courage. We view with admiration the man who is prodigal of life in an honorable cause, and who prefers death to the least stain of guilt. Now, these feelings surely indicate that the present is not our whole existence. Were this life everything to us, should we be so constituted as to be ready to cast it away in a sacred cause? Were death entire and eternal extinction of all our power and virtue, would the welcoming of it appear the height of glory? All these feelings which I have considered, which are inherent in human nature, and which prompt us to sacrifice the world and life to the purity of the soul, are so many attestations from God to the divine character of the soul, so many assurances that it is destined for higher relations than those which it now sustains to the body and the world; so many arguments to convince us that our soul is immortal, "that there is a spirit in man" destined to eternal existence in the heavenly regions of bliss with our Father and our God. Amen.

SERMON AT THE DEDICATION OF A NEW SEFER TORAH.

BY DR. M. SCHLESINGER.
(Of Albany, N. Y.)

It is a strange and uncommon ceremony which we are gathered here to witness—the dedication of a new book. What possible importance can there be ascribed to a new book in our days? In our days, to which the words of Ecclesiastes (xii. 12) are more applicable than they ever were before, " of making many books there is no end," when the world is flooded with books, one book more or less can matter but very little. It is true, there were days when the possession of a book was considered a fortune, when a book was bequeathed from father to son as a most valuable part of the ancestral inheritance, and was carefully kept and preserved as a family heirloom. But nowadays books are so common, within the reach of all and everyone, that a new book, we should think, ought not to create such a commotion in a community as this has done.

If the book we are here to dedicate were but like any other book, all this undoubtedly would be true. But in regard to this book, strange to say, the times have never changed. To this very day this book is considered the greatest treasure within the family to which it rightfully belongs—the family of Israel. To this very day it is bequeathed from father to son as the most precious part of the inheritance that came to them from their ancestors, and is most carefully kept and preserved. And well does it deserve all the care and love and reverence bestowed upon it, for it is indeed a great and wonderful book.

In the first place, let me remind you that it is not, exactly speaking, a new book; it is only a newly-written book. The book itself is old—very old—as old as Israël. It has been brought forth by the divine spirit, as manifested and revealed within this people, and, therefore, is eminently the property of Israel. But with the same right we may say, this book has brought forth, preserved and kept alive the people of Israel. Without this book there would be no people of Israel; we can not think of a people of Israel without their Torah.

This book, though but newly written, is as old as the history of mankind; yet it is not antiquated. To this very day it is the object of earnest study and research, the inexhaustible source of instruction, the living spring from which generation after generation has drawn the purest pleasure and delight, the surest comfort and consolation.

It is not only as old as the history of mankind, but has exerted an influence upon this history that can never be computed. More than anything else, it was this book that formed and shaped the thought and feeling of all people that came under its sway. And the more its influence, in all its simplicity and sublimity, will permeate the world—the more the divine spirit, which breatheth out of its every page, will become the spirit of the world—the nearer mankind will come to those ends it is longing for: to universal peace and good will and brotherly love.

This book, though but newly written, is as old as the civilization of the world, and was no mean contributor to, and furtherer of, this civilization. Yet, great as the progress of a civilization of more than three thousand years necessarily is, immense as the achievements, especially of our days, are, they have not left behind this book or made it superfluous. In many, many respects, which here to show would be too tedious, and therefore out of place, the civilization, even of our days, has not yet reached the high standard set forth in this book, though, of course, in many other respects it has gone beyond it.

It is an old, old book, which, different from all other books, always remains young and fresh and youthful. It is, perhaps, on this account that we Jews retain the old custom in multiplying the book, and reject the modern art of bookmaking. It is not printed, nor is the common writing material, paper, made use of. It is written on the skin of animals, on parchment—written in the old laborious way, by the hand of man, but written with a carefulness and minuteness which considered every little stroke of the smallest letter; it has been revised and searched for possible errors and mistakes again and again, that the old book indeed might be restored.

You see, the book we dedicate is an uncommon one; and if it be true, as it is, what the ancient poet says, "that books have their own fate," the fate of this book was also an uncommon one.

It was no other than that of Israel, the people, which brought it forth and always remained its responsible owner. On account of the contents of this book—that is to say, on account of their religion—Israel was hated and despised and persecuted by all the nations of the civilized world, who, strange to say, all accepted this book out of their hands as the most valuable and most sacred. Stranger still, with one hand the nations received this book from Israel, and the other they lifted up to strike at both Israel and the book. Out of this book the nations took the sublime doctrine, "Thou shalt love thy neighbor as thyself," "Thou shalt love the stranger as thyself," "Thou shalt love the Eternal, thy God, with thy whole heart, with thy whole soul and with thy whole might." Out of this book there shone forth to the world the true religion of love, and for the people which brought them this book they had nothing but hatred and malice and persecution. In one breath even now they praise this book as the holiest and divinest, and curse the Jew and blaspheme his religion, *i. e.*, this book, which, as they say, teaches a cruel and 'revengeful God; this book which, when it attempts to present the God idea to the human mind, utters the sublime thought: "The Eternal, the Eternal is merciful and gracious, long-suffering and abundant in goodness and truth, keeping mercy for thousands, forgiving iniquity, transgression and sin, and that will by no means clear the guilty."

Aye, as often as Israel was maligned, misrepresented and slandered, this book also was maligned, misrepresented and slandered. As long as Israel was persecuted and hunted out for extermination, this book also was persecuted and hunted out for destruction. A thousand times it was burnt and torn and trodden under foot, as Israel was burnt and torn and down-trodden; yet both survived their persecutors. Out of fire and water, from the rack and stake, Israel saved nothing but themselves and this book.

But all of this is passed, or mostly passed. Thank God! when we look for the scenes in which these terrible tragedies were transacted, we have to look over the wide ocean which separates this free and God-blessed new country from the old. Our country has no part in these horrible crimes. And in this new country, which at last has become the refuge of all that are oppressed, and has adopted the principle laid down in this new book: "One Father in heaven and one family of men here on earth, who are all equal before the law, as they are equal before Him"—in this country we again dedicate this book to the service of the All-good and All-loving, the Father of all.

Israel has carried this book whithersoever they wandered and whithersoever they were scattered; all over the world they have planted it as the עץ חיים למחזיקים בו—the tree of life for those who take hold of it. They have planted it among the nations, and to them all it has proved the tree of all spiritual life, the precious fruit of which has never failed to those who understood to pluck it therefrom; those who leaned upon it were ever richly blessed.

It was the banner which Israel has unfurled to the breezes

of the world, and which they have kept unfurled in the midst of all the storms and tempests that accompanied the advancing ages; under it they have fought for humanity and progress and enlightenment; to it they ever remained true and faithful, ever looked up for renewed strength and encouragement when disheartened and discouraged by the ill-will and tardy understanding of the world.

So may this book, now dedicated, prove to be a tree of life in the midst of this congregation; may its fruit ennoble the heart and enlighten the mind; may it strengthen the faint and support the weak; may it comfort the sorrow-stricken and unburden the heavy-laden; may it be a banner of light under which all shall do good battle for the enlightenment of the world, for love and peace and good-will among all men, that they may help to bring about the day when ה' אחד ושמו אחד, as the Eternal is one, so His name shall be one among all men, who shall stand united as one family of brothers, all looking up to their common Father, the All-merciful and gracious. Amen.

SERMON AT THE DEDICATION OF A BURYING GROUND.

BY DR. M. SCHLESINGER,
(Of Albany, N. Y.)

ברוך אתה ה' אלהינו מלך העולם שהחינו וקימנו והגיענו לזמן הזה

Praised be thou, Eternal, King of the Universe, who hast preserved us and kept us alive to see this day. We render thanks and praises to thee, O Lord, for life and health, as well as for all the innumerable benefits which thou daily bestowest upon us; but daily we remember that in life and health we have to prepare for death. Therefore, O Lord, we have gathered here together to dedicate these grounds as the last resting-place of the body after the soul has been called to thee, whence it came. In thy name, O God of Israel, thou Eternal One, Lord over life and death, we dedicate these grounds as the בית עולם gates which open out of this finite world into the infinite, where thy spirit dwelleth eternally. Amen.

My friends, it is a solemn occasion which has brought us together here. It is the truth as expressed by Ecclesiastes (ix. 5), החיים יודעים שימותו "The living know that they shall die," which has moved our co-religionists of this town, though but a small band of Jews, to acquire, not without pecuniary sacrifices, these grounds, and set them apart as the last resting-place for them and theirs. It speaks well of the moral character of our Jewish brethren in this place; for, though it be true that the living know that they shall die, there are but very few who think of it and act accordingly. On the contrary, most men live and act as if the thought that they shall die would never enter their minds. Our ancient teacher said: התקן עצמך בפרוזדור כדי שתכנס לטרקלין " Prepare thyself here on earth as in an ante-room, which shall lead thee to thy real habitation, which is eternity." By acquiring these grounds our co-religionists have shown that the adage of our sages has become their guiding star. We rejoice to see that they have not waited until the Angel of Death has entered one of their houses and thus reminded them of the shortness of our journey here on earth, but that in health and life, yet on the high ocean of their journey, they have looked out for the still, quiet haven where their broken vessels might once be safely stowed away; have secured the place which shall once become their habitation of eternal peace and rest.

This occasion, therefore, though solemn and full of awe, is not without its joys. Undisturbed by any lamentation and wailing, we can rise to a higher standpoint from which we may calmly and serenely look upon this well-prepared field which shall once receive the seed of immortality, once be filled with those little but so very significant hills, called graves, the tops of which in reality reach the heavens.

This will be a *Jewish* burying-ground; and if no thoughtful man can pass a burying-ground without being touched to the quick, without casting an affectionate glance into the past, so that the city of the dead, as it were, was opened before his spiritual eye, and he behold the realm of which, sooner or later, he, too, will be a citizen: a Jewish burying-ground must do all this in a still higher degree.

Here will be the resting-place of the descendants of Abraham; of those who, at the behest of God Almighty, the Lord over life and death, wandered from one end of the earth to the other, all over carrying with them his holy word, all over being witnesses of his greatness and goodness, all over adoring and worshiping the one sole God of heaven and earth; of those who, by reason of their unflinching faithfulness to their great mission of the Eternal One, found no rest nor peace during their wanderings through the ages and centuries, had no country and could do without any, because the whole earth is the Lord's, and all over they found themselves under his protection. The only possession they were allowed to take of this earth was the four yards of ground where their bodies were interred, the only resting-place that was not begrudged to them was—the grave. The descendants of this wonderful people have now prepared here, on this free and God-blessed soil, unstained by any persecution and injustice of this kind, this their last resting-place.

Very remarkable! Our father Abraham, when, at the behest of the Almighty, he had gone out of his father's house to the land which the Lord showed him, and was sojourning among the sons of Heth, had to tell them: " A stranger am I with you, have no possession in the country; the only possession I crave is a sepulcher where I may bury my dead."

Of the land of his promise he acquired first the cave of Machpelah, with the surrounding fields. And during all the thousands of years after him, whithersoever his sons and daughters were scattered, often hated and persecuted, always misrepresented and misunderstood, though they brought the light, the spiritual light which illuminated the moral and spiritual world—wherever a little band of Jews, the descendants of Abraham, gathered and founded a home, their first and special care it was and is to acquire a sepulcher, the ground where once their bodies shall rest in peace. It seems that, as long as they have not acquired this last resting-place, they retain the feeling of strangers and sojourners. But this place once acquired and the soil on which they live is holy ground—is *their* country, to which they cling with the undying affections of a warm and enthusiastic heart. And, indeed, is not the ground on which the cradle of our children stood, in which we have laid away the earthly body, so dear, the remains of those we love and can never cease to love, a holy ground? On such a day, therefore, on which we dedicate such a field for such a seed, the country becomes in a higher sense *our* country. This place is a connecting link which binds man most effectually not only to the world to come, but to this world also, to his fellow-man.

Our fathers and mothers had a peculiar way of naming such a place; they called it " the good place." To-day, as long as this place is virgin and empty of graves, has not yet seen and witnessed the sadness and unspeakable sorrow which comes over us when we are called upon to take leave of a loving and beloved soul, and intrust its body to the cold, dark pit; to-day, as long as this ground has not yet been watered with the bitter tears of fathers and mothers, who weep for their seemingly lost children, nor witness the still bitterer sadness of helpless children, who cry for their father and mother, the protectors of their infancy and childhood, has not yet seen the grief of brothers and sisters and friends and relations, as it once surely will—to-day we may be inclined to call it a good place. But our fathers always called it "the good place," and they were right.

In the sight of Judaism the burying-ground is not the house of death, but the בית החיים the house of life, of eternal life; it is not only the בית הקברות, the city of graves, but the בית עולם, the gates which open into eternity. Judaism shows that our Redeemer, the Everlasting and Eternal, liveth, liveth forever to redeem us from the dark shadows which death seems to spread over the soul of man (Job xix. 25). It teaches (Ps. xvi. 10) לא תעזוב נפשי לשעול that He will not let our soul go down into the pit. It brings conviction to the heart of man that the divine within him can never die. Thus the burying-ground could be to the Jew nothing else but "a good place" and "the house of life." As soon as we rise to the heights of this conviction the thought of death is no longer full of sorrow, but full of anticipated joy, no longer depressing, but elevating. Our faith in the salvation which is sure to come from the eternal, infinite goodness and mercy makes us endure the earth, even when she becomes a valley of weeping and sorrow, makes us endure the separation from those who are near and dear to our heart, because we know they can not be lost to us forever. Only where the faith in immortality has not taken root in the heart, will the sorrow for the deceased grow into despair.

Therefore, let us calmly overlook these grounds. Peering into the future we behold grave rising by grave and monument by monument, all showing and speaking of the love of those who were left behind. We behold children stealing away from the noisy bustle of life and wending their way hitherward to weep themselves into peace at the graves of father and mother. We hear the sighs and groans of the bereaved widow and widower, sad and lonely, sitting by the hill which holds the ashes of those who were nearest to their heart; how they whisper to the breezes the beloved name which once answered to so much love and affection! We distinguish the sorrow-stricken features of fathers and mothers, who had to give up the idols of their soul, all their hope and expectation of the future, and lay them so low. We see them all coming hither and looking up to the stones which mark the sacred spots, and they are consoled and strengthened, for each stone is but a finger-post, pointing upward, where they have to seek for their departed ones. They are comforted and strengthened by reading the words which are never missed on the grave-stone of a Jewish burying-ground: נשמתו צרורה בצרור החיים; their souls are bound up in the bonds of everlasting life, for which, we, too, have to prepare ourselves. This ground, therefore, is not only the connecting link which binds us to our country, this world and the world to come; it is also a sacred temple, in which voiceless sermons will be preached, more eloquent and sublime than human tongue can utter. The burden of these sermons is: Be ever ready and prepared for the time when thy soul shall be called away to give account for thy doings, while thy body will be laid into the ground, to return to the dust from which it was taken.

And thus, in the name of God, the Eternal One, be thou dedicated as the good place, the house of everlasting life, the gates of salvation! Be thou the field in which the seed that decays is sown, that the immortal fruit may rise heavenward. Be thou a place of comfort and consolation to all those who will once lay away within thy bowels the most precious they had on earth. Be thou a temple to all of us, that the tombstones which shall rise within thy precincts may be but so many fingers pointing upward, heavenward, to the Eternal, our Father and Redeemer. Amen.

ROSH HASHANAH.

BY ISAAC M. WISE,
(*Of Cincinnati, O.*)

צא ועמדת בהר לפני יי "Go out and stand upon the mountain before God." These are the divine words addressed to the Prophet Elijah, when he abode in the cave of Mount Horeb in a state of despair over Israel and his cause. He had seen the fire come down from heaven upon Mount Carmel to demonstrate to all the worshipers of Baal that the One and Eternal God is the Lord and King and Rock of Israel. He had heard the congregated myriads of Israel exclaim in accents of liquid fire: יי הוא האלהים, "God is the Lord." But the wicked Queen of Israel, hearing of the discomfiture of the priests and prophets of Baal, and the havoc made of them, sent forth her messengers to slay Elijah. He fled for his life to the wilderness, and there in that cave cried painfully: קנא קנאתי וג', "I have been very zealous for God, the Lord of hosts; for the children of Israel have forsaken thy covenant, have thrown down thy altars, have slain thy prophets with the sword; I am left alone by myself, and they seek to take my life." Poor man! poor enthusiast! He was neither the first nor the last victim of mighty enthusiasm. But then God commanded him to go out of his dismal cave, to stand upon the mountain before God.

Brethren, this is Rosh Hashanah, Israel's New Year. God bless you all, you and all who are near and dear to your hearts, this day and every day of your lives, all of which may be sweet and happy. May all of you feel the presence of your God in his holy temple, to fill your hearts with golden hopes and heavenly joys, to forget the combats and sorrows and tears of life, and behold the pleasantness of God; so the King of Glory may enter in you and with you into the portals of the new year. This is Israel's New Year, brethren; and what a mountain is in space that is the New Year in time. It is an elevation, and those who stand on its summit may survey the area below. New Year is an elevation in time, and those who place themselves upon it may look backward and forward, to the right and to the left, to survey the past and cast a glance upon the future. Therefore, in the divine words of Scripture, I call on you: "Go out and stand upon the mountain before God." Come out of the dismal cave of self-delusion, self-conceit and sinfulness; out also of the vulgar habits of indulgence, self-gratification and self-forgetfulness; also out of the dismal cave of grief and affliction and fear and apprehension; and stand high upon the mountain in the clear and transparent atmosphere of truth, light, godliness and holiness; and stand before God, the Eternal and Omniscient, who looks into the recesses of the heart and beholds the very motive of your volitions; the All-just and Almighty, who gives to man according to his ways and the fruits of his doings. Come out and stand upon the mountain before your God; come out and hear the message of the Most High to his servant Elijah.

Elijah came forth from the cave, stood upon the mountain and complained bitterly: "I have been very zealous for God, the Lord of hosts, for the children of Israel have forsaken thy covenant." Stop! here we must pause. The children of Israel have forsaken thy covenant, he said; not all of them, indeed, but many, very many, of them; not those, perhaps, to whom I speak, but many to whom I speak not, because they studiously and persistently desert every moral influence, and kneel spell-bound before Baal and Astarte, the Baal of a bewildered imagination and the Astarte of wicked and debauching propensities; not those, perhaps, of this city, but those of many cities and localities, who listen to no admonition, the name of God is never on their lips, they never think and never feel a sublime thought or profound sentiment;

to whom indulgence, gratification, pleasure wild and inebriating, is life's sole object; or perhaps these and those, here and there and anywhere, as none but the eye of the Omniscient penetrates into the secret dens of corruption, to know exactly who is and who is not of those children of Israel who have forsaken His covenant. One thing, however, is certain also in our days—a large number of Israel's sons, and, alas! also of his daughters, between the confirmation and wedding days, never show by one word or deed of theirs that they stand within God's covenant with Israel. In the most dangerous time of man's life, when youth matures to manhood, the passions are fresh and strong and the understanding insufficiently developed to govern them, those young people are withdrawn from every moral influence of the school and synagogue, science and art, elevating and invigorating literature, the society of men and women of culture, moral and intellectual ambition, or, what is perhaps an equally efficient educator, work, sufficient work to engage body and soul; yes, in many instances they are withdrawn from the moral influences of the virtuous family, the softening and humanizing affections of mother and sister, to live together in clubs or gilded saloons, with magnates of frivolity or champions of lewdness, left to drift unguarded, unheeded, unnoticed upon the wild current of life, to swim or sink, to live or die. Who can close his eyes to the fact that they have forsaken His covenant, many, many, of the sons and daughters of Israel, and kneel spell-bound before Baal and Astarte? Who can doubt it that a grievous sin has been committed on the rising generation, permitted to grow up without a God and the watchful eye of religion? Who will deny the necessity of saving our own sons and daughters from under the destruction of this age of gross materialism, which seeks pleasure. gratification, pomp, ostentation, tinsel and toys more than truth, light, happiness and true manhood; this sensual, scandal-loving and excitement-seeking generation, that has no aim beyond crude selfishness? Therefore, the divine words addressed to the Prophet Elijah are also directed to us, and now "Go out and stand on the mountain before God;" survey the location, take in the whole situation, and remember that you stand before your God, the Lord of justice, the God of righteousness. To you, young men in Israel, and to you first, those divine words are addressed. Have mercy with your kin, your companions, your brothers. You who are not sold into the perpetual slavery of sensuality; you who are not damned to sit with the cards, the cues or the goblets in your hands in order to be amused, who know and understand that there are higher duties, higher aims, higher pleasures, especially for the conscientious son of Israel; have mercy with your kin, your companions, your brothers; rouse them from that deadening slumber; rouse them in the name of truth and mercy; save them from the poisoning looks of basilisks; rescue them out of the iron grip of the forlorn and sinking victims of wickedness. Come out and stand upon the mountain before God. Save those who in a few years will sorely repent, and, perhaps, will discover it to be too late to amend, to restore the wasted time, energy, manhood, intelligence and human happiness. Hear the divine injunction, listen to the solemn admonition, save your kin, your companions, your brothers.

Standing upon the mountain, brethren, let us look around to discover why this is so. Why is it that while on the one side there is manifested in our days so sublime an enthusiasm for the cause of Israel, there is on the other hand so deadening an indifference to all that is of a religious, moral or even an intellectual character; so that the same people who care not for your religious belief and practice care for nothing else which offers not either gain or pleasure, sensual gratification or amusement? The prophet in the bitterness of his soul, answers this momentous question even before it had been asked. He exclaimed: "They have thrown down thy altars," not the one on Mount Moriah, but many other altars have they thrown down, so Elijah complained.

Here, methinks, the fault lies. The altars of ceremonial religion, the heritage of the Middle Ages, have been thrown down by advancing culture, liberty, intelligence, wealth, contact with the human family, the revolution of opinions which upheaves all strata of society. Mere observances and performances, however ancient and venerable, would no longer satisfy the heart of man. The ancient forms were broken asunder, and Judaism on this continent had become a weak shadow of the past, an exotic plant without the ability to strike roots in this soil. Honest men, men of inspiration and enthusiasm, raised their voices as did Elijah on Mount Carmel: "How long halt ye between two opinions (hobble on two clefts)? If God is the Lord, follow him; and if Baal, follow him." Let us reform, *i. e.*, let us adopt other forms, better forms, modern forms, æsthetical forms, to rescue the spirit of eternal truth; to give adequate expression to the sublime doctrines and precepts of the divine religion, which is the heritage of the congregation of Jacob. As in all political revolutions, the transition from despotism to freedom is understood by some, and misunderstood by many as a signal to violence, robbery and general lawlessness; as in social philosophy, the idea of independence is grasped and valued by many, and misconstrued by others into communism and libertinism; so the idea of reform in Judaism was understood and duly appreciated by many honest and enthusiastic men and women, even those who built up all these glorious temples of divine worship, schools of religious instruction, asylums for the sick, the needy, the orphan and the widow, associations of charity and societies of benevolence; even those who love and support all those institutions with their treasures and personal attendance, have built up a Union of the American Israel and a College to educate expounders of the Law; even those who have deeply implanted Israel in the American soil, in the hearts of good and intelligent people, in the esteem and respect of our neighbors, who have removed from our heads the prejudices with the superstitions and have rejuvenated with life and energy the declining spirit of despairing children. But it was misunderstood and misconstrued by many into a communism with the lowest class of God-forsaken worshipers of Mammon, and a libertinism common to the scum of society. They have thrown down thy altars and adopted the culte of Mammon, Venus and Bacchus. They have thrown down thy altars and returned to a loathsome heathenism. "This is nothing, that is nothing, all is nothing," is their crude motto; "let us eat, drink and be merry, for to-morrow we die," is their moral doctrine; knowledge and learning are good for professional men, they say; intelligence and enlightenment are necessary for public writers, orators or comedians; we live, we take life as it is, we are practical men. "And the superiority of man over the beast is naught, for it is all vanity;" it is the Darwinian baboon with two hands and no hair.

They have torn down thy altars. They would not go into the old synagogue, and do not show their faces in the new temple, which is too civilized a place for those used to dens and hovels. They did not pray in Hebrew and do not pray in English, because they can not pray unless Providence smites them with misery. They could not listen to the old melodies of the old-fashioned precentor, and have no ear for the sacred music of our choirs; it does not afford them the right kind of excitement. They did not read the Bible or any other religious book, and do not read any book now unless, perhaps, it contains a sufficient amount of scandal or crime. They worship not on Sabbath and propose now to deceive God and man also on Sunday. There is no God in their hearts, therefore none in their houses and families, none in their children, none to sustain a moral character. They boast of what they do not and believe not, although they would not care for telling what they do and believe. Next *Yom Kippur* you will hear again how many have taken illicit dinners here and there; but they would not tell you what else they have done on that occasion, nor will they tell you of anything good, generous, noble, humane or wise they may have done instead. You will hear of those who do their daily business to-day and do it on *Yom Kippur;* but nobody will tell that on that account they are better, more respectable, honorable or more trustworthy than you are.

I do not exaggerate, you know I do not. There are quite a number of people who have become libertines in this respect and appear to believe they could be good, moral men, who deserve honest men's respect without any religion. They also appear to believe they could raise children to be good and happy men and women without the moral influence of religious instruction. They think a man might be rich and fat and do a lucrative business without any religion; therefore, they have torn down thy altars, and also, alas! the altars of their children, the altars of a rising generation. The fathers have eaten sour grapes, and so the teeth of the sons are blunted. The fathers imagine they could do without it, and so the sons do without it. One wicked man leads many astray; one Satan consumes many victims; one debased ring-leader leads many to hell. So reform was abused, so the altars were torn down; so good morals, intelligence itself was defied, so they have deserted thy covenant, the children of Israel. They had outgrown the forms of the Middle Ages and had not grown high enough to understand the lofty principle of a purely spiritual religion. They escaped the fear of hell without learning the fear of the Lord, therefore, they scorn with infidels and laugh with the frivolous; but they have not learned to think and reason with earnest men. They have forgotten everything and learned nothing. They have thrown off the burden of the Sabbath, the yoke of divine worship, the restraints of the law without submission to the dictates of reason, the imperative decrees of ethics, the demands of humanity, self-control and self-perfectionment.

For the sake of my brothers and my friends, let me speak peace, I beseech you, men and brethren in Israel; for the sake of those who sink, go under, and drag others down into the whirlpool of self-destruction, let me cry out, heal, rebuild the altar of God, which is overthrown. You, the better men and better women in Israel, who stand to-day upon the mountain before your God and Father; you who do not bend your knees before Baal, who love truth and righteousness, God and humanity, you must do something to reclaim the fallen and the falling. You must make up your mind to give honor to God by the strict observance of his laws, honor to Israel by adherence to his precepts, and honor to human nature by going before others with good examples and inspiring deeds. "That they may hear and may see and deal presumptuously no more," you must set the example by a stricter observance of the Sabbath; you must honor your sacred cause by attending to it personally in all public meetings of the congregation, in divine worship or any other occasion; you must be strict at your homes as well as in public that the words of God be made known to the young and the old by all means at your command. To be brief, you men and women in Israel must be Israelites of the nineteenth century, as you can be Israelites no longer of any previous date, and set the example to others that there is a God in Israel who is our Judge, our Law-giver, our King and our Savior forever.

"And thy prophets have they slain with the sword," Elijah complains furthermore, as if he intended to say all hopes of reformation and restoration appear to be lost; they have deserted the covenant, have destroyed the altars, the doctrine and the deed are perverted, and the only men who could bring about a change for the better, the prophets, have been slain with the sword. Might we not utter the same cry of despair? אין עוד נביא, "We have no more prophets?" but that is not yet the worst, that Psalmist continues, ואין אתנו יודע עד מה, "And none of us knows to what, whereto all this will lead." The prophets are gone and ignorance has increased. Those who are appointed to replace the prophets are "Your prophets," who reveal unto thee messages of falsehood and seduction. Anybody almost appears in our days to be deemed competent to replace Moses and the Prophets, their precepts and the eternal truths of history. Any young man of a common school education in our days, any bankrupt man who has failed in his ordinary profession or trade, any common man who perchance has read a book and was lucky enough to become wealthy, any common howler or public crier, nay, renegades, apostates, abject impostors, political demagogues, eccentric croakers, anybody almost has become a substitute for the prophet, to tear down and uproot, to scoff at all things sacred and laugh at the teachings of reason, to begin history anew and close our eyes to the holiest treasures of man in all history of the past; and a blind multitude, pleasure-loving and amusement-seeking, worships this idol or that fetich, is bribed and corrupted by a laugh or pleased by scandal. May we not exclaim, "And Thy prophets have they slain with the sword?"

"Your prophets" who tell you privately you need keep no Sabbath, you need not worship your God, if you are yourselves artists, scientists, philosophers, free thinkers or something like it; "Your prophets" who are always ready to please you in your houses or even to laugh with you or for you over things sacred, over persons of earnest conviction; but when they come before the public they always appear in the sacred cloak of godliness and with a false face of holiness; these, "Your prophets," are the dead men slain by the levity and hypocrisy of this age of masquerades and burlesques. Do not accuse them, although they are damnable, as long as you must accuse yourselves of the cause thereof. If you do believe in God and truth, why do you run after priests of atheism and darkness? If you believe in moral principles, why do you prefer printed scandal or spoken indecency to the products of reason and words of purity? Why do you desert genius and run after comedians? If you believe in Judaism, and think the Sabbath must remain as ordained in the Decalogue, why do you not keep it? Why do you not distinguish the day in this or that manner to demonstrate to your families and your neighbors that, yielding to necessity, you sell out principles for dollars and cents? Let me stop here or else I might go too far. These are a few of the questions which I ask, not of you assembled in this temple, which I address to this age of levity and hypocrisy, this generation of masquerades and burlesques. We might, I think, say the same thing to-day, as did Elijah on Horeb, who exclaimed: "They have forsaken thy covenant, the children of Israel; they have overthrown thy altars and slain thy prophets with the sword."

And yet, however just that prophet's complaint appears to be, it did not appear entirely so to the Almighty. God admonished that zealous man to know and understand that he was not in fire, storm or earthquake, that he was revealed in soft and benign whispers. God admonished him that the world will not die out when Elijah dies, and charged him to anoint another king and prophet. God's promises must be fulfilled, however wicked this or that generation may be. God's word is eternal, but generations come and go. The *Midrash* adds to this: "Whoever depreciates Israel, let him beware lest he be depreciated himself. Isaiah said, 'And I dwell among a nation of impure lips;' and he was told with a burning coal to purify his lips. Moses said, 'Hear, ye rebellious ones,' and he was told, 'Thou shalt not bring this congregation into the land of promise.' Elijah said, 'The children of Israel have forgotten thy covenant,' and he was answered, 'Go and anoint Elisha ben Shaphat a prophet in thy place.'"

Well do we understand all this, and history repeats it very frequently. Whatever individuals, whatever a class of individuals may do or say; of Israel, as a community of all ages and generations the Holy One has said, "Verily, they are my people, children who lie not." Israel always was and is now faithful to his God. The minority must not be taken into consideration to condemn the majority. One man, one class of men, yea, one generation, may fail and fall, yet "The word of our God will last forever." The holy religion of Israel is beyond human power; it can not be injured. Well do we know how the large majority of this congregation, in fact of all our congregations, are faithful to God and Israel. But he is my God whom I humbly worship; they are all my own people, my own flesh and blood, whom I love; this law of God is my law, before which I meekly bend my head. Therefore, I mourn, I weep for those who fail and fall and disappear in the current of popular vices, and cry, with the bereaved mourners, "Horrid deep, give back my children!" Therefore, I mourn with mourners and weep with the wretched; with Mother Rachel in Ramah do I cry: "Woe over our children who run to self-destruction!" Therefore, I call from the recesses of my heart, to you, men and brethren, fathers and mothers, sons and daughters in Israel, on this holy day of memorial; I cry, go out, come forth and stand on the mountain before God. Neglect not my children, my kin, my brothers, the dear ones of my soul. You must do something to save, to rescue them. Resolve resolutions, devise means in your minds, on the mountain before the Lord. And with such resolves let us open the portal of the future and enter with the King of Glory, who will bless, protect and guide you all. May the year open with the light of truth, the sunshine of prosperity and happiness to all. God grant you life, peace and happiness. God grant you contentment, satisfaction and joy. May God protect your health, increase your wealth, enlarge your sphere of usefulness, pervade your souls with heavenly light. Amen.

THE CROSSING OF THE JORDAN.

INAUGURAL SERMON BY THE REV. DR. E. G. HIRSCH,
(Of Chicago, Ill.)

ע"רה'. ח'ר'מ'א לפ"ק.

In this hour, for me so momentous, allow me, first of all, to obey the promptings of my heart and return thanks to you for your kindness and confidence so signally evinced in calling me to the leadership of your congregation, so deservedly renowned among the sister congregations of the land. I know the great responsibility which to-day I assume, and I am painfully conscious of my inability to do it justice in its wide scope. But every petty fear is silenced, every hesitating doubt is hushed, if, as I do, I bear in mind what high vocation to-day becomes mine. To be privileged in your midst to work for the consummation of mankind's highest ideals, in the sense and according to the tenets of progressive modern Judaism, is a calling which may well lend new wings to my soul, and brace even such weak powers as are mine with perseverance and courage, never to tire in the effort to attain the noble end, which, under the trusty guidance of my honored predecessors you have recognized as the goal of your congregational aspirations. Indeed, to be the banner-bearer in the battle for Israel's and mankind's lofty interests, may be in our age, so strangely moved by the conflict of divergent tendencies, a difficult task, but is surely one that can not fail to bring in return a rich reward.

We are standing at the threshold of a new year. The weirdly mingled emotions with which we usually greet the birth of this youngest daughter of time can not but be intensified to-night by the reflection that not only as individuals but also as a congregation, are we now brought face to face with the uncertainties of the future. The message which this pivotal hour of years announces comes home to us laden with double import, and more urgently than perhaps ever before are we admonished to see to it that we be "*registered unto life.*" For to him who can rise above his own individual desires and apprehensions, regrets and anticipations, the quaint Talmudical legend that to-day the book of the dead and the book of the living lie open before the divine arbiter of human destinies must find a well nigh startling application. He must observe that the genius of the times is busy recording unto death views and conceptions of a defunct part, that he stands ready to unclasp the volume of the living, wherein to chronicle the hopes and aspirations of the nascent future! The advent of the new year to him must be symbolic of the coming of the new era, the rosy dawn of which even now colors the horizon; the lengthening shadows of the sinking sun are emblems to him of the parting salute of an old world of thought and sentiment, which is taking leave of us!

Yes, friends, a world of thought and sentiment, in which our fathers moved and lived, is taking leave of us, the children. There is no sphere of human activity, no field of human energy, but displays the portents of the revolution. No age before ours was swayed by such burning desire after knowledge, was ruled by such ardent longing after truth as is ours. Carried along and aloft irresistibly by this craving and yearning, we have explored the highest and the lowest, have traversed the immensities of celestial space, have unsealed the mouth of mother earth, have lifted the veil from off the countenance of nature, and wrenched from her many a secret of her work and working. And though much still remains unknown, and many a question is wafted back upon the wings of laughing echo, unanswered, perhaps unanswerable; yet the inheritance bequeathed to us by our fathers has proven too narrow in its restrictions. The old temple of knowledge has lapsed into ruins, even though the new one still awaits its architect.

And the reflex of this movement is most clearly felt in the province of the religious. Conceptions which to those that lived before us were among the dearest; ideas which in all the vicissitudes of life were to them staff and stay; hopes which in genial sunshine or chilling rain were their trusty companions; thoughts which braced their arms for the contest and work of life, all these no longer convey to us messages of divine peace! With those that cherished them, they are recorded unto death. In the book of the living about to be unclosed, we shall have to learn to read new inscriptions with which to adorn the portals of our heart's sanctuary.

That Judaism, too, is undergoing a similar process, no one can deny; no one can wonder at! As the German poet so aptly has styled it, it is the "heart of mankind!" It was, at all times, the first to respond to the impulse of cotemporaneous mental life; and to-day, it has not lost this characteristic function. It, too, appears before us to-day, bearing in one hand the book of the dead, speaking of a Temple which our fathers pilgrimed to, then majestic in its architectural completeness, now in ruins; in the other, the book of life, many of its pages still to be unraveled, but the signs of which Reform Judaism is destined to read! Thus, turn whithersoever we may, one world is sinking, another arising! In this, the first hour of my ministry among you, no question, therefore, presents itself to me with greater urgency than does this one: "How are we, a Reform Congregation, to build up this, our new world?"

In turning to Biblical literature for guidance to find answer to this question, no crisis, therein related, impressed itself so vividly upon my mind in its similarity to our own position as did the condition of the tribes, encamped along the banks of Jordan, after Moses' death under the command of Joshua, the new leader. The order is given to proceed. The river seems a formidable obstacle to further progress; and the conquest of the land, therefore, almost an impossibility. But nothing daunted, the leader's voice calls out to the hesitating multitude: ואתם תסעו ממקומכם forward from the spot you are encamped at. The river's rushing waters can not impede the onward march of the Lord's host. Let the priests, bearing the ark of the divine covenant, plunge in courageously, and a path will open in the very midst of the gushing waves. Take, however, twelve stones from out of the river's bed, whereon rested the feet of the priests, and on yonder shore erect with them a memorial column for your children after you! Such, in brief, the marching order of the new general. Its details, I think, are also well adapted to show us the way, and teach us the method, how we should proceed to perform successfully the work before us!

I.

ממקומכם חסעו ואתם Forward! from the spot where we are resting! This the first essential. Of one fact to-day we are too prone to lose sight. The praises of the Reform movement have been sung so loudly; the benefits which have accrued from it to Israel have been so frequently urged, that we too easily forget that, after all, much still remains to be done before the land of the future is ours. For, if we have succeeded in throwing off the yoke of Egypt, if we have crossed the Red Sea, if even in the desert we have received the tablets of the law, and feasted on heavenly manna,—we have, at best, but traversed that desert while the Jordan still remains to be bridged, the land of our promise has still to be conquered in many a hotly contested battle. In saying this, no one can accuse me of ingratitude toward those great leaders that during the past fifty years and more have directed the Reform movement; no one will charge me with underrating the scope or the effect of their self-sacrificing efforts. But as Moses could only lead his people to the brink of the frontier river; as he could but from the summit of the towering mountain behold from afar the shaded hills and laughing plains of the country, for which he had so ardently yearned and to which he had consecrated every sentiment of his pure heart, so also the Moses of our second liberation could but show us paths and tracks in a howling desert, bring us to the very border of the land of our future habitation, but they could not marshal the triumphal march of conquest. The mission of Reform is twofold, *critical* and *constructive*. The remark has recently, and very rightly, been made that hitherto it has been the bane of liberalism to have been too exclusively critical. That this observation holds good as to Jewish liberalism, no one acquainted with its history and development can gainsay. If to-day we hear so often the complaint and the accusation that the Reform movement has been fraught with disastrous consequences to the truly religious spirit, and if seemingly the charge is substantiated by facts patent and incontrovertible;—those consequences adduced and those facts harped upon are, in very reality, not so much the outgrowth of the Reform movement in itself as the necessary result of that exclusive criticism which unavoidably has hitherto swayed the liberalism of the day. Criticism, certainly, has its legitimate function. It is the pioneer that marches in the van of slowly advancing civilization, and the pioneer's work, too, at first blush, seems destructive. His sturdy axe cuts down the mighty oak of a thousand years; his reckless daring blasts the rock, nature's original fastness. He bids the waters take new direction, and disputes the dominion of their native soil to the original owner of the forest. And in return for all he destroys, he can but hastily timber a rough cabin of logs—a temporary makeshift, giving neither promise nor pledge of stability or security. And yet his destructive work is necessary. Without him the constructive civilization of those that follow after him is impossible!' So with us criticism had first to prepare the way, and its seeming destructiveness is an earnest of the solidity of the construction, which we now *may*, nay *must* rear. And still another consideration will show us that the much deplored criticism of Reform was necessary. Criticism is essentially aggressive, and all great and beneficent movements of human progress are aggressive in their first stage. So is the sun when he first bursts open the portals of the East; the first hour of his triumphant course along the horizon is one of conflict, waged against the sullen vassals of darkness, that fain would hold dominion forever. The peaks of the mountain summits, indeed, eagerly accept the morning's kiss, but the valleys beneath reject for a time the conquering hero's loving salute! So did the mission of

Moses begin by aggression, and his whole career, his constant attacks upon the heathenish propensities of his cotemporaries are but typical of the aggressive, critical spirit that animated the leaders of the Reform movement. They, too, found their people not only politically, but also spiritually enslaved. The God of the Fathers, Israel knew no longer; intolerable oppression had crushed out every recollection and consciousness of Israel's priestly mission. The present, so dreary, held out no promise for the future; and the past with its ruined temple, its overthrown Davidian State, its sacerdotal and sacrificial ritual, seemed the Paradise lost—miraculously to be regained. And more than all this! While, like Moses of old, the hearts of many burned with indignation because the lash of the task master cut deep and dire furrows into the back of the poor enthralled, while many dared resist the emissaries of the cruel Pharaohs, alas! many and many again, swayed by ambition and the desire for political preferment, joined the ranks of Israel's tormenters, and had but scoffing words for those that expostulated with them. Under such circumstances, from the midst of the burning bush of their love for their people, the Moses of our times received the divine appointment to go and reclaim the enslaved. And the fetters were rent asunder, the people liberated, led out of the house of bondage, the land of their fathers, the mountain of the Lord the goal of their journey. But the generation that left Egypt could not encounter Canaan. In the stony waste of the Sinaitic peninsula, the people had to undergo a purifying process. So also in our modern exodus from mediæval Egypt. The generation that bore the yoke of Pharaoh could not conquer the future. The flesh-pots of Egypt and the golden calves had, as yet, too many charms for them. During this period of conflict with these constant hankerings after the past, Reform had, of necessity, to be aggressive, and consequently wield the sword of criticism. The claim to eternal authority on the part of Talmudical Judaism, the legitimacy of tradition had to be investigated. The rock of the past had to be struck, and lo! we found the limpid waters wherewith to quench our thirst.

Like the geologist, we succeeded in separating stratum from stratum, and assigning to each period its peculiar formations, we discovered traces of gradual growth and unfolding everywhere, and thus vindicated our right to discard withered leaves for green buds just springing into life. The conflict, however, is now decided! Criticism has performed its function: it becomes our duty to leave the desert, for הבא דור המדבר אין להם חלק לעולם Those that forever would stay in that arid wilderness can not expect to be participants of the future. We must now begin the work of construction. The sword and the book, so relates an ancient Midrash, were given together, and in Reform Judaism criticism and construction should henceforth be firmly joined. Thus then, we, too, are ordered ואתם תסעו ממקומכם: Up! forward from the spot of your encampment! Yes, friends, perhaps louder than ever before does to-day the genius of the time call upon us to march forward. Who is there among us that does not know, that *life* to-day *with its many problems*, its *many doubts*, its *many claims*, is the river מלא על כל גדותיו full to overflowing, that rushes and gushes with sweeping current between us and the land of the future? Yes, life to-day more urgently and more piteously, than ever it did since man began to breathe and move under yon arched sky, clamors for an answer to its questioning. The solutions offered by the civilizations before our own, have lost their value and potency. If in antiquity the mere accident of birth—a sign of divine favor or displeasure—stifled every doubt, and compelled man to accept as inexorable the decrees of fate, under which he could groan, but which he dared not question, to-day the spot at which our cradle stood, and the circumstances by which it was surrounded decide naught, and are often but a fresh source of burning dissatisfaction and galling unrest. If in the Middle Ages the Church, while retaining the theory of divine grace and preferment manifested at birth, held out to the weak and lowly, the troubled and perplexed, the hope of a future compensation and retribution; to-day, the hidden regions of beyond the grave are quick with no incentive to endurance and patience. In one word, the world has lost the compass whereby to steer life's fragile bark. "Is life worth living?" this the harrassing problem to which no response will come; and the times are big with volcanic energy; social upheavals multiply in number, increase in horror, and the whole fabric of our boasted culture seems out of joint. And for this very reason, it becomes the sacred duty to-day of modern Judaism, *to construct on the eternal principles of Judaism an all embracing philosophy of life*, to study man in his ethical relations, to listen to his doubts, and to confirm him in his hopes, to brace him for the struggle of life, and show him the palm of victory to be striven after. Mere negative criticism can not do this. Therefore, like Joshua's host of yore, חסע *forward! onward!*

II.

But, friends, let us recollect here, at the very outset, one essential point. The very river of life which it is ours to ford, will open its sweeping current only to the priests bearing the "ark of the covenant." If we do not wish to be swept away by its swift waters, we, too, have to take with us that ark, emblem of the covenant, which obtains between man and his Maker. In other words, the adamantine rock, upon which we are to rear the temple of the future, must to-day, as ever in Judaism, be and remain the living consciousness of the sublime relationship that links us to God! Perhaps the sciences refuse to adduce proof of this covenant. The telescope and the spectroscope are both silent on that score; and the astronomer, when computing the orbits of the stars, will not take account of this factor. And even so the geologist, tracing the developments of the earth's incrustation, successively through all its periods, will not point out in the fossil remains of the buried epochs or in the formations of the present day evidences thereof. Nor can we hope, in the laboratory of either, chemist or physiologist, to succeed better. But what of that? The covenant which we are to cherish is not an outward one. "Not in the heavens and not in the sea, but in thy mouth and in thy heart to do it." The raging ocean of fire, the whirling tempest failed to bring home to the prophet of old the knowledge of his God; the soft voice of his own heart revealed to him what he could read neither in the stars above him nor in the rocks around him! Philosophy has, indeed, demolished the so-called evidences of God's existence deduced all from the outward work and working of Nature. But the lessons which the life of man and mankind teaches—these no philosophy can controvert or render nugatory. What if without phosphorus there be no thought—the mind which works through the instrumentality of the brain will ever remain more than a mere secretion oozing from brain matter. The heart will ever be more than a pumping apparatus, the tear more than a chemical salt—man more than an automatic machine; and the man of science who would deny his own manhood. —is at best a giant Samson, blinded by his prejudices, laying hold of the pillars of the sanctuary and in their fall working his own destruction. What makes man a man is the eternal prompting which he alone of all creatures feels, down in his heart, to rise above his finite surroundings and soar up to ideal heights, to enter into close union with the infinite. How far soever we may follow the footprints of man's work on earth, we find this power operative within him. True, often, very often, the flight of his aspirations took a wrong direction, but as the erratic course of erring stars confirms even in its irregularity the laws according to which the others are held in their even paths, so still in its errors the human heart reveals the eternal law of its constitution. Nor can the infinite remain for man an abstract idea; he ever feels it as a living reality. Conscience and virtue are its ministering angels within him. And virtue is not a euphonious sound for selfishness and policy. The little child's eye, whose mind is certainly free from all guile of utilitarian calculation of its own interests, involuntarily sparkles with holy fire of enthusiasm when it beholds the noble faces and figures of those who devoted their lives to what is good and noble; and even the criminal, steeped in the most abject mire of moral depravity, can not stifle the plaintive voice within him, "Man, where art thou?" and escape the chiding of his conscience, and must quake under its lashes, he, for whom neither dungeon nor gallows had any terrors. That virtue and conscience partake of the characteristic trait of all that is human, that from small germs, with changing standard, they, too, have shared in a progressive process of evolution—this fact does not disprove their reality and universality. For they are not merely *individual*, they are *cosmic forces*.

History is the Sinai from which, if shrouded in clouds and trembling with fiery commotion, above the peal of its thunders and by the glare of its flashing lightning, we hear the jubilant declaration, "I am the Lord, thy God!" On the tablets of the Law, there promulgated, we may read, that if *virtue be a policy* it is *a divine policy;* that nations as well as individuals only then flourish when in accord with virtue's dictates; that they perish, if they dare oppose its behests, which, notwithstanding human opposition, will be carried out to a successful issue! *Yes, Virtue, or better, God, with conscious purpose rules the world!*

And this idea, this covenant must also be the corner-stone of the system we have to construct. Otherwise it בנין נערים והוא סתירה it will be a child's card house, which can not endure! Otherwise the fate that awaits us will be similar to that of those daring Titans that raised a tower to storm the heavens, but to find their undertaking end in dire confusion.

For the thoughtful history points out one lesson: Atheism has ever been the grave-digger, never the architect, of civilization. Look at Rome, in the first century of our era; contrast her with Jerusalem! The seven-hilled city, then at the zenith of her power; Zion and Moriah, but faintly aglow with the rays of the setting sun of their decline. Both had opened their gates to Greek thought and culture. But, though the mistress of the world gladly patterned her own songs after the strains that once filled with their sweet music the Olympian arena; though she sat an eager disciple at the feet of masters full with the lore of the Stoa and the Academy: could she touch with new life the genius of Hellas?

She became its tomb, because *atheistic, frivolous*, she had lost all comprehension of, all love for the ideal. Not so on Palestine's sacred soil! There Greek culture was quickened into new life; the God-idea of Israel endowed it with potencies hardly conceivable; and Christianity went forth from thence, not merely to bury a world, but also to construct one. And again, when fourteen hundred years later, Greece stepped out once more from the ruins of Byzantium, where long she had been secluded, and in Italy and Germany found willing adepts: when the "eternal city" at the bidding of a Medici on the papal throne, saw rise in stately proportions St. Peter's majestic dome; while, in yon little Saxon town, a much less stately cathedral began to resound with the burning eloquence of an iconoclast, a monk but recently emerged from the cloister's solitude; which of these two, Rome or Wittenberg, proved the Mecca of the New World, then spreading? The papal court, *frivolous* and *atheistic*, though fostering the new arts and sciences, could but erect sad monuments over the grave of a civilization, the last remnants of which it was, while Protestantism, the Bible as the word of God in its hands, called up to life, energies and tendencies, the beneficent rebound of which we even to-day yet feel. But why go so far? Follow me to the dying decades of the eighteenth century! A hurricane is sweeping over both hemispheres; America and France are in the throes of a new era. But where does the storm bring in its fold life, where death? Beyond the ocean they deify reason —but she can with bloody hands tear down, not build up; here, on this side of the Atlantic, with the God of their fathers a living presence in their heart, the sturdy champions of the Revolution, not only *tear down, they build up*. Let these instances suffice! Let us, too, heed their warning: Forward! that is, indeed, the order of the day; but only when the ark of the covenant leads the way. But, on the other hand, let us not forget that this idea of the covenant which makes us kin to the Infinite must ever remain a *living thought*, not degenerate into a *dead dogma*. If Judaism protests with all the fervor that strength and truth of conviction can elicit against the *dogma of materialism*, it does no less raise its voice against the *materialism of dogmas*. Our religion never was dogmatic. Liberty of conscience, untrammeled by any restrictions of a formulated creed, was the treasure which all ages watched over with never flagging zeal. Its greatest men could never dare reduce to authoritative articles the ever-living principles of our faith, without encountering a jealous and always successful opposition! While the synagogue, here and there, perhaps pronounced the ban of excommunication against men bold enough to emancipate themselves from the mandates of practical custom and ceremony, it very rarely, if ever, made theoretical dissent from prevailing opinions the basis of the decree of exclusion. Some are ready to see in this a symptom of inherent weakness. "What is Judaism?" so they exclaim, "no one knows because no one can formulate it." They forget that Judaism is not *confession* but *conduct;* that it is a life, and life can never be formulated; it is no crystal but a constant flow. Indeed, not the tongue that glibly repeats articles of faith, not the lips that are ever ready to pronounce the name of the deity, are the tests of how deeply we are conscious of our relationship to our God within us, around us, above us, but the heart aglow with love of all that is true and beautiful; a hand ever ready to do what is good and noble. This characteristic trait of Judaism is not an element of weakness, it is its tower of strength. It alone spares it the futile and frantic efforts under the necessity of which all dogmatic religions are smarting, to reconcile with *new standards of knowledge, old standards of belief*. It alone steers clear of the cliffs upon which dogmatic religion is in constant danger of foundering, the assumption of two kinds of truth—*the one scientific, the other religious*. No, keeping pace with the advance of mankind, it scaled round after round of the ladder-reaching from the earth up to God, with its hopes, the ascending angels, but also its doubt, the descending angels, its steady companions. And so to-day, whatever the cosmogony we accept, whatever the views we entertain as to the character and composition of our sacred literature—if our theism be a principle of action, rather than dogmatic assertion, these opinions do not conflict with our Theology. In the land of the future the manna may cease falling from above, but the ark of the covenant, with the eternal tablets of the Law, the ever blooming staff of life, is still with us, because within us.

III.

And finally a third essential is suggested by our text: "Take from the river twelve stones, erect with them a memorial column, so that when thy sons ask thee about their significane, thou mayest be able to acquaint them therewith." In constructing our new system, we can not break the *historical nexus* with the past. Whatsoever is truly human is historical. The distinction between instinct and reason, beast and man, manifests itself mainly in this, that instinct has no history, while reason has. In our day the claims of what is historical are often overlooked. Idealism to-day attempts to build the shrine of the future without remembering that the future can only be a continuation of the past, through a living present, and thus in vain delusion the edifice rises upon the quick-sand of individualism. Where the thread of history is rent asunder, the bark of idealism carries only sails, no anchor. The physical universe is held in equipoise by the conflict of two forces, the centripetal and the centrifugal; so the moral universe loses its balance when it refuses to submit to the operation of the centrifugal, the historical force. And pause one moment, and reflect, what history is that with which we are to retain connection! We see there before us as a people, swayed by one idea, and often martyrs to that idea: "It is the priest people of the world, banded together for the purpose of marching in the van of true humanity." And this claim to this privileged position is well substantiated. It is easy to show that in Israel the issues of humanity were first recognized and first solved; and that the solutions victoriously stood the fiery test of actual life! Nor can *we* afford tó-day to give up our priestly mission. The levitical purity laws and dietary regulations, indeed, we may discard; but the priestly robe woven with bitter tears and dyed in the life-blood of thousands of martyrs—this we can not resign, for our task is not done, the victory of true humanity not yet won. Thus, we, too, have to take the stones and erect them into a memorial column! We will preserve our historical organization, observe our historical holidays, chant in our services the old songs of the Jordan and Euphrates, and address our petitions before the throne of grace to a certain extent, at least, even in the language which our fathers spoke. But I can not forget that the memorial stones are not an end unto themselves. They are but means to acquaint the young with the great lessons and truths of our history, imbue them with the spirit of our past, instill into their hearts the love of our task in the present. Have we been able to carry out this intention heretofore? Who would say, we have? Certainly, I am the last one to detract one tittle from the historical value of the historical Sabbath. But we live under such circumstances that it has, indeed, become a historical reminiscence, not a living institution. Certainly, I am the last to desire a schism in Judaism. But I can not shirk the duty to provide for such as can not observe the historical Sabbath additional services on such a day, as it is possible for them to attend. I deny that this step is a surrender of Jewish principles. Nay, furthermore, I insist upon the introduction of these services on the general civil day of rest in the name of the priestly mission of Israel, which is sacred to us all. The great prophet of the captivity, living in a time when, like in ours, a new heaven was spreading, and new earth was founding, held out to his contemporaries the goal: too insignificant it is for עבד לי מהיותך ונקל me that thou shouldst be a servant unto me יעקב שבתי את להקים for the mere purpose of raising the tribes of Jacob and bringing back the guarded of Israel: I have given thee as a light for the nations לגויים אור ובתתך Our efforts can not confine themselves to-day to our own circle; the world, thirsty with the thirst of knowledge, claims our services. Our salvation is to become also its salvation. In the words of my honored predecessor, "Judaism has to express its views on all the vital questions of the day ; and the forum for this is not the Sabbath trampled upon, but the civil day of rest!"

These then are the principles which shall guide me in the administration of my office in your midst. A great work lies before us. Like Reuben and Gad, our congregation is commissioned and pledged to march the advance guard of the army and bear the brunt of the battle. Let us be true to this trust! Let us in the new year all rally with old enthusiasm around our flag! Then, indeed, our names will be recorded in the book of life and God's blessing be with us. Amen.

RELIGION OR NO RELIGION?

YOM-KIPPUR SERMON,

BY THE REV. DR. LILIENTHAL,

(Of Cincinnati, O.)

Text.—מִי יְהֹוָה אֵלָי—"Who is with Jehovah, come to me.—Ex. xxxii. 26.

In my sermon on the second day of Rosh Hashonah I promised to discuss on this morning of Yom Kippur, the Sabbath of Sabbaths, the grave and momentous question—Religion or no Religion?

Of course, when on New Year's Day or on Yom Kippur we look around us and see the House of God filled to its utmost capacity—when every seat is occupied, and the aisles are almost thronged with eager visitors—then it might seem preposterous, nay ridiculous, to put the question—Religion or no Religion? When every one listens to the summons, when every one appears before the Lord to do homage to the God of Israel, to renew his allegiance to our sacred creed, to proclaim this evening with us: עברי אנכי "I am a Hebrew, and fear the Lord of the Universe, and hence with soul and heart I confess: Hear, O Israel, Jehovah is our God, Jehovah is One." Then who should seem to doubt that there is still alive in our midst a sentiment of religion, a sentiment which reminds us of our higher duties and nobler qualities?

O, I gratefully invoke the divine blessing on you all, the ones who attend the divine worship regularly, and the others who come to the House of God but once or twice a year. We all feel to-day that we are brethren and sons of one holy covenant; present or absent during the year, somewhere and somehow there lurks in us the thought that we all bear and share the same responsibilities, and have the same task and the same mission to fulfill; and, like the people answered Joshua, the servant and successor of Moses, we all say to this holy day of grace, love and mercy: "All that thou commandest us we will do, and whithersoever thou sendest us we will go."

Be blessed, thrice blessed, therefore, for the sentiments which animate and prompt you to-day, on this Sabbath of Sabbaths, on this day of holy convocation.

Let us be frank, sincere and true; for this day is devoted to truth, which despises all deception; it is consecrated to rigid, careful examination. Let me ask: How many in this vast assembly are here merely by force of habit and custom, or out of reverence for their elders, whom they do not wish to grieve and to offend, or out of regard for public opinion, which they do not like to challenge, and with which they do not wish to have an open rupture? and how many are here from clear and sincere conviction, from a rational understanding that the day and its summons are not a mere farce?

And again hear the next one. "What, have you joined a congregation? Do you attend that thing which they call divine service? Are you willing to contribute your mite toward its support? Indeed, I had a better opinion of you. I did not think you were so fickle-minded. Do you not know that all this is a mere nursery tale, an obsolete allegory from man's and mankind's childhood; that these ceremonies are petrified mummies; that only such people who do not think and do not read and do not understand the spirit of the enlightened nineteenth century will cling to them; but you and I who are advanced, who know better than these so-called religious people—we should join them, and even assist them with our means, instead of trying our utmost to break it down and to level it to the ground?" And what do we answer to this charge? We shrug our shoulders, laugh in our sleeves, that they can read our inmost heart; and before ourselves we feel ashamed that we have yielded to the persuasion and solicitations of others.

But these points, as much as they may come home to you, are still of minor, very minor importance. The real pressure against religion comes quite from other outside quarters. There come the men of science, master minds, giants of knowledge, and take the Bible and prove its mistakes and tear it to pieces, and fling its torn leaves to the four corners of the compass. They stand there—a Darwin, a Huxley, a Haeckel, a Tyndal, and a hundred others—with their incontestible, irrefutable proofs of science. Instead of reading the antiquated books, written thousands of years ago, they read the book of nature, decipher its alphabet, discover its power and its eternal laws, put reason against blind faith, array science against superstition, and the ever-living fountain of knowledge against the petrified mummies of creeds and doctrines, and state with crushing earnestness: "Vanity of vanities, all is dream and vanity."

And the cry is caught up by thousands and tens of thousands, and is re-echoed: Vanity of vanities! What do we know? what can we know? How can you stake the creed of your church against the stern proof of science and against real, tangible knowledge? Oh, how bitterly has the human race been deceived! How shamefully has it been enslaved by the selfish trickeries of the clergy! Down with it; the sooner the better. Let us break down these follies. We want no religion. We are men, and scorn and laugh at these old follies and mummeries.

Well, all right; no religion! Let us abide for a moment by this verdict. We know nothing; we can not know anything. All we have to do is to live, to eat, and to drink, to support our families; everything else is mere sham, a bubble that will burst sooner or later. Let us suppose they are right, and let us join the grand chorus: "There is nothing of interest to ourselves but we ourselves, and be done with everything else."

Right, all right; but let us examine this standpoint from the social, the scientific, and lastly, from a religious point of view.

All is nothing; and with the last shovel of earth they will throw upon our coffin, or with the ashes which will remain in the furnace of cremation, there is an end, an absolute end of it. Dust to dust, and ashes to ashes, that is all, the real philosophy of life, and there is nothing behind and over it.

Now, if this be the case, I would like to know for what reason I should not try to make the best and most agreeable out of this short lease of existence. I would like to know why I shall govern my passions and restrain my lusts and curb my pleasures and desires, and shall not try to gratify and to satisfy them to the utmost of my capacity.

I would like to know why, for what reason, I shall respect property. What common sense, in the name of common sense, is there in the fact that you count your fortune by the hundreds of thousands, not knowing even how to use the interest of your capital, while your fellow-man near by starves and leads a life of care, anxiety, trouble and misery?

What sense is there in your living in a house, finished and furnished in the most elegant style, occupying perhaps to the utmost five or six rooms, and using the others for mere show and display, while that poor workman, with a wife and six children, is crammed into one or two little, damp and musty rooms? Why this arrangement? Why this injustice?

Come here. I love that woman there whom you call your wife and the mother of your children, and she loves me, too. Dust to dust and ashes to ashes! Why shall we go around and about, fretting and longing one for the other? Why not gratify the desire of our hearts, the longing of our souls, and enjoy the hour of sweet intoxication which love's golden cup offers to us so temptingly, so alluringly?

"Oh," I hear you exclaiming down there; "you exaggerate, you talk in the pulpit like a man who has lost his senses! What shall become of society, what of the family, what of property, if such principles are taught, proclaimed and recognized? Do you wish to bring on another Babel? Nobody dreams of such teachings, of such principles! These are only the scarecrows, the nightmares, with which you priests try to frighten the people into submission and obedience to your caste!"

Nobody dreams of those principles, you say? Stop a little and let us look around and listen to the voices of our age. There was a book published in Paris which created intense excitement; it is entitled *Properte c'est le Vol*, "Property is Nothing but Wholesale Theft." There is stern logic in that book; and it calls on the masses to redistribute the goods on earth, and to realize the teachings of the fraternity and equality of men.

"Ah!" you say, "we know that Proudhon, that eccentric visionary, who wrote that book, who was known and laughed at all over Paris. He was but an individual, and who cares for him?"

Well, if you do not wish to look at an individual, then look at the Internationals, who spread their meshes all over Europe, and hear their teachings. They say, Why do you respect property? You answer, justice demands it. We say it is injustice. You cling to such ideas only because you are used to them, have been reared and educated in them. We will give you another education and another instruction, and you will soon learn to see otherwise, and to conceive and to judge otherwise.

But, you will answer, how can the human society, the State, the community, exist, if you undermine the family and every other human institution? They shall not exist as they now exist, is the sharp and quick reply. They are founded upon might above right; upon the supremacy of capital against labor, of the privilege of the few against the suffering of the masses. The State and the community and human society have to be reorganized, have to be reconstructed; we have a new code of laws, written by Fourier, and St. Simon, by which we shall change this vale of tears into a Paradise of pleasure. Down with the present fabric of lie and injustice, and let us rear the temple of fair and unbiased equality.

Oh! you say, these are only dreams, never to be realized. Ah, do you see there the lurid flames of the Commune; do you hear the petroleum balls exploding; do you see the scum of humanity reveling in blood and wine? Dust to dust and ashes to ashes, is their cry, and the hour we have enjoyed is ours and everything else is a lie.

And the family? They do not want wives and husbands, they do not wish for parental care and love, for filial gratitude and affection. Children? The community must take care of them. Come, ye Apostles of free love, and preach your new gospel; come, ye communities of free love, and set us the example of general prostitution; come, now ye Mormons, and teach us, as the man may indulge in fifty wives, so the woman may indulge in fifty men; it is only the logical reverse of your premises. The moment rules and egotism governs, and he who enjoys the most acts the best. Down with every other principle; they have no reason, no foundation, and no answer to the question: Why shall I restrain and curb myself?

This is the point we will come to: this the direction we are steering in. You shudder at it; but there is no reason, none, why it should be otherwise. Of course the final result will be a war of all against all, a stepping back from civilization into barbarism. For after all there still will be the strong and the weak; the enterprising and daring and the lazy and cowardly, the scheming and ambitious and the inert and the peaceable; a new kind of oppression will follow, worse and bloodier than we dream of; and such a one as Robespierre and Marat and the guillotine have taught us. But it is the logical consequence of the sentence, dust to dust, and all else is crack-brained, wild fancy!

So much from the social point of view; this is the logical and matter-of-fact answer to the question. "Religion or no religion?" But let us now put this picture aside; and coolly and calmly consider our subject from the scientific standpoint.

There you now hear a continuous talk about Darwin, Tyndal, Huxley, and their eminent compeers. Did you read the great speech which Tyndal delivered before the Belfast Association, in Ireland? Did you peruse the other lecture, delivered before the same association by the great Huxley? They are no scoffers, and no Internationals, and no Communists; they are the men of calm, stern, irrefutable science, they are men who assert nothing but what they can prove. They show you by the handwriting of nature, that the history of creation, as recorded in the Bible, can no longer be sustained. They analyze the human mind and all the intellectual faculties, and from the animal world upward they prove that we are but a higher evolution, a higher manifestation, but not the Lord's as we have dreamt. They take the Bible, and tear it and cast its leaves to the four winds of heaven; they show you, by their sharp reasoning, that all your theology is nothing but a visionary falsehood. Educate mankind, they say, and they will outgrow your follies, and a new and better era will dawn upon the deluded, cheated and derided human race.

This is the opinion, the superficial one, which man outside of the pale of science, entertains of the new discoveries and the new discoverers. This is the new-fangled Hosanna, which here is whispered in the neighbor's ear, and which there is proclaimed with wild enthusiasm. Down with your religious mummeries. It is all folly, and the sooner we get rid of them the better for us all. Science, and no more religion! this is the motto of our enlightened, progressive age.

Well, now let us look into those doctrines, and, with the unbaised frankness and impartiality with which we have scrutinized the social question, let us see where we will come to.

First comes the history of the creation, and it is asserted that it did not come to pass as the Bible relates it. Granted; what do we care for that? Our religion does not consist of a book, and is not composed of mere letters. We all know now that the books of the Bible were written at various times and by at least fifty-two different authors. We know that the theories and systems of the various nations and religions surrounding these authors were not without influence on the compilation of the books and their writers, though they all inflexibly and invariably maintained the sublime principle of One, nay One. indivisible, spiritual and eternal God.

We all know that the letter killeth and the spirit reviveth. We cheerfully subscribe to this sentence, which the prophet already had laid down, when he said: רוחי אשר עליך ודברי אשר שמתי בפיך first the spirit, and then the letter. We are fully aware that the Bible can no longer be read and taught, as we have learned it, and have been taught it. We must divest it of the language used at that distant time, of the expressions which were customary, of the figures in which they dressed their thoughts and ideas. We must translate all this into our own language; we must change it into our strain and mode of thinking; and then and only then shall we begin to understand the real meaning and the real intrinsic worth of the Bible. We shall then, of course, be constrained to give up many cherished ideas, many a prejudice, long and tenderly nursed; but we shall not lose anything by it, neither shall religion and the Bible; nay, we all shall merely gain by it.

Well, the men of science say, the creation followed another process than that described in the theory of six days; if they prove it, all right. Our old rabbis, with their usual sagacity, already in the remote times of thousands of years ago, have laid down the principle אין דורשין במעשה מרכבה אין דורשין במעשה בראשית knowing but too well, that science and progress and continuous investigation would change the literal tenor of the Bible. Hail, then, hail to science, which dispels superstition, does away with mere fables and fictions, and teaches us, as Kepler glorified himself in saying: I am permitted to rethink the divine thought of the Creator!

The men of science assert: " Evolution instead of successive creation; eternal laws instead of successive changes." I like this idea; it is grand, glorious, sublime, and by far more corresponding with the infinite wisdom of the Creator than a successive patchwork. It displays a power beyond the reach of human conception; it exhibits a plan as immense as the universe, with its immeasurable time and space, into which the human mind can not follow—no, which the mind can not even imagine. Push on, onward and upward, thou divine spark that illuminates the mortal clay, the frail frame of man. The book of nature is a book of revelation indeed, written by the finger of God, and we like to read and to understand it.

So far so good. But they go too far. In analyzing the human mind and analyzing the human consciousness they reduce man to a mere machine, to an exceedingly well-constructed engine. We are here neither in an academy of science nor in a college of medicine to discuss subjects of anatomy, physiology and kindred sciences. But the result of all this investigation is, that there are nerves in the human body which, like the keys of a piano-forte, must give such a sound if touched in this way, and another sound if played in another way. All will and must be reduced to a certain mathematical formula, and soul and mind and conscience being thus shriveled up in a living skeleton, we are, as Huxley says, mere automatons, and every moral responsibility will cease, and every moral liability has to be cancelled. Whatever can not be dissected by the scalpel, or weighed on a physician's balance, or analyzed in a chemist's crucible, is nothing, is fancy, is imagination, and has to be blotted out from life's stern reality.

I recollect having delivered in this city the funeral sermon by the side of the coffin of one of our Jewish physicians. The men of the various medical colleges crowded the gloomy room. I knew many of them, sound and stern materialists. When I had spoken but a few minutes, the poor widow and the children began to wail and to cry aloud. I asked them: "Is it true that this corpse is the last? Dust to dust and ashes to ashes and be done with? Come, ye medical men, bring me one of the tears shed by those mourners who are bereft of father and husband; bring me one of those tears; let us analyze it even under the microscope, and show me where is the grief, the sadness, the bitter emotion, which made out of those tears more than a mere drop of salt water. No spectrum, and no balance, and no crucible will show it, and still we know, we feel, that it is therein and must be somewhere."

But I say these discoveries carried on beyond their legitimate sphere must destroy all moral liability and responsibility. I shall now read you a short leader, published in the *Tribune*, the most liberal paper of the Eastern metropolis on the same morning on which it brought Huxley's last oration. It says: "If we are to push to ultimate conclusions the theory that the acts of the lower animals are purely automatic, we shall be immediately confronted by the extension of that theory, which is demanded by the similar anatomy of man. If this point is yielded, we are brought face to face with the problem presented in the case of the wounded French soldier, who is scrupulously honest when the sound part of his brain is acting, but who is an inveterate thief when under the influence of its wounded portion. In the latter condition he is plainly an irresponsible being, who knows not whether he is eating beefsteak or asafœtida, whether he is smoking pine shavings or tobacco; whether he is handling a cane or a musket. Yet he is the same, being who at other times exhibits no lack of ordinary reason or sensibility. Not only theological dogmas, but our entire criminal jurisprudence, nay, the structure of society itself must be affected by these problems. A murderer brought before a court of justice might admit that he struck the blow, but allege that the murder was simply a piece of unconscious cerebration. Certainly no court of to-day would accept such a plea; but the plea is in full harmony with scientific teachings."

That is the verdict of the liberal press. Our entire criminal jurisprudence, nay, the structure of society itself, will be endangered by these theories. Here we land, here we come into a pandemonium of hell, in which the wild passions of the rabble and the ignorant masses are aroused by the crackbrained leaders of the Internationals and Communists to a general destruction and desolation, and where their wild theories are sanctioned and approved by the scientific teachings of our modern savants. It is no dream and no scarecrow. In the German Parliament in Berlin, one of the members, the noted delegate from Saxony, elected and sent by the Communists, openly declared: "Why these palaces? why these treasures of art and beauty? why these splendid halls? Down with them; huts will do for us; modern civilization is a lie." This is the haven, this the port, into which the principle "no religion" must and will finally steer its ship surmounted with the red flag and driven by its black, rugged, wind-torn sails.

But some of you will say: "We assert 'no religion,' and are we guilty of these excesses you so vividly depict? Do we advocate those extravagances you are exhibiting?" To this I answer: I have shown you only the signs of the times, of which you can read in every morning paper. I have shown you only the logical consequence, to which the principle "no religion" must inevitably lead. It will not be carried out at once, as little as Rome was built in one day. And lastly, you all have more religion than you are dreaming of, as almost every man has more religion than he is aware of. He can not help having religion, no matter in how many various forms it may manifest itself, and this point leads us to the other question: Shall we, must we, have religion?

Man is not responsible for more than what is given unto him. The elements which constitute the man we can easily find out and work accordingly. They have manifested themselves in the history of the human race and the individual; they have assisted in organizing human life in its domestic, social and political sphere; they can not be denied, unless the world is to be decried as a lunatic asylum, as a farce, without sense and without meaning.

These elements must be listened to; disobedience will be punished by the eternal laws which govern them; they may for some time be diverted from their regular course; but the action is followed by reaction, and these elements surely regain the supremacy. Just as the physical man will starve himself to death if he refuses the food which his physical nature peremptorily requires, so do the intellectual, moral and emotional elements in man claim their rights; they are innate and can not be denied, unless disorder disturbs the organization of the individual, no less than that of human society.

These elements are clearly indicated by the short sentences: we think, we feel, we act. No man of sound reason will deny or dispute these facts; or, in other words, we are endowed with mind, with conscience and with affections. Now, what is the function of these elements?

The mind thinks, investigates and wants to know the cause of every effect and every event. By an innate, irresistible force, and partly by all the needs and wants of the outside world, it is continually driven to look out for the connection between the various links of life and nature. The questions why and whence and how, are already on the lips of the child, and linger still on the lips of the old man. From the visible it presses on the invisible, from the tangible it stretches its feelers to the spiritual, and always wants to reach higher on the ladder of the universe. It stretches, it longs, it pushes on for the unfathomable, unreachable, and longs for a final cause in which it can rest; it can not hover in the bottomless space and time; it longs for a foundation, on which it can settle with its tormenting questions.

But to the question, Who art thou, what art thou, how art thou? there comes no positive answer. The finite mind can not grasp the infinite. "No human eye can see me and live," says the Bible in its figurative language. We are surrounded by a world of living wonders, which excite our curiosity but refuse to still it. There are millions of visible worlds above us on the starry horizon; we see them, we calculate their orbits; we measure them, we weigh them, but when we ask: Are you inhabited, ye million of suns, what is going on upon your surface? they move on in majestic silence unmindful of our inquisitive mind; and sing only their hymns of the sphere melodies; and there remains the eternal conundrum in all its grandeur, majesty and sublimity.

Man would be lost in this vast ocean that stretches

around and above him; he would not know in what direction to steer the tossed boat of his life were it not that a magnetic needle is given unto him, that points out his way and his journey. You see order around you, it says, and order is required of you; you see eternal laws around you, and laws you have to obey; you see harmony around you, and in harmony and for the purpose of harmony you, too, have to watch and to work. No disorder, no destruction; no self-willed, uncontrolled and uncontrollable passion; as these immense orbits follow their own ways and still by gravitating one toward another keep up the heavenly harmony, so you, too, must follow your own road in such a manner that it will harmonize with others; as the elements of nature aggregate and form the substance of the sun, and the leviathan and the worm that writhes at your feet, so, ye men, shall aggregate and co-operate with each other to work out your task. This is the language of conscience, the magnetic needle in the stormy bosom of man and mankind; and it teaches, and it demands and commands order and justice and equity, and advances the harmony of human history and human society.

But that is not all, that is not enough. More has been given unto us, and for more we are still answerable and liable. Conscience teaches us mere duty, solemn and stern obligations; but there is more, something better, something nobler in man, the human heart, with its affections, with its sweet, dear and blissful emotions. The heart is not satisfied with compliance with stern duty, the heart is not contented with mere obedience to imperative obligations; it wants more, it thirsts for more, it gives more, it wants and desires and gives love. Wendel Philips truly says the heart has its own logic; and the German Poet truthfully sings:

> Im unermeſſenen Weltſyſteme
> Die ſchönſte Perle der Natur,
> In ihrem Strahlendiademe
> Der reichſte Demant an der Schnur,
> Das höchſte Wunder unter allen,
> Das Meiſterwerk in Raum und Zeit,
> Das iſt das Herz in ſeinem Wallen—
> Das Herz in ſeiner Trunkenheit.

There is no egotism, there is no selfishness, there is only the unquenchable desire to make happy, to propagate joy, to multiply gladness and felicity, and there come descending and ascending on the ladder that reaches from earth to heaven and unites heaven with earth in the holiest and sweetest bonds, the angels of charity, benevolence, kindness, goodness, forbearance and love, the best and greatest of all, and wipe away the tears of sorrow, and smooth the furrows of care and anxiety, and heal the wounded and broken-hearted, and they call their brother angel, "Hope," to their assistance; and light breaks into darkness, and a rosy dawn follows the gloomy night, and the golden rays of the day the heaviness of despondency, and the human heart shouts in exultant joy: Man, that is thy work, thy task, thy charge, and be thou blessed, for thy creation, the creation of love, is better, nobler and grander, than the mute, silent, sternly obedient universe!

This, my friends, is religion: truth, justice and love. This is the religion revealed here in the heart, taught here, inscribed here on the tablets that can not be broken, and stand like the rocks of eternity. This is not the wild, destructive passion of the Socialist, the International and the Communist; this is not the automaton of the scientist; this is life, and love, and hope, and order, and light. It is a *sanctum sanctorum*, before which mind and conscience and heart bow down like the high-priest before the holy ark when he blessed his people and mankind.

But now comes your turn again, and I hear you say: "Yes, we cheerfully subscribe and acknowledge allegiance to such a religion. But stop a little; look around you and compare therewith the teachings and doctrines of the various churches, creeds and denominations. Instead of light you find blind faith; instead of truth you find creeds, that defy all common sense and reason; instead of love you find prejudice and sectarian arrogance. Thank God that man in general is better and more enlightened than his church or his creed, or else human society could not live and could not exist together. This is the religion against which we protest, which we dislike and disapprove of. If you please, what have you to answer to this objection and exception?

I have not to answer for other creeds and other religions. I do not wish and do not intend to meddle with them. We are both too tolerant for that. I have merely to answer for my religion and your religion and I am ready to do that whenever called upon.

What does our religion say to the mind, the conscience and the heart? To the mind first. Let us open the Bible and it begins with the sublime words: "Let there be light." Our language, says Weaver, no language can afford an expression of grander force. Rhetoricians pronounce it the sublimest sentence in human language. "Let there be light," this is the first and supreme command for the mind. No blind faith, no submission to feigned, infallible authorities; there is but one mediator between God and man, and that is common sense and reason.

Yes, work on, ye scientists; unravel the mysteries of creation; rethink the thoughts of the Creator; we follow you, and still we stand on the ground of Judaism; it approves of your indomitable researches, it encourages you, nay, it commands you to carry on your investigations, for it says: "Subdue the earth and have dominion over it;" or, as the German poet says:

> Ergründe die Gesetze der Natur,
> Erforsche ihres Waltens mächt'ge Spur;
> Verfolge sie auf jeder Bahn,
> Mach' sie dem Menschen unterthan.
> Das bringt dir Ehre und Verdienst,
> Hier ist's, wo du den Lorber dir gewinnst.
> Doch halte weise still an dieser Grenze,
> Denn Jenseits blüh'n dem Forscher keine Kränze.

The poet was right. For here stands the eternal mystery, the eternal problem. And Judaism does not try to solve it. It does not pretend to prove more than can be known. And to the great question: What art thou? It has no other answer but אהיה. "I am, what I am," and you, mortal, frail man, take off the shoe from thy foot, for the ground upon which thou standeth is holy ground.

But this sublime, unknowable and unfathomable mystery is not such a mystery that stands in no connection and in no correspondence with man. No, Judaism says: Here is thy conscience, and here thy innate sense of duty, and I am the Lord, who has created and endowed thee with these faculties; and thou hast to live up to that which has been given unto thee. It does not say with the scientist, thou art an irresponsible automaton; no, it says, the sin lies at the door; unto thee is its desire, but thou shalt and canst conquer it. It does not indulge in the visionary dreams of the Red Republic and of Communism; there stand the ten sacred commands which teach us to respect life and property. It knows too well that men are not all born on one level; it knows too well that Communism and Socialism would undermine the individuality of man and break down his title and the intrinsic excellence of humanity. Hence it says צדק צדק. Righteousness and justice shalt thou pursue; that is my warning given to human conscience.

And what does it say to the heart? What does it teach it? Oh, if love could be commanded, if it were not in itself life's end, life's wealth, life's reward—it is enjoined on every page of its Bible. Love thy God and love thy fellow-man, love the poor and the needy, the stranger and the homeless, the widow and the orphan, so it commands from the beginning to its end. No feast and no enjoyment, no pleasure and no blessing, but they are remembered who appeal to our heart and to our affections. And as the Bible speaks so continue the Rabbis. Charity and benevolence are of more worth than all the observance of empty ceremonies, says the one. The basis of the Law is, love thy fellow-man like thyself, says the second. רחמנא לבא בעי Heaven begs only for your heart, says a third. And a fourth, the great Rabbi Yochanan says לב טוב give him a kind, loving heart and man will accomplish his mission to its fullest and noblest extent.

So speaks Judaism, so teaches Judaism; such is its answer to your questions, to your objections. It is in harmony with the mind, the conscience and the heart. It is in harmony with the progress of the age, already made; with the progress yet to be achieved. And proudly do I exclaim: Thank Heaven that I am a Jew, and that I can answer with the prophet, עברי אנכי ואת אלהי השמים אני ירא I am a Hebrew, and adore the Lord of Light, Truth, Justice and Love. And now, when in conclusion I put the question to you: מי לה׳ אלי who is on the Lord's side, let him come unto me, will you not follow the summons of the day? Yes, you have come and you will answer, עברי אנכי and Heaven's best blessing on you and your good children for this answer; and when the evening of our life will come, and when the evening of this day comes, we call in our holy congregation, as did the people around Elisha, ה׳ הוא האלהים Jehovah is God and the Lord, and there is none besides him. Amen.

THE FESTIVAL OF THE SPRING.

BY REV. ISAAC S. MOSES,

Of Milwaukee, Wis.

The beautiful feast of the spring-time, the day of glorious memories of the past and of cheerful hopes for the future, has appeared, and we Israelites, with renewed love for the faith of our fathers, celebrate an event which testifies to God's love to us and of our trust in him. Centuries have passed since that event, nations have risen and vanished, humanity has changed its appearance, nay, we ourselves have undergone such strange mutations that our very existence is a riddle to the historian, and yet we commemorate every year this ancient occurrence with so great an affection as if we meant to merge all our historical experiences in this one event. And why? Because it is more than the single event marking the beginning of our history which we celebrate to-day: the principle underlying our feast is not merely a remembrance of the past, it is a state of experience, it appeals to every heart, to every mind, to every soul. And as such it is befitting that it come to us with the coming of spring. For what we celebrate as the doings of God in history, the spring-time reveals to us as the doings of God in nature. It is the same lesson differently told, and easily understood by those whose hearts are filled with love and whose minds reach out after the truth.

How wonderful is the process of nature in the spring-time! Where but a few days ago everything seemed dead and barren, the promises and forerunners of life are appearing. Awakened by the loving glance of the sun, the earth shakes off the bonds of sleep, the fetters of the winter, and clothes herself in beauty; the dry branch on the tree assumes a brighter hue, and the tiny buds that were hidden beneath the sheltering snow, kissed by the warming ray out of their slumber, begin to unfold their blossoms. From the depths beneath, from the heights above, the unfettered powers of nature begin the work of re-creation, and every heart and every soul feels the strong pulsations indicating new strength and vigor of life. Even the feeble, the frail and the sick draw fresh hope from the overflowing fountain of promise, which the spring-time opens for all.

Does not every plant that now gladdens our eyes silently proclaim the providence of God, saying: "I have slept beneath the cover of the dreary winter, and God protected me while I had no strength; darkness and death were around me when God poured his light over my grave and awakened me to new life. I was fettered with the bonds of destruction, and God opened my prison, calling me forth to joy and liberty." And while nature thus speaks to us, in the language of beauty, a voice within us echoes her words and thrills us with strange agitations. We, too, have experienced the protection of God; we, too, have felt his light and his truth; we, too, have been liberated from the bonds of a slavery with which no earthly servitude can compare.

As we stand in the midst of a reawakened life, seeing the signs of nature and understanding their deep import, our ancient faith holds out, too, similar signs, symbols from the past, that speak to us of the lessons of the present. And these symbols are: The *Paschal* offering, which, though no longer sacrificed upon the altars of Jerusalem, is, according to its original meaning, a symbol of God's protection to our fathers, "when he punished the Egyptians, and our houses he *saved*," the unleavened bread reminding us of the haste in which our fathers left the land of their degradation, not even having time to prepare leavened bread, "so suddenly did God *reveal* himself to them and redeem them," is a symbol of God's revelation to man; and bitter herbs, signifying the bitter life, the hardships of servitude from which God liberated our fathers, and led them forth to a life of freedom, is a symbol of progress and freedom. They are not dead, these symbols; and, like the signs of reawakened life in nature, their meaning is not exhausted because they refer to one particular time, but they speak to everyone of us the intelligible language of our own experience. Let us, then, try to understand their meaning, which is so beautifully reflected in the mirror of the spring-time.

I.

During the months of the winter, life in nature seemed dead or sleeping, but the power that now awakens the dead and reanimates the slumbering, hovered over the silent fields and did not suffer the children of nature to see destruction; an invisible hand protected the helpless, until the luminous days of spring appeared to call them forth from their hiding-place.

Long and dreary was the slavery under which our fathers sighed in Egypt; the yoke that was put upon them was calculated to crush out their life. But He who rules in history "did not sleep nor slumber;" He watched over Israel and protected them against destruction, to preserve them for the time of liberty. Thus we see the protection of God in nature and in history alike; and, turning our view from the outward experience to our own inner world, we can not help acknowledging the same fostering hand of God.

Do you remember the time of your trials, when you toiled, and your powers began to fail, when you trusted and your confidence was abused, when you hoped and were deceived, and you stood stripped of courage and bereft of hope and the world seemed dead around you? Or have you forgotten the days of youthful error, when by your own follies you broke the round on which you stood and were sinking away into the depths of uselessness, when you mistook the aim of life and extinguished the light that was to guide you through the darkness of passion and error to the beautiful spring of a noble character? Who has saved you from this misery of soul? who so ordered it that you did not bury your hopes, that you did not stifle your love, that you did not lose your belief in man? Who saved you when you stood at the brink of destruction, and you were like a frost-bitten plant, a tree untimely broken? Who saved you from the horror of your self-contempt, and preserved and strengthened you for the beautiful time of the unfolding of your powers and your striving for the better and the higher? It was *God*, who watches over the helpless; it was the divine power in you that aided your battling soul and healed your aching heart—the divine hand that upholds with tenderness the soul of erring children, and reaches out to them the loving hand of a father.

And not only has God protected us, but also those who are dearest to our hearts—our children with whom he has blessed us. No one can look upon these tender plants of ours without feeling the deepest sympathy toward them. Helplessly they come to us, helplessly they depend upon us, and all the richness of our nature and the fullness of our love to them is inadequate to their need of help from us. Numberless dangers, countless perils surround the feeble child. Who can look upon the suffering of a child without being touched to the heart as with the pang of some great woe? In such moments we feel more than ever our dependence upon the protecting love of God for watchfulness over these feeble plants. Happy fathers and mothers, when you look upon the blooming faces of your children, remember that God has watched over them even as he has watched over the children of nature. But why do I see tears? Do you remember some flower that bloomed so beautifully in the autumn, which the spring-time can no more awaken? Be still, throbbing heart! "Why dost thou writhe my soul, why dost thou complain?" Like a faithful gardener, God has trimmed the tree that it shall bloom the fuller and be adorned with a richer foliage. He woundeth and healeth, and even his wounding brings salvation, that the richer life, the deeper sentiment, struck by the rod of sorrow, shall, like a living spring, fructify those plantlets which alone bear the fruit of immortality. Yes, God has protected our children, those that are with us, and those that await us. And more than that, God also protects our work for the future. Like the husbandman who scatters the seed in the autumn and patiently trusts through the whole dreary winter time, waiting for the returning strength of the sun, and hoping to reap the rich fruit of his labor, so do we, day by day, throw out the seed of our work upon the field of humanity, and trust God to protect our endeavors, to watch over our deeds of love and our efforts for the realization of some great ideal, that our strivings and our yearnings shall be justified by the result, that the fruit of our labor shall be rich and wholesome, and be sufficient for those who come after us to live upon and to plant for the future harvest. What are we working for, but to still the gnawing hunger, to clothe the freezing body and to have shelter from the ruthless play of nature? What a pitiable existence ours would be! When we look upon our children, is it not they for whom we work; is it not they of whom we hope that they shall take our place and look back upon us with gratitude and bless our memory because we have left them the rich harvest of our soul's experience and our mind's endeavors? Or, when we look around us and see the struggles of humanity, and notice the combat that is going on between the lower, selfish interest and the higher aims of mankind toward the unfolding of freedom, the spread of truth and the development of purity and justice; is it not there where we find our work to be a work for eternity, no matter how great or small our strength lies in this, that we enlist for the victory of the nobler and the better? Or, when we notice the hunger for love, and the thirst for sympathy, of those who are near us, is not the satisfying of that hunger and the quenching of that thirst a nobler work than all our earthly avocations? To plant the trees of genuine friendship, so strong and indestructible that no winter of sorrow, no hail and ice and sleet of fatal misunderstandings can deaden their vitality; to reach out the cup of consolation to the mourning heart and the light of hope to the distressed and downcast; to lift up the lowly, to uphold the sinking, to reinstate degraded humanity upon the throne of usefulness and honor; is not this our work for life? But who guarantees us that our best powers shall not be spent in vain, that the plantlets of our heart and mind shall not be destroyed by the worm of ingratitude, of envy and hatred? It is God who protects our work; it is the divine conscience within that tells us no seed of goodness can be destroyed, and as long as you *know* that you are sowing seeds of love and doing works of humanity, fear not the cold winter of envy or malevolence, God protects your works for the future.

II.

Again: the spring-time is the bringer of light, which, by its gradually increasing rays, draws forth the slumbering plants from darkness and death to life and growth; or the sun comes with sudden strength and rends asunder the graves of the plants and causes them to come forth in their blooming garment of beauty. Our fathers in Egypt, through the long night of misery, had lost that all-sustaining power, hope and confidence in God; they could but sigh and groan over their labor; they had only complaints and tears, but no uplifting of the eye to him who is absolute justice and love. And yet their groanings reached up to God, and his help came so suddenly that they could not even prepare leavened bread for their march to liberty. And thus the lesson to us is equally suggestive, for it teaches us *the revelation of God to man* through experience.

It is through our own experience that our religious consciousness begins to dawn, that the God of our fathers is revealed to *us* and becomes our God. As in the dim distance of the past men's minds were awakened from their lethargy through the pressure of their surroundings, at first dimly groping in the dark, and then gradually seeing more and more clearly the light of divine power over them and in them; so we are awakened, day by day, by the wonderful occurrences that make the warp and woof of our life, until they become the very texture of our consciousness, so that we fully realize the truth: "Not only our fathers, but also us has God redeemed in his love."

And as it is with the individual, so it is with entire nations; the experience of the individual man is the experience of humanity. When we look over the traces of antiquity or examine the crude notions of uncivilized races, we are struck with amazement at the almost incredible progress of the mind which leads us up from the first stupid glance at the brilliant sky and the wonderful scenery of nature to the latest interrogation of inquiring intelligence. There stand before us the nations of the past, trembling before a fleeting shadow and cowering in fear before the rolling voice of thunder, seeing in every sight of nature a magnified monster, an image of themselves, and bringing crude sacrifices to the horrid creatures of their misguided imagination. And we see them growing into a clearer perception of the surrounding world, into a finer sense of that Infinite Power, which is the cause of all causes. What explains this growth? Historians tell us of influences from without, of teachings that penetrate a nation, changing and moulding its conceptions. No people has ever been tutored into the idea of a God, or into the doctrines of morality: *they found them out by their own experience.* When calamities befell them and they had lost their confidence in their gods; when they were struggling for liberty and acquiring strength through the combat for their highest interests, divine truth dawned upon their consciousness, the truth that there is a power that breaks the chains of slavery, that hates tyranny and oppression, and punishes the injustice of the oppressor. Such events in the life of a people are the true revelations of God, and they are sufficient germs for the growth and development of the purest and clearest ideas, of the richest and ripest sentiments that make up the sum and substance of a people's religion. The redemption from Egypt was such an event in the life of Israel; it was the seed of that mighty tree whose fruit has nourished the mind of humanity, the tree of Judaism, and its great importance as the beginning of a glorious future is, therefore, divinely expressed in the first commandment: "*I am the Eternal, thy God, because I have brought thee out of the land of Egypt, out of the house of slavery.*"

Nor is it otherwise in our times, especially when we notice the present development of Judaism. There was a time when the beautiful garden of our religion was surrounded, not by a protecting fence, but by high and thick walls that shut out the light, and under whose long shadows the plants became pale and sickly; briars and brambles covered the most fertile portions and were declared trees of life and trees of knowledge. You still remember what absurdities have been forced upon our minds, what meaningless forms and old, unintelligible ceremonies and foreign customs that had their origin in superstition and fear, have been taught to us as religion, as the effluence of divine wisdom. During many centuries the Jewish mind labored under this terrible bondage, and all the great men of genius, with whom the history of Israel so richly abounds, were unable to break the shackles of this spiritual slavery. How then comes it that we have a religion purified from the dross of superstition, and a beautiful form of worship, worthy of the time in which we live? Whence our courage to break with the traditions of the past and create that new spiritual phenomenon—Reformed Judaism? Are we wiser and better than our fathers? Oh, no! but we have found by experience that all these forms and ceremonies did not satisfy our religious nature, that they did not still the cravings of our hearts nor bring us nearer to God. Who taught you the great lesson of spiritual freedom, the liberation from the thralldom of authority? Was it not *your own common sense* that had been awakened by the luminous time of this century? Yes, God reveals himself to us, not in clouds and thunder, or in visions and dreams, but through the powerful influence of our own experience.

III.

Lastly: the spring-time is the time of joy and good tidings, when our breast expands more freely and we draw a deeper breath in the warm and pleasant air. Like the plants at our feet, we raise our head with courage, for we know that the dreary winter is gone and that nature is busy in preparing a feast for us. In such days of cheerfulness we love to speak of the unpleasant time of the winter, when our movements were hindered by reason of the cold or the snow and the ice. Thus our fathers, when the time of their liberation had come, loved to revert in their thoughts to the time of their misery and oppression; and when the day of their spring of freedom returned, they placed bitter herbs on their festive boards as a remembrance of their sorrows and humiliations in the land of slavery. For, as there is no greater agony than to remember happier things in the midst of our distress, so there is no greater satisfaction than to recall our troubles and misfortunes in the days of our happiness.

Mankind began its career with brutal force; to be powerful was to be virtuous, and the most reckless tyrant based his authority upon divine origin, while the people suffered under the lash of despotism. Yet the blasphemous theories of tyrants could not protect their blood-stained thrones against an outraged and desperate people that was longing for liberty. Hence the changes and continual redistribution of power that characterized ancient history. But humanity was not destined forever to simply change one tyrant for another; a higher development of freedom was taking place—the development of political independence, which, passing through many intermediate stages, has at last borne its ripest fruits in England, France and America. But while the nations thus struggled for the light of liberty, Israel, the first banner-bearer of freedom, was made the target of intolerance, and all the bitterness of an enraged nation was heaped upon the scattered remnants of a people who celebrated every year a feast of liberty, as a protest against the narrow-mindedness of a priest-ridden humanity. Those were bitter times of persecution and humiliation for the people of Israel when the sovereign's will and the people's rights waged war against each other, while the poor, degraded few had to pay the cost of the battle. It made no difference to the unhappy Israelite under what government he lived, exclusion and shame awaited him everywhere.

At last the spring-time of liberty dawned even for Israel. The long abuse which he had suffered from the hands of those who were themselves yearning for liberty, and his firmness and unbending trust in the redeeming power of God gradually awakened the conscience of the nations, who began to see in the fate of Israel their own fate and became ashamed of their narrow-mindedness, which till then was a sign of patriotism or of piety. The emancipation of the Jews wherever it took place was the unmistakable sign that the spirit of genuine liberty had taken hold of the heart of man. Thus the remembrance of our liberation becomes a source of joy for the friend of humanity, as it proclaims the old Jewish principle so ardently sought by the best and noblest minds: "One law and one right for all, liberty for every individual!"

Israelites, do you know the importance of the ancient symbol that is to remind us of the bitter, cruel experiences we have undergone in history? It is the symbol of progress that leads up from the dark time of despotism, of spiritual and bodily bondage, to the bright, luminous day of freedom and tolerance, of equal rights and equal duties, of mutual respect and mutual assistance; the time when man is weighed by his worth and not by his creed, when he is esteemed for his love to all and not for his hatred against a helpless class of people. Rejoice, Israel, on your festival of liberty when you recall the memories, the long and dreary way you have traveled; it was the way to freedom, not for yourself alone, but for humanity. Rejoice in this time of freedom, when the heart of mankind is turned kindly toward us, when every barrier and distinction is being broken and the voice of humanity is bringing good tidings even to those who still bear the yoke of intolerance. But remember that this joy implies a sacred duty, the duty of showing yourselves worthy of this time of liberty. As we have been contributing toward the progress of freedom by our suffering and endurance, so we must contribute to its maintenance and growth by our activity and zeal, by our earnest participation in everything that leads to the emancipation of the spirit and the spread of culture, so that everyone of us may say בעבור זה עשה ה' לי on this account has God done this to *me* when he liberated me from Egypt.

Let us rejoice and offer thanks to God on this day, when the signs of nature and the symbols of the past recall to our minds the wonderful doings of God, for we see that he is guiding us, through our hearts' experience, to the knowledge of his protection; through our minds' endeavors to the acquisition of truth; and through tyranny and oppression to freedom and joy.

Thank the Lord, for he is good, his kindness endureth forever. He leads mankind onward and upward to higher aims; humanity is rising and progressing toward a nobler and better state, its symbol is the spring-time, the everlasting regeneration of nature. Amen.

MEN MORE INSTRUCTIVE THAN WORDS.

(Sketch of a Hanukah Sermon.)

BY ISAAC M WISE.

השמת לבך על עבדי איוב.

It is reported in the good book that the Almighty asked Satan, "Hast thou put thy heart on my servant Job?" Satan evades the question, and instead of an honest reply to a direct query, comes out with an argument against Job. The Almighty had asked him, Hast thou put thy heart, hast thou thoroughly and impartially searched into the deeds and motives, feelings and wishes, sentiments and intentions of the man Job, who is my servant, innocent, straightforward, God-fearing and turning from evil? and Satan behaves satanically, telling him as much as: I do not care for that, I am engaged in fault-finding, and I will try. Upon life's journey you will find many such a Satan. The better the man the more eagerly will Satan scan his shortcomings.

Perhaps the passage before us contains this idea: The Almighty in his benignity asks Satan, Hast thou put thy heart on Job, that thou, admiring and truly appreciating a good man, mightest be ennobled thyself? But Satan feels no such desire. He is Satan because he is not impressed with the necessity of becoming better, wiser, nobler, more enlightened and more generous. He sees not the good; he has an eye for evil only, and so is his reply to the inquiring Deity. At any rate, these words convey the beautiful lesson that in the earnest contemplation of great and good men, with their deeds, sufferings, and triumphs, there is a more instructive lesson than the savant's words can convey. It is plastic speech; it is dramatic doctrine; it is telling.

It is maintained in the Talmud that when man after his death appears before the court on high he is asked the question first, "Why hast thou not engaged thy mind in the Law? Why didst thou not pay more attention to divine lessons, to moral and intellectual improvement?" If one then answers, I was too beautiful, hence too much exposed to worldly allurements, too much engaged in dressing and pleasure-seeking, in balls, theaters, operas, concerts, calling and receiving calls; he (or she) will be answered, Thou wast not more beautiful than Joseph, the son of the beautiful Rachel, who withstood all the allurements and remained faithful to the God of his fathers, the sacred cause of his race, the teaching of his venerable sire. If one shall answer, I was too poor, I had to work to earn my daily bread to support my family, I had to work also on the Sabbath and holidays in order to earn a livelihood—and you know there are such men in this world—then he (or she) will be told, Thou wast no poorer than Hillel, who split wood for a livelihood in the city of Jerusalem, yet did he appropriate half of his wages to pay the door-keeper at the academy in order to gain admission and to hear honored sages expound the Law. If one shall answer, I was too rich, too much engaged in business and speculations, the rise and decline of prices and stocks, higher and lower percentages, I had no time to attend to ideal affairs when the reality of materialism engulfed my whole life, he (or she) will be answered, Thou wast not richer than Eliezer b. Harsum, the high-priest, who succeeded his brother Simon the Just; he had sixty cities on land and sixty ships on the seas, and yet he was always engaged in the study of the divine Law, in moral and intellectual advancement.

The author of this beautiful parable quotes no words; he quotes men, more instructive than words. The mind more easily retains and actualizes such noble types as Joseph, Hillel and Eliezer than it can the book of impressive lessons which these names suggest. By admirable deeds the heart of man is moved to admiration; the sublime in the human character moves man and child to veneration. This admiration and this veneration are the best teachers of morals, the most efficient preachers of religion. It is the greatness of the book of Genesis, and many other chapters of the Bible, that it teaches its lessons by classical human figures, in plastic and dramatic language. This method was imitated by the rabbis of old in their parables and allegories, the teaching of men instead of words, of deeds instead of sounds. The most useful reading for the purpose of self-culture is history and biography, if one understands how to put his mind and heart into the great traits in the characters of great men; and this it was which the Almighty asked Satan, "Hast thou put thy heart upon my servant Job?" and Satan said no, as do many human beings, who have eyes and see not the good, the beautiful, the sublime, the imperishable and eternal.

As this is *Sabbath Hanukah*, says the man at our elbow, we will be told again the old story about Antiochus Epiphanes and his edict to make an end of Judaism, the heroic suffering of pious *Hassidim*, old Eleasar, Hannah and her seven sons, and the other martyrs; the heroism of old Mattathia and his compatriots, of Judah Maccabee and his valiant brothers, the battles fought, the victories won, the temple and its service restored, the lamps lit—old stories so often told, so commonly known, known to the children, it is of no use to repeat them. Friend, we reply השמת כבך על עבדי איוב, "Hast thou put thy heart on my servant Job?" Have you ever sufficiently contemplated, admired and venerated those ancient classical figures which look like lofty snow-capped mountains, swimming in an endless sea of mist? If you have indeed contemplated them sufficiently, then you can not help seeking their company again and again. The man who has gone one hundred and three times to see Shakespeare's "Hamlet" gave us a satisfactory explanation of this extravagance: "Did you never have a dear friend whom you heartily admired and loved?" said he. "Well, then, did you ever get tired of that friend's company? Did you not rather yearn to meet him again when he was absent? Were you not glad to welcome him home after a long journey? Did it not do your heart good to hear him tell his story? Well, then," said he, " I love and admire 'Hamlet'; I have put my heart in his excellencies, and could go and see him many hundred times more, especially as the world around me shows so many commonplace people."

Alas! the man may be right, for we have often done so ourselves. When we see so many people creep and crawl along in the dust with their heads scarcely above it, creeping and crawling along so cunningly, so hurriedly, without leaving their resting points, so sagaciously, without thought or consideration, and so busily without doing anything; when we see so many ants rolling a grain of wheat and then fighting over its possession; ever so many frogs leaping lustily in and out of stagnant, green swamps and croaking as though they had conquered a world or solved the mysteries of existence; when then misanthropy chilling and stinging, threatens to beleaguer the heart, and Satan whispers into one's ear the whole family of *homo* is not worth an honest man's day's work or a sleepless night, what then? Are there not, must there not be thinking men to whom sometimes thoughts like these occur? What then? Then we hurry to our library, close the door behind us, and take from the shelf the Bible, Josephus, the old *Zemach David*, the Talmud, or the dust-covered *Yuchasin*, to read the stories of great men. Plutarch, yes, old Plutarch, we take from the shelf to converse with great men, towering among these human ants; and old Ossian must sing his songs to the music of David's harp. Then the room fills with a stately procession of classical and sublime figures, who sing the songs of seraphic fire and speak of heavenly wisdom and celestial beauty. Then they move along with psalmody and hallelujah, with psalteries and timbrels, and you move along with them, and the heart is healed, and the mind is refreshed, and love to God and men returns, admiration and veneration lift you up on mighty pinions and you behold God's eternal wisdom and goodness manifested in human nature. Thank Heaven that there is a past, and that there are great men in the past to refresh and to elevate the present generation.

Therefore we ask once more, "Hast thou put thy heart upon my servant Job?" Have you put your hearts upon those sublime figures of Mattathia, his five heroic sons and their valiant compatriots? Have you contemplated the patriotism, the holy zeal, the divine enthusiasm, the deathless love to God, to Israel, to God's law and God's truth, which distinguished those men? Have you caught fire from their fire, sparks flying from the ancient rocks? Have you sufficiently admired and venerated them to become like them? If you have not, they ought to be reproduced a thousand times before the feeble memory of this lazy-busy generation, till the lethargy and indifferentism of the masses be overwhelmed, and the spirit enliven these dead and bleached bones. If you have, then their company must be welcome, a thousand times welcome, to you, those old friends of humanity, those glory-crowned children of the Living God, those brilliant diadems upon the head of the human family. You must be desirous of seeing "Hamlet" a hundred and three times.

Perhaps we have forgotten that not all men like good company, but we speak to those who do. Perhaps not all men wish to be instructed, but we address those who seek divine lessons, search after truth, and wish to improve and advance; to those who want to have a satisfactory reply to make when they appear before the court on high. To them we say, "Men are more instructive than words." Amen.

ISRAEL'S INFLUENCE ON CIVILIZATION.

A SERMON

BY REV. DR. FALK VIDAVER.

(Of Evansville, Ind.)

TEXT:—"Look unto Abraham, your father, and unto Sarah that bore you; for he was one when I called him, and I blessed him, and I increased him."—Isaiah 11. 2.

There is an old Talmudical saying האבות סימן לבנים " Parents are a pattern to their children. Indeed, nothing leaves as indelible an impression upon the mind of the child as the deportment of its parents. There may be some exceptions to this rule, yet in the majority of cases you will find that sons and daughters take after their fathers and mothers with regard to virtue, modesty and respectability. And not only do the open conduct and action of the parents impress themselves upon their children's minds and contribute to the formation of their characters, but also the inner passion and hidden proclivities and propensities of father and mother are generally propagated to their offspring. Therefore, if you are desirous of discovering the primitive source of the good or ill-behavior of individuals, scrutinize closely the life of their parents. Such, my friends, is also the case with a whole nation, the character of which is generally moulded by that of its first parent.

Cast a look upon Israel, whose father was Abraham, as the prophet in our text exclaims: " Look unto Abraham, your father," and, as his name in Hebrew signifies a father of a great nation, you will be fully convinced of the truth of my assertion. Like a golden thread does Abraham's character run through Israel's life. Let us see what were the distinguished traits in the patriarch's character. Our wise rabbis remark עין טובה וכו׳, "he who has a kind, good and pleasing aspect, an humble spirit and contented soul, is a disciple of Abraham. That the patriarch had a pleasing aspect and was good and kind to all, we may infer from the Scriptures, which tells us the story of the three strangers that visited Abraham. This story gives us an idea of the patriarch's kindness and benevolence, how he was devoted to the cause of humanity, that even when feeling indisposed he could not rest without extending a helping hand to the poor, and therefore he placed himself at the door of his tent in order to offer his hospitality to the weary wayfarer. The disciple of Abraham does, therefore, bestow charity upon the poor without any distinction of nationality, religion or race; he breaks his bread with hungry people without searching into their nature and character. That Abraham was humble and meek, we learn from the Scriptures, which relate that Anar, Eshkol and Mamre, three idolaters, were intimate friends of the patriarch. In spite of Abraham being a chosen servant of the Most High, he did not feel proud and haughty, nor did he look with contempt upon others who held different religious views and who did not recognize his God. The disciple of Abraham does, therefore, love, honor and respect his fellow-men, not because of their piety, or because of their concurring in his religious opinion, but because they are human beings, created in the Lord's image. That Abraham had a contented soul we conclude from the fact the Scriptures speak of, namely, that he refused the invitation of the King of Sodom to share in the spoil which he took in the battle which he fought against the kings for the liberation of his nephew, Lot. The disciple of Abraham does, therefore, never covet the possessions of his neighbor, and never questions the will of God, nor asks why others are richer than himself, but feels satisfied with the share that has fallen to his lot, and rejoiceth in the least which he receives at the hands of his Creator.

Now, my friends, as the patriarch possessed the aforementioned three noble qualities, who would be justified in maintaining that Abraham can not be put up as our model and pattern because he lived in an ignorant age and he himself was not irradiated with the light of civilization? And yet such an assertion is being made in our present day. But how unjust, how perverted, how illogical is such an assertion! It is true that Abraham, as well as all great men of the biblical age, lacked a knowledge of geography, physiology, astronomy, and all other modern sciences; those people were no philosophers or merchants, but husbandmen and shepherds. Yet I am sure that you will acknowledge that neither geography, nor botany, nor any other natural science constitutes civilization. One's mind may be enriched with deep erudition, his body may be adorned with elegant and costly attire, yet with regard to manners and deportment toward his fellow-men, he may not be superior to a savage; while on the other hand again, one may be ignorant of natural sciences, yet his own nature may be noble, he may be clothed in rags, yet beneath those rags there may be a large heart throbbing with the pulsation of love and sympathy toward his fellow-men. Now, my friends, which of those two would you call civilized? Surely the latter and not the former. Civilization is synonymous with refinement, and does not consist in the acquisition of learning, but in the realization of good and humane deeds, in being just, upright, charitable and benevolent. Science as well as religion is but the means whereby to attain civilization. Abraham, therefore, did reach the acme of civilization, because he was kind to all, an humble spirit and a contented soul, and to be so is to have scaled the summit of humanity and gentleness.

We may, therefore, assert that Israel was the first civilized nation in the world, for the noble qualities of Abraham were implanted in the hearts of his posterity. Like Abraham did Israel enter into the world with עין טובה pleasing aspect, yes, with a mission to bestow spiritual charity upon the nations, to endow them with a religion of truth, with the idea of the Lord's unity, aad thereby to dispel from their life's horizon all mists of savagery and fanaticism, and to kindle in their midst the refulgent light of true civilization. But alas! Israel's calling met with strong opposition; many obstacles and impediments were interposed in his way, many plots were hatched in the dark against his security. This Bible, which contains a treasure of godly teachings and edifying principles, which Israel brought to the nations, was maltreated by them; the truthful lessons which it contains were perverted and misconstrued, and conclusions were drawn from them tending toward Israel's injury and destruction. The Romans and Greeks, in spite of the rapid strides with which they marched on in the field of art and philosophy, lacked the spirit of humanity, the knowledge of refinement; they were unconscious of the intrinsic worth of man, because they believed not in the great God, the Creator of man; they were a sensual, material people, hence they persecuted Israel, in whom they found a people that placed spirituality above materialism, and whose life and works were devoted to an ideal, namely, to their Heavenly Father.

Israel, like Abraham, was humble and meek. Israel's motto was שלום peace. Peace in his own midst, and peace unto the nations. And thus did Israel settle in his land with desire to dwell therein peaceably, quietly and undisturbed. But soon the nations invaded his land, twice destroyed it, and robbed him of his possessions, and left him homeless and forsaken. Yet he did not despair and abandon his hope and trust in God and in a better future. Israel was also endowed with the great virtue of contentment, and therefore he felt satisfied with the little that was left to him, as long as he could pursue his avocation, namely, to foster faith and belief in the Almighty and to realize the noble qualities which he had inherited from Abraham. By so doing did Israel indirectly and unobtrusively contribute to the civilization of mankind. And indeed, after innumerable tribulations and trials, Israel had the satisfaction of seeing his God and his Bible taken up by the nations as objects of worship and respect. Israel saw millions of people recognizing the God of Abraham and acknowledging the worth of the sacred Scriptures, and thus could Israel rightly expect a different treatment at the hands of the nations. But Israel was sorely disappointed in his expectations, for the idea of God as well as the spirit of the Scriptures were not perceived by the nations in a pure and correct sense. Instead of an incomprehensible and invisible Creator of the universe, instead of the God of the decalogue, an incarnated Deity was invented, and instead of the wholesome book of the Scriptures other books became the guiding stars of the nations.

These new inventions, of course, did not fall short of their object. They blinded the eyes of the nations, so that they regarded the darkness of superstition and ignorance as the light of a true civilization. They boasted of possessing a religion of love, but in the name of that religion the most cruel and atrocious acts were perpetrated. Inhumanity, injustice and all kinds of evil were concealed under the cloak of that pretended religion of love. Israel, as a matter of course, could not be considered the parent, the originator of such a religion, since Judaism distinctly prohibits the bearing of suspicion and hatred against one another, and impresses upon our minds to "love our *neighbor* as ourselves" and the word *neighbor* implies every human being. Israel, therefore, fell a victim to the nations' rage and groundless animosity, because they considered him a renegade, denying the truth of their religious principles; yet did Israel never cease to foster the noble qualities of Abraham and to look upon the patriarch as a model. While the nations rejoiced in barbarism, Israel, although having been secluded and immured in ghettos, practiced humanity and utilized the great virtues bequeathed unto him by Abraham. It was but toward the fifteenth century that science began to accomplish that which the religion of the nations could not accomplish. Science began to break the ice of civilization. The nations then began to arrive at the acknowledgment that the virtue of love, which they considered the basis of their religion, was adopted from Judaism. And this word love, in its original sense, expresses the noble quality of Abraham, namely עין טובה a good aspect, yes, kindness to all. The nations since then have begun to appreciate Israel's worth, to recognize his merits, and to grant him civil rights and liberty. And if in our present enlightened age, in some places in the old country individuals like Treitschke and Stoecker, and their equals, exhibit hatred and enmity against Israel, we need not wonder at all, for these individuals have not yet emerged from their old state of savagery, they are not irradiated yet with the light of true civilization; their actions and thoughts are in conflict with the religion of love which they profess. These enemies of Israel revive old complaints against the Jewish people. The Talmud, they say, contains places which speak disparagingly of non-Israelites. This is true. But these places in the Talmud are to Israel now a dead letter; and again it would be unjust to blame the child for the wrong actions of its parents. And, apart from all this, we could easily justiy those aforementioned places in the Talmud, if we considered the age in which and the people among whom they were written. They were written against the Romans, the destroyers and degraders of Israel. Shakespeare was right in putting in Shylock's mouth the words: "If you prick us do we not bleed? if you tickle us do we not laugh? if you poison us do we not die? and if you wrong us shall we not revenge?" Indeed, our wise rabbis only revenged themselves on their enemies in uttering against them sentences of reproach and disgrace. Israel's enemies of our present day do further complain that the world is becoming Judaized. To this I would answer, in the words of Lessing's "Nathan the Wise," when the cloister brother says to Nathan, "You are a Christian," Nathan rejoineth: "Happy are we indeed, for the very same qualifications which make of me a Christian in your eyes make of you a Jew in my eyes." The world become Judaized! Would that all human beings emulated Jewish charity, Jewish benevolence, Jewish true faith and belief in One God. Would that they strove to realize the great virtues of Abraham. They could then boast of being good Christians. We would not then hear of persecution and hatred against any human being, love would reign supreme among the family of man, and every one would look to Abraham and follow in his footsteps and become a blessing to mankind. Amen.

HEBREW MONOTHEISM.

A DEDICATION SERMON.

BY ISAAC M. WISE.

שמע ישראל יי אלהינו יי אחד

"Hear, O Israel, God is our Lord, God is One." These are the mysterious words which accompany every son and every daughter in Israel, from the first dawn of cognition to the last breath of life. It is the first lesson which the mother teaches her child, and the last farewell addressed to the departing soul by surviving friends. Like the atmospheric element, always and everywhere, these solemn words went with Israel from yonder wilderness of Sinai, through all ages and climes, all revolutions and changes, to this very day and place; to every place where Israel has found a home. These words are older than Moses, the Talmud maintains. The sons of Jacob addressed them to their father in his dying hour, as a solemn vow of fidelity to the one eternal and sole God.

I call these solemn words mysterious, not only because they contain the mystery of all mysteries, *the sole contents of absolute truth, reason's grandest theme, ethics' primeval rock, and man's most sacred hope* on earth and in heaven, as I shall attempt to expound; but also on account of their marvelous effect upon the heart and soul of the Hebrew. Young or old, religious or frivolous, learned or illiterate, living or dying, you address to him these wonderful words, and they sound to him like a solemn admonition from on high, like the fresh element of vitality poured into his veins, like angels' salutation, like eternal melodies from the Rock of Ages.

Therefore, brethren, on this gala-day of the Congregation Anshe Chesed, when we are assembled to dedicate this magnificent sanctuary to the glory of God and the promulgation of eternal truth and divine light, to invoke the blessings of the Almighty upon this new monument of piety, this congregation, a faithful mother in Israel who has erected it, her officers, committees and supporters who have sacrificed time and treasure so profusely to rear and embellish this gorgeous temple, the artists and artisans who have accomplished it, and all the brethren and friends who have come to worship and rejoice over it,—on this solemn occasion, let us expound and pronounce over this temple and congregation the solemn words, "Hear, O Israel, God is our Lord, God is One." May they be deeply impressed on every heart, and engraved on every stone in this structure—may they permeate the very atmosphere of this santuary forever and aye. Amen.

I have said the sublime words of our text contain the mystery of all mysteries, the sole contents of absolute truth and

I.

REASON'S GRANDEST THEME.

Let us first investigate this point. God is the most sublime word to be a proper equivalent of the ineffable name of four letters, which, in Hebrew, represent the GREAT I AM, being, essence and substance, without limitation, the cause and substance of all that is, was, or will be, the life, love, might and intelligence of all that lives, loves and thinks, the infinite goodness, wisdom, justice and power, manifested in this universe and far beyond all human conceptions of universe,—He who said, and it was, who commanded, and there it stood. So Moses and the prophets, Talmudists and philosophers, all great teachers in Israel, knew and understood the inscrutable and ineffable ADONOI. This is absolute truth, and the foundation of all derivative verities, as far as conceivable to the human mind.

Reason has no means to proceed beyond the GREAT I AM. Here is the universe, mutable and perishable in all its phenomenal parts. The mutable can not exist without the immutable; the perishable must rise from the fountain of the eternal; the universe must be the revelation of the immutable and eternal God. No waves without ocean, no finite beings without the Infinite, no universe without God, none of which can be either thought or imagined.

Again: here is the universe with its hostile forces, crossing orbits, and perpetual antitheses of functions, beautifully harmonized in its grand totality, with its co-ordinations and subordinations of all that is, real or latent, to one sublime and unfailing unit, in revelation of Him whom Job calls "He who maketh peace in his heavens high," whom the hosts on high glorify, "Praise to God's glory from his place," and of whom the chorus of seraphim sing, "Holy, holy, holy, is God Zebaoth, all the earth is full of his glory." Without the one Almighty and All-wise there could be no unity and harmony of the universe. Without one God there could not be one cosmos.

Furthermore: Here I am, says man. I live, I love, I think, I know that I know and what I know, and reason on reason's functions, laws and substance. That which is not in the whole, can not possibly be in any part thereof. I am a part of this whole, therefore it must be life, love and self-conscious intelligence, and I am but a miniature revelation of the Eternal God, as the ray is of the sun, the drop of the element of water, the visible and finite manifestation of the invisible and infinite Deity.

And here is the history of man, and especially Israel's history, with the hand of Providence perpetually manifested, with its ever-revolving wheel of justice, and its triumphal car of progressive truth, light and happiness. And here the conscience and consciousness of man with his universal knowledge of godhead, to read with reason's eye in conscience's depth—" And thou shalt know this day and reflect in thy heart, that God is the Lord: in heaven above, and on earth below, there is none besides." So we know and understand and utter with veneration and awe, with adoration and love, "God is." I can not see him, yet I know him

I can not imagine him, yet I love him. I can not comprehend him, but I adore and worship him. I can not utter his praise, his greatness, his majesty, his glory, his unsearchable immensity, but I kneel in the dust and rise to heavens high, knowing that he is, and therefore am I. This is reason's grandest theme.

Truly, this is no God accommodated to the gross conceptions of thoughtless men; no God to be located in some corner of the universe or outside thereof in the realm of imagination. This is the living God of Israel. Therefore we say, "Hear, O Israel." The nations, the individuals, in fact, made their own gods. Therefore, they were ideal men at best; oftentimes fantastic beasts. Israel made no god; God made Israel. In Israel, God's nature, law and will were manifested and made known to the nation by the inspired intelligence of her own sons; therefore, he is called the God of Israel, known, so known, in Israel only.

Therefore, while the nations, starting out from the basis of small, narrow and localized gods, necessarily remained narrow, sectional and fettered in their ideals and principles, as none excel their own ideal of deity, Israel, starting from the broad principle of absolute truth embodied in the doctrine of the Infinite Deity, had always the most high, the most sublime and universal before his mind, and grew up in the broad conception of the God of the universe. So all conceptions, ideas, doctrines, principles, hopes and expectations of the nation became large, wide, broad and deep, sublime and divine. Therefore, Jews only could write the Bible; and they only could defy all revolutions, outlive all changes, and stand unmoved at their divine banner. So that intelligence was cultivated and enlarged, so that the children in the streets of Jerusalem understood well what in substance was communicated to the select few in the heathen mysteries and academies. So Israel preserved a deathless fidelity to God and truth. A great God makes a great people. Small souls have miniature gods. As long as man worships small gods, he remains narrow, fettered, intolerant and fanatical. Whenever all men will worship the eternal, absolute, infinite and sole God, the human family will be redeemed, fraternized and free, intelligent, just and liberal. The Eternal, the Living God of Israel, shall be enthroned and worshiped forever in our temples, as in the tabernacle of Moses and the sanctuary on Mount Moriah. There shall be nothing small in our conceptions, narrow in our principles, absurd in our observances, superstitious in our beliefs, illiberal or exclusive in our hopes and prayers, where in the name of truth and reason, we exclaim, " Hear, O Israel, God is our Lord, God is One!"

I have also said this is

II.

ETHICS' PRIMEVAL ROCK.

Let us explain this second point. It is maintained that monotheism was the theology of many or all nations of antiquity. The Bible maintains: "From the rising of the sun to the setting thereof, the name of God is praised." It maintains nowhere that either Moses or Abraham invented or discovered the great principle of monotheism. On the contrary, it is maintained that God was known to Noah and to Adam, suggesting that man's knowledge of the existence of one God is innate and universal, and his desire to worship him is spontaneous. Error came in the train of corruption, in the time of Enoch first, and in the time of Nimrod later. One thing, however, is certain, if monotheism ever was the theology of Gentiles, this sacred heritage has been preserved by the people of Israel. This was sufficient cause for Israel to say, " God is our Lord," and to exclaim, " This is my Lord, and I will adore him: the Lord of my fathers and I will extol him."

There was and is another reason for this claim. It is this: The Bible teaches no revealed God; it teaches God revealed in his own works and words, manifested as Providence in his dealings with man and mankind, and as the supreme ideal of moral perfection. The glory of God, or God himself, we are told was not made known to Moses. He was told: " No man can see me and live." God's ways, his mercy, benevolence, love and grace, providence, were revealed to Moses and expounded by the prophets. God, as the perfect ideal of morals, was made known in Israel. "God is our Lord," aside of all theocratic doctrine, because his will as manifested in his works and words is our law, our moral code, prescribing to us how to live, to be righteous, humane, pious and happy, here and hereafter, now and forever, in this and every other generation.

In this point Israel's theology and faith are superior to all religious systems known in history. Morality is the offspring of truth. Corruption and degeneration are the children of error and fiction. Truth redeems and unites; error enslaves and sows discord among brethren. Neither the God nor the gods of the Gentiles are represented as free, wise, just, benevolent and merciful. Slavery and fatalism were characteristics of all Pagan theology; because their gods were natural forces and natural objects deified and fantastically magnified; and their one and most high God is an abstraction, a collective idea of their gods. Their lords are no God, but their God is an ideal abstraction of their lords. There is no foundation of ethics in their theology. Neither their God nor their gods are types of holiness.

In Israel, God is and always was the most sublime ideal of moral perfection. Our *Elohim* Providence, our national God, individual God, tutelar God, particular God, is the one eternal and sole Deity, the Father and Ruler of all men, the Preserver and Governor of the universe, and the most sublime ideal of moral perfection; so much so, indeed, that the rabbis of the Talmud could teach that to walk with God or after God signifies always attempting to imitate God's moral excellencies, to become wise, just, benevolent, merciful and gracious as God is. Therefore, Israel's theology and faith are the primeval rock of ethics, and outside thereof no religious system is known whose votaries can look up to God, as they teach him, and say we will do as God does in order to be righteous, pious and happy. There is moral freedom in Israel, because God is free. Our *Elohim* is God himself; hence not the ruler of a section, or the Father of any particular people. Our Lord is wisdom, intelligence, reason itself, hence demands not of us that we sacrifice our individual reason on the altar of uninquired faith in human dogmas. No person in Israel can be pious at the expense of his or her intelligence, humanity, or morality. To be pious signifies to be rational, wise, just, free, charitable, humane, useful to man, and a blessing to the human family, because so it is the will and such is the nature of God. Therefore, there are in Israel equality, fraternity and humanity in the name of the Father of all. There can be no favored classes before God, no blazing pyres for the infidel, no burning hell for unbelievers, no dungeons and no hangmen for theological sinners. There must be mercy for the sufferer, bread for the hungry, assistance to the weak, protection to the helpless, forbearance to the sinner, justice, mercy and love to all. Therefore, Israel preserved with his religion also his intelligence and his morals intact, the fraternity of all, and charity to all, freedom, justice and love for all. The Jew could not be stupidly pious and barbarously religious, his God being reason's grandest theme, and the primeval rock of the most sublime ethics. When we say, " Hear, O Israel, God is our Lord," we say it all: the highest intelligences, wisdom, love, grace, justice, freedom, humanity and piety, righteousness and philanthropy, in the most sublime sense of these terms.

The Eternal, the benign Father of all men, shall be enthroned and worshiped in this temple. There shall be nothing selfish and sectarian in our worship. No pious criminal, no barbarous bigot, no misanthropic fanatic shall find shelter at the corners of this altar. Love, purity and humanity shall be sanctified here before the Eternal God who is our Lord; and human nature shall be elevated to the unselfish service of God and man. Let us dedicate this temple to God, reason and humanity, and it will be a sanctuary in Israel.

I have said, lastly, this is

III.

MAN'S MOST SACRED HOPE IN HEAVEN AND ON EARTH.

Let us briefly expound this point. On earth it is certainly the highest hope of all good men that the most sublime principles of ethics be victorious in all our social and political relations, that truth be triumphant, love unite all, justice sway a universal scepter, and there be no more wrong, suffering or misery on earth which men can prevent or heal. Brethren, when we utter the sublime words, " Hear, O Israel, God is our Lord, God is One," we take upon ourselves the burden of the kingdom of heaven—to obey the law and will of God, to do as God does in wisdom, justice and goodness, to love as God loves all his creatures, and to establish upon earth the eternal kingdom of righteousness, freedom, justice and love. This is certainly man's most sacred hope on earth. But what has our text to do with man's eternal hopes in heaven, in life eternal? And it is common in Israel to repeat these sublime words, solemnly and devoutly, at the dying couch of the Hebrew. Why is this? Every religious Israelite hopes to hear these words in his last hour. Why is it so? The closing words of our text, "God is One," fully reply to these queries.

"God is One" signifies, first, the eternal, absolute and sole God and Israel's Elohim, King and Ruler, the sole Sovereign in the kingdom of heaven, are not two or more gods. There is but one God, and none besides him. This certainly is the primary signification of the words, "God is One." It is numerically first.

But aside of all other significations attaching to these words, we must emphasize especially the fundamental, namely, "God is One," hence there can be nothing outside of him. All perceptible and conceivable beings are in him real and formal ideas, of whom he only is conscious, as man's ideas are actual in his mind. How these infinite progressions of beings are a unity in God, I know not, but I know that they are because they are a harmonious cosmos. We know that the progressions of ideas are a unity in the human mind although we know not how.

Man is not only in God, but God is also in him, for he is conscious of God and his works. Inasmuch as God is in man, he is "a portion of the Deity from on high," as the Talmud has it, or "the image of God," as the Bible expresses it. Man is a formal and self-conscious idea of the Deity. Self-consciousness distinguishes him from the rest of God's creatures. The purer and brighter his knowledge of God and his will, and the holier this consciousness, the purer, brighter and holier will be his self-consciousness, and in the same ratio will he stand in relation to God as a self-conscious being. Therefore, the correct cognition of the fact, "God is our Lord," the thorough comprehension of truth, and the practice of righteousness as the necessary sequence of this absolute truth, rouse men to self-conscious immortality in God.

Self-conscious immortality in God, I have said, and I repeat it. For God is One, eternal and infinite by himself, subject to no change, no increase or decrease, no growth and no decline. He is, was, and will ever be the same. But God is One, therefore all things are immortal in him. Nothing can perish. Forms change, the substance remains. There is no death, it is all eternal birth. All things unconscious are unconsciously immortal in God. Self-conscious man must be self-consciously immortal in the One and Eternal God, as self-conscious indeed as he has become by his self-culture in the knowledge of God and the practice of holiness. God is One, hence this self-consciousness of man is in God and of him, and imperishable as is the One and Eternal God. All of us were in God before we became individualized beings, and will be in him after the dust has returned to the dust and the spirit has returned to the Lord who gave it. This is the signification of the words, "God is One;" and therefore we address them so solemnly and devoutly to every dying man. They contain man's highest hope in heaven and on earth.

Therefore, brethren, when we exclaim, "Hear, O Israel,

God is our Lord, God is One," we have said all that man can know. Here is God and eternal truth, God in his infinite glory and majesty, absolute truth in beautiful harmony with reason's loftiest and deepest research. Here are holiness, human perfection and happiness, wisdom, love, freedom, justice, humanity divine and divinity humane, one God and one human family, the primeval rock of all ethics. Here are hope and consolation, trust and divine power, the highest and holiest hopes in heaven and on earth, the eternal kingdom of heaven.

Therefore, with these sublime words we dedicate this temple, consecrate this congregation, and sanctify every soul to the service of God, truth and humanity.

Lift up your heads, ye gates, and be ye lifted up, ye everlasting doors, that the King of Glory may enter! Let us feel in this solemn moment our immortal nature, the King of Glory entering this tabernacle of flesh and blood. In this moment of holy inspiration, let us feel our union with God, and our reunion with all the good and pious fathers and mothers who have gone home to eternal life. Brethren of the Congregation Anshe Chesed, in this holy moment let us remember the founders of this congregation, who have been called away from this earthly pilgrimage and now rejoice with you over your success, to the glory of God and the honor of Israel. So, with holy feeling, let us dedicate this tabernacle to the eternal and one God; to the progress of truth, freedom, justice and humanity; to man's eternal hopes; to the blessing of its founders; to the immortal faith and cause of Israel, with the ever holy words, "God is our Lord, God is One."

THE
MAIN LESSON OF ISRAEL'S SANCTUARY.

BY ISAAC M. WISE.

The Lord of Hosts may bless you all
Assembled in this sacred hall
  To seek your God enthroned above,
Enthroned below in Israel's praise,
In nature's light, in wisdom's rays,
  In souls inspired with fervent love.

The Lord of Hosts console you all
Whose sighs and tears for mercy call
  To him who knows his creatures' woes,
With whom the good, the true prevails,
Who is our Rock that never fails,
  The tree of life that ever grows.

This house, O God, this holy shrine,
We reared to praise thy name divine,
  Accept in grace and fill with light,
The light of wisdom, truth and cheer,
From heaven high to mortals near,
  Revealed for aye on Sinai's height.

Give ear, O Lord, to our appeal,
Respond with love, thy grace reveal,
  To bless this house be ever nigh;
Let's feel thy love in joy or grief,
To hear our thanks and grant relief,
  To raise each soul to thee on high.
      Amen.

A solemn occasion, brethren, convenes us in this noble structure which you have reared, a monument of piety and devotion to God and Israel, to beautify this city, to testify to your fidelity to the religion of your fathers, and to consecrate this particular spot to deathless truth and imperishable hope from the unfailing fountain of Sinai. And now you have come with grateful hearts to render praise and thanksgiving to the Almighty for this signal success, inspiring you with holy joy, and to rejoice before the Lord over your sacrifices of time and treasure cheerfully made before God and to the glory of his holy name. And now you have come with impressions solemn and feelings sublime to dedicate your beautiful handiwork to the worship of the Most High, the promulgation of truth, the elevation of human nature, and the perpetuation of Israel's light, charity and solidarity, to extend over the entire family of man. It is a solemn occasion, indeed, and we feel that it is.

Among all the holy edifices of the past and present, none is as wonderful and marvelous, as suggestive of lessons most sublime and verities truly divine, as is the temple of Israel. Its history is a broad streak of light across the entire horizon of human knowledge, from the first records to this present moment, telling with irresistible force there is an Almighty Providence preserving and governing this human family. The flame of its perpetual lamp, from which all religious lights in the civilized world have been lit, the lamp never extinguished, the light never obscured, teaches the self-sustaining and indestructible vitality and energy of truth, whose growth, advancement, progression and final triumph no power on earth can prevent or restrict; for truth is God's and God is omnipotent. The tenacity, consistency and unshaken fidelity of its congregation under the sorest of trials and bloodiest of afflictions prove that man is not the lord of truth, but truth holds dominion over him; he must obey its behests, must bear and promulgate it in spite of sufferings and afflictions, of misery and death. Such is human nature, such are the decrees of Providence. Most wonderful, probably, and most suggestive, is the inscription upon the keystone of Israel's temple, which all philosophers must indorse, all religions must adopt, all codes of ethics must confirm. There are two gorgeous pillars upon which Israel's divine structure rests; the one is, "Hear, O Israel, God is our Lord, God is One," and the other is the commandment, "Thou shalt love thy neighbor as thyself." Upon these two pillars the arch of perfection in its pristine beauty rests, the divine law, concerning which the Psalmist said: "The law of God is perfect." Upon the keystone of that arch, in bold relief, in indelible characters, is the sublime inscription: "And thou shalt love God, thy Lord, with all thy heart, with all thy soul, and with all thy might." This contains all which true religion and philosophy, all human codes of laws and ethics have ever said and will say in all eternity.

This motto on our keystone, in the first place, points heavenward, not to A God, but to THE God, the only and sole God, the cause of all causes, the force of all forces, the Almighty, who is the intelligence, life and love of the universe, whose wisdom and freedom are manifest in this cosmos, with its beautiful order and harmony, and whose holiness, grace, justice and benevolence are revealed in man and the totality of his history. It points not to an *unknowable* God, hidden in the mists of phantasts or the sophistries of unripe thinkers. It points to "thy Lord," the omnipresent and ever-living God of Israel, whom we see perpetually in his works, hear forever in his words, in all words of genuine intelligence; who is in us, with us, about us, everywhere, whom we seek, feel, conceive, know and worship; after whom we yearn, long and pant in life and death; of whom we are, and in whom we live forever; "thy Lord," who is providence, ruler, preserver and Father, the cause and the law, the substance and the harmony, in me and in all, gracious, just and true forever.

Next, the motto on our keystone points to the only means of placing man in perpetual communion with the Eternal God, of uniting the individual spirit to the universal spirit; its name is Love. "Thou shalt love God thy Lord." To love God is human perfection. To love God means to be united with him. To love God signifies to have entered the portals of heaven and to live in the Father's glorious presence, in bliss everlasting and unalloyed. To love God means in love to be God-like. Then, our motto tells us how to live, how to practice this great lesson, in order to reach this human perfection, this undisturbed and unalloyed bliss.

Man is, in the first place, an emotional being. He has instincts and passions, propensities and inclinations, which become feelings, desires and volitions. Without the emotions, and the effects they produce, man could not be man; he must be either angel or rock. They are the mainsprings of his earthly enjoyment, pleasure and happiness; in them the cause of self-preservation rests, and from them the impulses to intellectual, ethical and religious ideas and ideals, seeds and deeds issue, as the sweetest scent of odoriferous flowers depends on the roots imbedded in vulgar soil.

Man's emotions may be naturally kind, generous and noble, as I believe they are; they may be, as the ancients personified them, the *Yetser Hat-tob*, "a good genius," to make of one a nature's nobleman or a noble woman. Such, however, is the influence of society, the force of ungoverned passions, and the delight in their frequent gratification, that abuse and misuse violate the Creator's law, and disturb the beautiful harmony. The main-springs of enjoyment, pleasure and happiness are violently turned into abject sources of misery and wretchedness, to clog the intelligence and to benight the religious and ethical nature of man; the servant is elevated to the master's place, and brutalized man loses his freedom, nobility, dignity and happiness, and the emotions have become, as the ancients personified it, a *Yetser Ha-rah*, "an evil genius," which, as they say, is also *Satan*, the demon which hinders man from doing good and being true; *Semael*, who poisons human nature with wickedness and corruption; and the *Maluch Ham Maveth*, "the demon of death," to finish his own work of destruction. Judaism knows of none besides this personified Satan, which is a mere personification. In human nature, these two demons have their latent existence in perpetual combat for preponderance and dominion, and man's will decides which shall reign and which obey. What supports the will in regulating the passions and emotions correctly? Which particular force has the Creator bestowed upon the human being to govern his emotional nature? "Love," our divine motto replies—love, the most powerful of all emotions, must regulate and govern them. Develop, strengthen and invigorate this passion of passions in your family relations first, then gradually extend it to your fellow-man, to all the children of nature, to nature itself, to nature's Lord and Maker, to embrace all, which is to possess all, in expanded and invigorated love. "Love God, thy Lord, with all thy heart," with all passions, emotions, feelings, desires and volitions, regulated and governed by the mighty passion of immortal love, expanded and extended to all of God's creatures and creations, and culminating in himself; that is the omnipotent guardian angel of the emotional man, with his *Yetser Hat-tob* and *Yetser Ha-Rah*, to protect, elevate and perfect him as man made in the likeness of his Creator.

Let all your emotions be under the control of love, our sacred motto teaches, and this will lead you upward to human perfection, to love God, your Lord, with all your heart. Whatever idea or ideal one may have of his God, he is always HIS Lord, his highest idea and ideal; love God, *thy Lord*, with all thy heart, always remains the standard of the ethical perfection of the emotional man.

Brethren, let this temple, first and foremost, inspire your hearts with love—love to God and man, love to nature and nature's God, and it has become your guardian angel. Dedicate it with the love of your hearts, and it is holy to man, sacred to Israel, and consecrated to the Eternal God, whom thou shalt love with all thy heart.

Man is an intellectual being. He ate of the fruit of the tree of knowledge, and the name of that tree was intelligence, and the name of the fruit thereof was self-consciousness; and the man ate thereof and lost his innocence and his paradise, for he was a child no more, no longer did he live the life of thoughtless security in emotional impulses and blissful enjoyment, his eyes were opened and he saw himself nude. He thought, he reflected, and his paradise was gone. "With wisdom vexation groweth, with knowledge affliction increaseth."

And yet man could not be man and remain a child. True, the days of childhood are paradisian, and the years of maturity full of vexation, trouble and disappointment, unknown to blissful ignorance; yet man would not be man without his intelligence, mankind would not have reached the high position of the civilization, freedom, enlightenment, knowledge and dominion which are the boast, pride and wealth of the nineteenth century. He who sees the end of everything in its first thought, all phases of being in their ideal state, he who is our Maker and our guardian forever, must have willed it so that man should make proper use of his intelligence, as well as of every other capacity or ability bestowed on him.

Intelligence, like love, is a divine power in man, and, like every other gift, it may be used well and properly to the blessing of man and mankind, or abused and misused to the misery and affliction of both. Intelligence in covenant with love, love in harmonious union with intelligence, disarm the Cherub, with the flaming sword, guarding the gate of Eden. and open wide the portals of paradise to God's intelligent children. The heartless and unfeeling savant is no less brutal than the deteriorated savage. The loving and visionary phantast is no less mischievous than the cold, selfish and calculating sage. The former is half man and half devil, the latter half woman and half statue; only half, and Sacred Writ commands, "Thou shalt be perfect with God, thy Lord." Those who are led astray by their intelligence to self-corruption, the violation of sacred duty, the destruction of human happiness, the perversion of truth, the detriment of human rights, and love none and nothing except their own dear selves, are no less miserable and wretched than those who are slaves of savage propensities and groan under the heavy yoke of triumphant passion; or those who are always under the influence of phantasmagorias to be forever displeased and disappointed, because they would not listen to reason's warning voice. Those who live in superstition, land in fanaticism; those who deny God, dread the devil. The emotional man is a ship without a rudder; reason a rudder without a ship. Love is a benign moon to the lonely traveler; intelligence is a majestic sun to furnish attraction, light and life. They must never be separated.

Here again our sacred motto speaks words of divine wisdom: "Thou shalt love God, thy Lord," not only with all thy emotions, with all thy heart, but also "with all thy soul," with all thy intelligence. Like the emotions, the intelligence must center in love. Your love shall be intelligent, and your intelligence wedded with love. Like your love your intelligence shall expand and extend to all objects within your horizon, to land and sea, to heaven and earth, to past, present and future. Nothing shall prevent you from knowing and understanding all which is, was or will be. There shall be no limit to your reason, and no boundaries to your understanding. Seek, inquire, search, grasp and comprehend all you possibly can; be the wisest of men and the most intelligent of nations; be not frightened from the path of reason by the superstitions of the foolish or the errors of the wise; rather avoid error and evade folly. God has not given you this divine gift of intelligence to be overawed by superstition, clogged by despotism, silenced by fear, or deadened by priestcraft. He has given you intelligence to use it wisely, fully and perpetually; but, for the sake of your life and happiness here and hereafter, use it properly in union and consonance with love, goodness, benignity, virtue, purity, and upright humanity. For the sake of your life and happiness here and hereafter, never lose sight of the objective point, the real aim of all reason, intelligence, understanding, wisdom, learning and intellectual glory, which is to know God and to be united to him by this knowledge, to know God in your love and with all your wisdom, to possess him and to be in him. This must be the guide, the path and the light; whoever leaves it runs into error, misery and self-destruction. The fear of the Lord is the beginning of and the impulse to all wisdom; to know him, to love him, with all the heart and with all the soul, is wisdom's perfection, beyond which there is none—is happiness everlasting, is human perfection and human greatness, beyond which no mortal can proceed.

Brethren, dedicate this temple as a home of intelligence and truth, wedded with love and benignity, and it will be a temple in Israel, holy to the God of Israel, as was Solomon's gorgeous sanctuary on Mount Moriah. Think of God and his greatness, think of God's love in true devotion, and this temple is consecrated to God and truth, to love and intelligence, to human happiness and life everlasting.

As you all know, some modern doctors maintain that the animal also possesses love and intelligence; only that it is not human love and intelligence, I feel compelled to add, is not manifested either in human words or human deeds, and without the manifestation we have no knowledge of the existence of a force. Besides, human love and intelligence are characterized by ideality. Man is inventive, creative; he conceives ideals spontaneously; he has ideality and the genius to realize these ideals in words, music, motion, paintings, statuary and architecture. This building, like all others, was first an ideal in the architect's mind, and became then a reality by the artisan's work. No animal has ever put into execution any of its ideals, because it never had any.

Ideality is the word which chiefly designates human superiority above all sublunar creatures. He alone possesses ideality, invents, creates, and looks far beyond all realities; neither one nor all of them will satisfy him, because his ideals are higher, and, in many instances, much higher than the realities. Ideality is not only the mother of religion, the cause of progressive ethics, the guarantee of immortality, the progenitor of art, the lever of industry, and the first cause of all progressive civilization; it is more, infinitely more than all that; it is the perpetual impulse in the human mind, compelling it onward, forward and upward, to reunite with the Eternal Deity, if we only correctly understand and properly use this heavenly gift. But, alas! it is only too often abused by want of love, lack of intelligence, or both.

The miser also possesses ideality, but it is led into the wrong channel. Mammon is his God, and wealth for its own sake is his ideal, which makes him and others miserable, and perverts his nature. The over-ambitious man, greedy for reputation or notoriety, fame, vain-glory and false honor, for reward without labor, and glorification without merit, also possesses ideality; the envious, the avaricious, the man jaundiced with morbid jealousy, the despot, the conqueror, the fanatic, or the proud chief of a band of bandits, each and all of them, possess ideality, but their ideals are satyrs, demons, devils, void of love and true intelligence: human nature is perverted, shorn of its glory, stripped of its nobility, dragged into the quagmire of the lowest passions, from which dark, dismal and distorted phantasmagorias rise; the mind is sick, its ideality obscured, and its ideals are *fata morgana*.

Therefore, our divine motto commands that not only thy emotions and intelligence, but also thy ideality shall be guided and controlled by this one great and glorious principle, by the eternal love to the Eternal God. This must be the touchstone for all your ideals, their perpetual moderator and governor. They must be in perpetual harmony with this divine love, in order to lead you onward, forward and upward to your destiny—onward to the human family and upward to God; love to the Most High be the controlling power of your emotions, intelligence and ideality. So man reaches human perfection and happiness.

Me'od, as the Hebrew text has it, signifies something exceeding, beyond and above all things known, and being the last of the three terms used in this connection, it signifies something higher than intelligence, which can be ideality only, as it corresponds to all these significations in this connection. "Thou shalt love God, thy Lord, with all thy heart (emotions), with all thy soul (intelligence), and with all thy might (ideality)," which is the highest might in the human mind, all of which must be controlled by man's love to God, the Most High. This is the path of life and light to human perfection and happiness, which all religions must adopt, all philosophies indorse, all true codes of ethics and law must reduce to practice. This is the keystone inscription in Israel's ancient temple. Time can not efface it, intelligence can not overlook it, all progressions of all sciences and philosophy can not improve it. The arm of eternal and supreme wisdom has impressed it on the rock of ages; no man can go beyond it.

Brethren, let us consecrate this holy structure with the deathless words of eternal wisdom: "Hear, O Israel, God is our Lord, God is One"; there is none besides him. "And thou shalt love God, thy Lord, with all thy heart, with all thy soul and with all thy might"; there is nothing above it. Here all human wisdom ends, and here divine wisdom begins. Brethren, let us dedicate this house as a temple, a sacred shrine forever, of these sublime and glorious truths. Love be the glory, the shekinah, of this house; love to the Eternal God be the fire from heaven to consecrate your emotions, intelligence and ideality whenever you enter into this holy place. So may the Almighty be worshiped forever; so may his children be enlightened and blessed: so may God's glory be enthroned in this house, in this congregation, in your hearts and your souls forever and aye. Amen.

THE FOURTH OF JULY.

BY ISAAC M. WISE.

TEXT.—"Then a spirit took me up, and I heard behind me a voice of a great rushing (saying), Blessed be the glory of the Lord from his place."—[Ezek. iii. 12.

The Prophet Ezekiel broaches the profound secret of prophecy, how a man becomes a prophet; how the soul reaches that higher state of intellectual existence wherein it can listen to the direct communication from on high, and understand it intuitively. "Then a spirit took me up;" the spirit bore him aloft, says the prophet; then he heard and saw that which he could not hear nor see before.

As long as the mind is subject to the dominion of the lower passions, it beholds and unravels, as the captive from his subterranean cell, only that which lies low in the same level—that which gratifies and intensifies the passions. Rising higher, the mind sees more; rising highest, sees most. When the mind has that power that governs and lifts up the soul-man, as the prophet says of himself, "And then a spirit took me up," then man may be a prophet, conceiving directly the will and law of the Most High.

Words and laws are latent deeds—actions in the abstract: deeds are concrete laws—words which have become flesh. History is the Bible of deeds. When we have before us the words of great men, we try to imagine how high the one or the other was lifted up by the spirit, and we call that altitude his greatness. If we have before us laws, we measure the greatness of the lawgiver by the same gauge. In the history of this day, the Fourth of July, when, in 1776, American independence was made a fact in history, we have before us a deed to be measured by the same scale.

Between two and three millions of human beings, by no

means united in their political opinions, and scattered over a vast territory from Georgia to Maine, and as far west as Central Ohio and Kentucky, without any of the modern facilities of communication,—these few and widely scattered men took it upon themselves, in the face of the mighty Empire of Great Britain, to declare the independence of this continent forever. It looks mythical, sounds almost fabulous now to contemplate it, although it is only ninety-eight years to-day that the Declaration of Independence was signed in the city of Philadelphia. Since the days of the Maccabees, history offers no parallel to this heroic resolution. How could a handful of men, representing a divided and powerless people, strike so high?—how could they resolve upon so daring a deed, which was to revolutionize all existing forms of government and open a new era in the world's history? If any one of those sires who set their signatures to the immortal instrument could speak now, he would answer in the very words of the prophet: "Then a spirit took me up." They saw and felt, they understood and set forth in plain language, that certain things were wrong, unjust, contrary to the laws of God and man. They felt the duty of asserting the rights of man, of appealing to the Divine Author of these rights for redress, and in raising the banner of independence to redress these wrongs forever. Being borne up by the spirit to believe firmly in their rights, and to confide implicitly in Him who gives, protects and executes them, they felt in themselves the power to strike high, regardless of consequences, and to perform a task which will forever elicit the admiration and gratitude of all good men. High-minded, or high in mind, are the Anglo-Saxon terms to name the state of the soul under the influence which the prophet describes, "Then a spirit took me up."

So history is made according to the will of Providence. Man is conscious of wrongs or evils existing, and he attempts to redress them, to remedy them. He sees that certain ideas are beneficial and to the blessing of man, and he seeks to realize and enforce them. He can not go beyond this. His consciousness reaches no further; his reason can not penetrate into the future and the combinations characterizing it. But those who do either are men lifted up by the spirit. Persons who worship their own interests, live in the narrow circle of their lower passions, seek gratification, pleasure, wealth, rank, fame, or the thin veil of false pride and fading vanity, thinking only of themselves and for themselves, they will never be lifted up by the spirit which they enslave; they never feel the necessity of righting wrongs, remedying evils, or redressing the wounds of humanity. Such men do not make history; they place obstacles in the path of progressive humanity, which good and high-minded men must remove that history can take its course. Those men, however, who, careless of consquences, fearless of probable results, heedless of their own interests, safety or condition, seek to overcome existing evils and to replace them by what is right and good and a blessing to the largest number of human beings, as those sires have done who sent forth the Declaration of Independence,—those are prophets in deed, as the prophets of the Bible are prophets in words. All of them are men whom the spirit has lifted up high above the littleness of every-day life, high above the small selfishness of little creatures, who are to themselves all in all; above dwarfs and pigmies, whose world is no larger than a dollar, and whose horizon is bounded by the few rays of their obscure selves. Those high-minded men see a world of life and love around them, a world of duty and conscience in them, a world of truth, light, justice and goodness above them; they are great, and everything about them is wide, high, large and grand. They are the men whom the spirit has lifted up; and so we opine were those who planned, signed and executed the Declaration of Independence. Those are the prophets of the Lord, either of words or deeds.

The prophet furthermore tells us, when the spirit had lifted him up, "And I heard behind me a voice of a great rushing." We can see of God and truth only that which is past, has transpired, has become a fact of nature or history. Behind—always behind us—we hear the voice which we understand; never before us. So when Moses desired to see God's glory, he was placed in the cleft of a rock, inclosed from all sides, and covered by the hand of the Lord till he was passed; then, after the Lord passed, " Thou wilt see behind me, but none sees before me." As long as events transpire before our very eyes we understand them not, because we can not penetrate the future to see the consequences of the events, and the consequences expound the events. Those who saw the lake which once covered this Mill Creek valley, before the Ohio broke through yonder hills, could not see or know that under the water a region of land formed to become once the arena of the city of Cincinnati and her beautiful environs. We who stand behind the scene survey the field now retrospectively, and say, So God worketh in the silent deep. So is all our knowledge of the footprints of creation retrospective, and the creative power at work right under our eyes—for creation never ceases—escapes our attention and evades the scrutiny of the best observer. We hear from behind.

The same is the case with human deeds, we understand them retrospectively only; for the great deeds are prolific germs — and that is their very greatness — of numerous events, all of which combine into one chain of facts, a unit in themselves, as the coral reef contains many millions of defunct creatures, and still is one reef. Neither Columbus nor those who ridiculed him, nor those who supported him, could form the slightest idea of what the consequences of his discovery might be. Those who saw the first emigrants land on the Atlantic shore of this country could not know how God works in the silent deep the inverted pyramid of events. We hear from behind; all our knowledge is retrospective.

Deeds, like prophetic words, must be expounded and verified by the course of events. When the prophecy came to Abraham, "And there shall be blessed all the families of the earth by thee and thy seed," there was none, not even Abraham, who understood the import of those words; none could understand the three currents of Judaism, Christianity and the Islam to come from that source, surround, water and fructify the world, and give to history its basis and character. When the prophet announced the words: "And God will be king over all the earth, that day God will be one, and his name one," none could think of the bare possibility of the universal republic, the universal monotheism, and the universal brotherhood of man, speaking one language, in all things divine, as we see all this approach now. Time expounds oracles as it expounds events. The words and deeds unconscious in speaker and actor, uttered and done on the strength of general principles and universal laws, of which man is conscious, are placed aright in the sublime consciousness of Providence; but we mortals see from behind, know and think retrospectively. Time enlightens us, whether oracles are divine and deeds prophetic and providential.

Now, let us step back ninety-eight years into Independence Hall of Philadelphia, and, with the enlightenment gathered from ninety-eight years of history, let us look upon the group of men signing the immortal instrument, and, like the Prophet Ezekiel, we will confess: "And I heard behind me a voice of a great rushing." Ask those sires: What are you doing in your solemn conclave? And we understand the answer to be, "We are laying the foundation for a future nation of forty millions of free and independent people, to become the ideal and pattern of free government, the palladium of liberty, equality and justice, the secure haven and godly refuge to all men and ideas persecuted and down-trodden by wickedness and despotism. We are planting the tree which is to bear the fruit with the seed therein, from which there shall grow the French Revolution, the revolution of all European institutions, from Sweden to Rome, from Spain to Russia, overthrow all mediaeval remains, conceptions and relics, and replace them by a new world of free men and women. We are destroying the old prejudices and hostilities of nation against nation, denomination against denomination, all the prejudices of color, race, tongue, and former condition, and unfurling the banner of the unity of the human family by and in its ethical nature. We are inviting all nations and tongues, all races and denominations, to meet on the broad plains of this continent, to become better acquainted with one another, to recognize the childhood and image of God in each of his children, to improve, elevate and appreciate one another, and establish the covenant of eternal peace under the reign of justice, and under the proud and mighty banner of Liberty." Now we understand the mighty deed performed in 1776, on the Fourth of July; now we know that it was a prophetical and providential deed, which time has expounded, and which the future will expound much more clearly. "I heard behind me a voice of a great rushing," and hearing it we admire, we look back with proud gratitude upon the framers and signers of the Declaration of Independence; hearing it, we kneel down in the dust and worship the King of kings, the God and Father of all his children, the invisible, benign and eternal Ruler of our destinies, whose name be praised and glorified forever and aye.

What are the words that the prophet heard, when the spirit had lifted him up, and he had heard behind him a voice of a great rushing? He heard the words: "Blessed be the glory of the Lord from his place." So we hear if we listen. If the spirit lifts us up into the region of the spirit, higher than our selfishness, loftier than our little interests of every day life, more eminent than the swamps of the lower passions, and we look attentively upon the divine words and events, to hear behind us the eternal voice of God's revelations like thunders loud, pleasant like melodious song, and continual like the harmony of the spheres,—then we hear and feel perpetually, deeply and indellibly, "Praised be the glory of the Lord from his place." Only the glory of the Lord can be praised by man, for God could not be revealed or expounded to human intelligence; his glory is revealed in his works, in the words and deeds of his servants, in the conscience and consciousness of man. The glory of Lord only can be praised, because the Hebrew *Baruch*, which we render to praise, or to bless, signifies growth and increase of what is good and desirable. God groweth not and increaseth not; but his glory may be praised: it may grow and increase among men by a better knowledge of his wonders, wisdom and benignity. The glory of the Lord is praised and blessed from his place, from nature's vast domain which speaks with a thousand tongues of the Creator's wisdom; from the uncountable millions of creatures which praise him with every instinct of their nature and every breath of their lives; from man's mind, which is the mirror of self-conscious Deity; from every place where law is revealed, wisdom preaches, love smiles or life rejoices in existence, the glory of the Lord is praised.

The glory of the Lord, however, is chiefly praised and most powerfully proclaimed by great and beneficial deeds performed unconsciously by good men, who merely obey the voice of duty, without knowing how great and important their deeds are. Good men listen to the voice of duty: this is the law to guide us. This obedience leads to the execution of deeds which abound forever to the blessing of mankind. This is the glory of the Lord revealed plainly, clearly and evidently. No philosophy under the sun can undermine this great teleological truth laid down by the prophet in a brief passage.

From this standpoint we look back once more upon the Fourth of July, 1776. Those sires who framed the Declaration of Independence simply obeyed the voice of duty to the best of their knowledge, and this is the greatest and the best man is able to do: he obeys the eternal law of his Maker. Those sires could not know the immense consequences of their deed; then God alone could know it. They worked out unconsciously a new scheme of salvation for the entire human family. We look with admiration and gratitude upon those men, whom Providence has selected as instruments of a great work. But who has done the work, and who does it now? None in particular, but all under the guidance of Providence. None has done it, for none was conscious of the work to be done; and now that we might be conscious of our destiny, now selfish interests and small considerations, political tricks and cunning falsehoods have more to do with the government of our affairs than the voice of duty and the consciousness of our destiny. Who has done and does it now? None of us; God has done it, and he does it now. It is the work of Providence.

Therefore, we hear the same voice now, "Praised be the glory of the Lord from his place." Our country and our history praise the glory of the Lord. The Fourth of July praises the glory of the Lord. All honest men who perform conscientiously their patriotic duties to obey, and merely to obey God's law, praise the glory of the Lord. Yea, the very fact that all the cunningness and baseness of some of our political leaders, all the bribes, embezzlements and public robberies, all the class legislation and party favoritism, all the corruption, degradation and dishonesty in some circles, and all the baseness among citizens who tolerate and indorse it, do not undermine our prosperity or check our influence abroad, do not destroy our prospects, blight our hopes and consume our strength, also praises the glory of the Lord, and shows that Providence jealously watches over his works.

Let us, however, not forget that God is long-suffering and all-just. Nations live and prosper on their virtues, and perish and decay of their own sins. While we rejoice and worship before God on this Fourth of July, let us be grateful to our Maker and mindful of his eternal laws. Like the fathers of this republic, let us jealously guard the sacred boon of liberty and equality. Let us be just and upright, true to honor and duty, in full sympathy with the human family, and in word and deed let us be free men and women, let us always be borne aloft by the spirit to higher aims to loftier aspirations, above selfishness, littleness and narrowness. Let us attentively listen to the voice of God's revelations in his works and words, and let us attempt perpetually to know and to understand what the Lord thy God requireth of thee. Let us live, feel, think and act in obedience to God's law, and always praise and bless the glory of the Lord from his place. Amen.

THE WORD OF GOD.

A SABBATH NAHAMOO SERMON.

BY ISAAC M. WISE.

Nahamoo! *nahamoo, ammi!* "Console ye my people." So the prophetic lesson begins, because this Sabbath follows the ninth day of Ab, the day of Israel's mourning over the fall of Jerusalem and its temple. But we can console those only who mourn. This congregation mourns no longer over events which took place eighteen hundred years ago—the fall of Jerusalem, the destruction of the temple, and the dissolution of Israel's political nationality; therefore, we can not console, and must select another subject for our discussion. It is before us in the same chapter of the Prophet Isaiah (xl. 1), which opens with the words spoken—*Nahamoo!*

It is admitted that the twenty-six chapters of Isaiah, from xl. to the end of the book, were written by an anonymous prophet, the Hebrew Demosthenes of the broadest cosmopolitan principles, who, seeing the downfall of Zabaism, the victories of Cyrus and Darius the Mede over the declining empire of Babylonia, and the approach of those armies to the ancient capital on the Euphrates, called upon his brethren dispersed over the East to return to Palestine and to build up again a Hebrew Empire on its classical soil, and upon the living principles of monotheism and its sublime ethics. The first speech of that prophet, from xl. 1 to xli. 17, is the introduction to all the subsequent speeches, and lays down the subject of his discussion, together with the arguments in its support, and the sublime theology and teleology upon which they are based. He begins with the main subject, announcing in terms of inspiration that Israel's national sins were expiated, and now highways should be leveled through the wilderness for the captives to return home, and the glory of the Lord should appear over them once more, so that all flesh should see that the mouth of the Lord had spoken. This is the main subject of all the speeches following. But right here, at the very threshold, it appears a number of objections were raised to the prophet's inspired message, and one of them, it appears, was this: All things are perishable; nations and systems of religion and government, like organic beings, are born, grow, flourish, decline, wither and die; why should Israel only make an exception to this rule? Having existed nine centuries and more, Israel declined, withered and died a natural death, like empires much larger and nations much more powerful; why should Israel alone resurrect from his ruins? This appears to be the import of verses 6 and 7: "A voice saith, Proclaim! [call, announce] and it saith what I should proclaim: All flesh is grass, and all its goodliness is as the flower of the field. The grass withereth, the flower fadeth; because the breath of the Lord hath blown upon it; surely the people is grass." Nations, grass and flower are subject to the same law of perpetual dissolution which admits no exception. Truly, Israel was the particular servant and messenger of the Lord, proclaiming the glory of his name, the beauty and wisdom of his laws; but " my way is hidden from the Lord, and my cause hath passed from the cognizance of my God " (verse 27); there is no justice in this law of perpetual dissolution, cognizable to man, and it admits of no exception. To all this the prophet replies, the argument is fallacious in its premises and conclusions. There are things perishable, and there are things eternal. " The grass withereth, the flower fadeth; and the word of our God will stand firm forever."

There is stability in the back-ground of all these changes, eternal life in perpetual death; there is something imperishable in this chaos of destructive elements, and that something is

THE WORD OF OUR GOD.

It must be said here at once, that words are articulate sounds expressing ideas by the instrumentality of the known organs of speech, lips, teeth, tongue, gum and throat. Wherever there are no ideas there are no words, therefore animals speak no words; and wherever the organs of speech are missing there can be no speech of articulate sounds. God is incorporeal, hence he has no organs of speech, and speaks not in articulate sounds as man speaks, or in interjections as animals do. He may let thunder, hurricane or cataract speak articulate sounds, but within the experience of man he has never done so. When the Scriptures narrate that God said, or God spoke, it must always be understood that he said or spoke as God says or speaks, and not as man does, by articulate sounds. It is language not bound to words as day speaks to day, as night instructs night, as the heavens declare the glory of God. It is thought conveyed to thought.

Again: God's speaking means creation. Man thinks ideas at certain intervals, and thinking, he becomes conscious of his self-consciousness, and at such moments he lives spiritually. God is the eternal, infinite and uninterrupted self-consciousness. He thinks always and continually, therefore he is always conscious of this self-consciousness. With man, ideas may become creative in the artistic sense as well as in the scientific, when the inventive idea is realized in concrete form; because his is a limited amount of power connected with his spiritual existence. God's power being as unlimited as his wisdom, each of his ideas is creative. God thinks signifies he creates, and God creates signifies he thinks; thinking and creating are indentical in God. Man thinks in words; the idea must become word before it is identified with his spiritual self. The first creation of the thinking mind is always the word. In imitation thereof, we speak of God's creation as God's word. "He said, and it was; he commanded, and there it stood." "By the word of the Lord the heavens were made." Therefore, in the first chapter of Genesis, "God saith"; and the ancient rabbis properly call attention to the fact that in the record of creation it is repeated ten times, "God said." The word has not become flesh; but the thought has become the cosmos. All that is, was, or will be in the universe, from the crystal to the sun, the infusiorium to the Hashmal—each is a word of God, all is "the word of God," the only Logos of which we can form a conception worthy of a Deity. The facts of creation are the Creator's dialectics: the world is God's real dialectics.

Whatever is, was, or will be, crystal or infusorium, earth or sun, fly or Hashmal, must have eternally had ideal existence in God before it assumed real existence in the cosmos; and after it passes away from the material realities it must remain forever and aye a fact in the eternal memory of the Almighty. No material is lost in nature although it undergoes perpetual changes. No idea can be lost in Supreme Wisdom, however often it may pass through the transition from ideality to reality or *vice versa*. Whatever is, is imperishable in its elementary material and its ideal existence. All things rest forever in the bosom of eternity, in the wisdom of the Almighty. "And the word of our God will stand firm forever," however the grass withers and the flower fades.

So the prophet refutes the premises in the argument held up against his message. You say change, dissolution and revolution mark the law of nature: whatever is must perish; I say, so it appears only to the superficial observer, but it is not so in truth and reality. All these changes are evolutions around the firm axis of stability, immortality and eternity. Whatever is, is imperishable in reality or ideality, in the body or in the spirit; therefore, he argues, further on (verse 26): "Lift up your eyes on high, and see who created these" [worlds]. There is eternal revolution and order, appearing and disappearing; still each girded with power. "Not one escapeth," none—nothing is lost. The word of God will stand firm forever.

Here we pause for a moment and ask: Why not I? If nothing can be lost, why should I? If all things are present forever in God's eternal self-consciousness, how could I escape it for one moment of eternity? The things which think not and feel not and know not and love not are imperishable; and I who think and feel, know and love, who am conscious of all, and think of God and universe, kneel in the dust before my Maker, and identify myself in contemplation and prayer with the GREAT I AM,—how could I alone, just I among all creatures, be perishable? And also to us the prophet says: "The grass withereth, the flower fadeth, and the word of our God will stand firm forever." There is no death in God's universe; it is eternal birth in the world of reality, eternal life in the world of spirit. The form changes, the substance remains in God forever. What is unconscious here is eternally conscious in God's self-consciousness. What is self-conscious here remains forever a self-conscious idea in the eternal wisdom of God. Whatever thinks, that is for itself, and whatever thinks not, that is in the self-consciousness of another.

What has been said already entitles us to the conclusion that the work of man, certainly no less than the work of nature, is the eternal word of our God. Man, his intelligence, and its various fruits, can not be imagined lower in the series of things than the other individuals of organic or inorganic creation. If the crystal, the infusorium, the earth, the sun, is the word of God, man and his ideas must be. Therefore, here again the same law of perpetual dissolution and eternal stability. Every page of history speaks the language of dissolution. Wherever we look ruins meet our gaze— ruins of great cities, mighty castles and ancient bulwarks. Wherever we go, we step upon graves—graves of individuals, graves of nations once mighty, prosperous and proud. In the little history of every person there are plenty of graves —graves of dear persons, cherished hopes, ardent wishes, intense desires. These ruins and graves demonstrate the law of dissolution.

Yet nothing is lost that is worthy of preservaion. Houses, castles and cities are destroyed by the preying tooth of time, but the arts and sciences of architecture are retained in the memory of man, improved and perfected by the work of passing centuries. The body perishes, the soul remains. The same is the case with all works of genius and all productions of reason. However carefully preserved they perish at last, but the ideas remain in the memory of man, and these are the words of our God.

In consequence of man's free volition, he is productive of illogical ideas; yea, his reason recognizes the logical by its contrast with the illogical. But the history of man is most wonderful. Whatever is low, small, mean, destructive of human prosperity and happiness, contrary to justice, freedom, or the progress of humanity; however mighty and prudent their representatives and exponents; however successful, feared and proud they may be, it lasts but a short time, and then they go under, and their ideas with them. History neutralizes the evil effects and buries in oblivion all that is mean, injurious or wicked, and their bearers with them. For a few years only, Alexander the Great could abuse his genius and opportunities to selfish purposes; then he died in the prime of life, and the conquered nations became the conquerors of Grecian culture and letters. Rome conquered and crushed down Judea; but a little while after Judea conquered Rome, and crushed out her gods, altars and temples.

Again, all that is great, noble, generous, sublime and divine in man's words and deeds; whatever advances human prosperity and happiness, elevates man's character, or fraternizes the human family; whatever is said or done in the service of truth, justice, freedom, and their advancement among men, is faithfully preserved in the human memory. Their authors die, their names are forgotten; but their words and deeds are stored away in the treasury of humanity and guarded jealously by a thousand different means.

Thus gem was added to gem, idea and invention preserved and increased, utilized and amplified, until the human family had amassed the wealth known now as the civilization of the nineteenth century, with all its arts and sciences, philosophy and religion, ethics and government, each idea of which was once original with somebody, and with him it was the word of our God. For with all our learning and experience, we have no means of accounting for the rise of original ideas in the human mind, every original idea being a new creation, except the connection of individual mind with the universal, which is God, and the perpetual influx of God's ideas into the human mind. God's ideas are creative in nature and creative in man; they appear there in the form of reality incarnated in matter, and in man they appear in the ideal form, incarnated in words,—the same word of God here and there. Again, the matter in which the human ideas are realized—houses, castles, cities, works of genius or reason, nations, forms of government, etc., together with the necessary appendages of the illogical, alogical, mean, small and wicked, like matter and its form generally, perish and are perpetually changed; but the word of our God shall stand firm forever, and not one iota thereof is lost in the memory of man. Here then is immortality for good and useful men also in the human family.

Therefore, the prophet could refute also the conclusion in the argument held up against his divine message. If all that is great, noble, generous, sublime and divine is imperishable, why not also the treasures of Israel, his sublime monotheism, his grand scheme of ethics with God as the corner-stone thereof, his message of freedom, justice and equality? If those elements in general must be called the word of our God, why not Israel's in particular? and if this word in general can not perish—must outlast time itself— why not also in Israel in particular? Nine hundred years of history had taught the lesson that in Israel the word of God lived prosperously, the divine light shone forth brightly and brilliantly, while darkness, wickedness and absurdity increased and thickened among the Gentiles; and yet the word of God must live forever in man, as in nature. Therefore, he called back home the children of Israel once more to build up the empire of truth and justice, on the basis of one God and one human family; having been the vehicle of revelation, why not also the means of preservation? And he was sure of success, for the grass withereth and the flower fadeth, and the word of our God will stand firm forever. Therefore, he tells them further on in his argument (xli. 8-10): " But thou, Israel, art my servant, Jacob, whom I have chosen, the seed of Abraham, my friend. Thou, whom I have taken hold of from the end of the earth, and called thee from the midst of its chiefs, and said unto thee, Thou art my servant, I have chosen thee, and not cast thee away. Fear thou not, for I am with thee; be not dismayed, for I am thy God: I strengthen thee, yea, I help thee, yea, I uphold thee with the right hand of my righteousness."

Yes, brethren, let us behold God in his works and hear him in his words, in us and about us. Let us prepare to meet our God and to receive his word in us, for the blessing of humanity, for immortality and eternal happiness. Whatever is godly is imperishable, is good and sublime. Let us be forever faithful children of our Heavenly Father, that he be revealed and his name glorified in us by his ever-living word. Amen.

SHEBUOTH.

A SERMON BY REV. DR. D. EINHORN.
(Of New York.)

Text.—Ezekiel xvi. 8-22.

Among the most striking pictures of the Bible, which mark the covenant made by God with Israel on Sinai, is the representation of a betrothal. It extols the bridal love of faithful Israel, even as it reproaches the chosen people for forsaking their God, and for their adulterous attachment to the worship of idols. In the books of the prophets especially we meet with this representation in various phases; but nowhere is this picture painted in as brilliant colors as it is in our Haftorah.

You have just heard the flaming words which compose the entire "Song of Songs." These words, with their joyful and plaintive sounds, must deeply affect us at the consecration of this happy band of children. What hopes and fears for the Jewish congregation are intimately connected with the consecration of their offspring, in a time of such widespread indifference and neglect of our sacred covenant! To each of these little ones, God exclaims: "Thy time has come, the time of love for me, and I will spread my mantle, the Thorah, about thee as a protection against thy nakedness and helplessness; I will solemnly consecrate myself to thee and make a covenant with thee that thou becomest mine. I will anoint thee with oil, the symbol of the light of my Thorah. I will attire thee in a splendid robe and will place a precious diadem upon thy head." Surely every true Israelite asks himself, Will this promise of God find a lasting echo in their hearts, will their short day on earth really be unto them a full day of love for God and for their fellow-men? Will the splendor with which they attire themselves to-day adorn them until their last breath, bidding defiance to every storm, or will it be squandered for useless tinsel, for empty trifles, for that deceitful display for which so many so-called Jews are now sacrificing their best and most sacred gifts, in order to stand exposed with all their gold and silver, and even then, when all their bodily splendor becomes food for worms, to reject everything which might serve them as a covering for their nakedness?

My dear children, your future and that of Judaism depends on your answer to this question, and therefore I will now speak to you in particular, and to the congregation in general, of the way in which God pledged himself to Israel on Sinai,—of the marriage ceremony, of the marriage adornment, and of the wedding-ring. I shall subsequently speak of the marriage witnesses, as well as of the gradual elevation from mere betrothal to actual marriage.

The marriage ceremony is clearly expressed in our text. On the part of God, it reads: "And ye shall be unto me a nation of priests," and on the part of Israel: "All that God has spoken we shall do." In this sacred marriage ceremony, introduced by the words, "Ye shall be unto me a *Segulah* among the nations, for mine is the whole earth,"— the idea of a national God is excluded. In it is most emphatically expressed the doctrine that the covenant with Israel is by no means to decrease God's love for the rest of mankind, but by it to procure the happiness of all nations. Israel was appointed from the very beginning to be the priests of God, to spread God's words unto every people, not to remain isolated forever, not to ossify because of aristocratic pride, not to cluster by themselves on the heights of pure monotheism; but to become the beacon light of truth to all nations, to carry before all of them the torch of morality, to pave the way through the heathen desert to the mountain of the Lord, and only then to abandon willingly and joyfully its special mission when this great aim shall have been fully realized.

We now come to the bridal ornaments, which our prophet pictures in all its Oriental splendor. There are splendid robes, chains, bracelets, ear-rings, and a crown for the head. The robes indicate בגדי כהונה the dress of the priests, the chains symbolize Israel's wonderful history, the ear-rings and the bracelets typifying the efficient energy in the struggle for God—the ready ear, the clear insight of our prophets for the religious needs of the various ages: finally, the crown, which symbolizes *The Decalogue*. The ceremonial law refers to the priestly robes of Israel. This was not bequeathed to all nations, but was given to Israel alone as a sign of its high mission. Its purpose is, partly, to separate the chosen people—living under the sway of heathenism—from the abomination of the idolaters; partly, to adapt to the service of the *Only One* the heathenish forms of worship (as has been done in the case of the sacrificial cult), from which the old world had not yet entirely severed. And also, just as the holidays with their various symbols have salutary effects upon our religion, so does the ceremonial law aid in strengthening us in the divine truths, in helping us to remember the holy mission of our race under the direct guidance of our God. This ceremonial law is by no means sanctifying in itself, but it affords a means of sanctification, It is subject, by its very nature, to such changes as are in keeping with the spirit of the age. These changes resemble those which we experience daily. The influence of climate, seasons and age necessitate corresponding changes of garments. It is an established fact that the ceremonial law of Moses has undergone most thoroughgoing changes during the time of the first and second temple, as also during all the periods following our expulsion from the holy land. Mankind, no matter what their degree of culture and civilization, will always stand as much in need of ceremonies as it does of language. These ceremonies, however, must not become rigid, nor must they be suffered to remain threadbare and dilapidated. They must be illuminated by religious thoughts, they must harmonize with the existing stage of the religious development, they must reflect the glory of Judaism, and must keep pace with those duties which are continually required of the chosen people. That religion which has been destined to assume the supremacy of the world, must never be permitted to walk about tattered and torn, or turn its priestly garments into a mummer's garb. No! When the urgent necessities of the time require it, it becomes a duty to stand prepared to reform religious ceremonies. So has it been done by the best and greatest men of our history —by our old prophets, who never ceased to oppose with flaming words those mere outward ceremonies, forms which, when left unheeded, would tend to impair our religious principles. Was it their aim to tear down and destroy? No; they wished to rebuild the ruins, to save, to glorify the internal life of Israel, to prevent those frivolities which sought by means of ceremonies to cloak their vices. Is it possible to kill those efforts for reform which are now in progress? Surely the death of these reform movements is the funeral-knell of Judaism; and yet the most bitter enemies of Judaism within and outside of the fold of Israel are incensed against reform because they see in it, not a glorious reconstruction of the ceremonies of our religion, but despair and death.

The chain typifies our history, in which are linked together most wonderful events, under Divine guidance, encircling centuries. Name the historian who has been able to solve this riddle of the wandering Jew, this riddle of an existence under the oppression of countless years, and nameless suffering, and the clanking of the chains of slavery. The nation had no center; it was scattered throughout the earth in all directions, and, though despised on all sides, its life permeated all nations; it nourished the world with its spiritual treasures; it encircled the whole people of the wide earth as one endless golden chain. A nation it is, which, though but a mote among the nations, traces its existence back into the dim obscurity of antiquity. This nation has wandered on and on to the present, encountering the storms and hurricanes of fate, tossed hither and thither, yet is nevertheless closely linked together by an impervious spiritual chain, that for the very reason of its dismembered condition, became, a bond of union for all human families by means of its Messianic activity, and celebrated the proudest triumph of the world's history, and still stands to-day full of life and vigor, fighting for the same glorious principles. Such a people is a living Bible. If our so-called Jews knew more of their own history, they would see, although they possessed but a little common sense, a golden chain which the Almighty has lent as an ornament only to that people whom he has selected, to be the blessing of all mankind, and whom he therefore crowned on Sinai with a refulgent halo. There he bestowed upon them the ten words—the soul of the holy Law, for in them are contained the eternal principles of all true religion, all true morality and all true prosperity in individual, family or national life, not for Israel alone, but for all reasoning beings; the doctrine of the one spiritual, holy God, who hates oppression and recompenses every one according to his deserts. This doctrine, to the the rugged height of which millions among the civilized people of the world have not been able to elevate themselves, is the foundation-stone of all purely spiritual devotion to God, of all self-consecration in word, deed and sentiment. This doctrine inculcates the sanctity of the oath and of the Sabbath, the honoring of father and mother, the inviolability of the marriage relations and of all personal rights.

According to Moses, all human sanctification must be patterned after Divine holiness. From this incontestable premise a new moral order was deduced and inscribed upon the two stone tablets. Here is a moral law which, through Israel, has been recognized and submitted to by the whole world. Do you really think that a moral order could exist without God, without a highest judge and legislator? Is not that which we call possession meted out to us from worldly possessions? Whence shall we derive a safeguard from communism? Whence derive security for our titles to that which we possess—that which is so often not even the fruit of our own labor? Is wealth anything else than a robbery of the hungry and needy? Is man nothing more than a two-legged creature, who, according to a custom among certain people when he dies, is thrown into a pit as any carcass, without a word of prayer or consolation? What higher right has man over the animals in his social relations? What higher claim have you for life and fame and honor?

Honor the crown of Sinai, O Israelites! instead of smiling at those who drag it in the mire. God has placed a terrible responsibility upon your shoulders in making you its bearer. This crown is the highest possession of all mankind. Consider the words of our sages. God is said to have called unto Israel from Sinai: "If you reject my Law the world shall sink into *tohu vevohu*."

One gem, one precious gem, taken from this crown, must be especially regarded, particularly since it is so sadly neglected,—it is the Sabbath, the gem set in the bridal ring. The Midrash (Bereshith Rabboth, 10), speaking of the divine Sabbath in the history of creation, says that the creation resembled a ring of the king of the world, upon which the seal was not yet fixed until the Sabbath made the declaration of the conclusion of the good work, and thus set the seal to the ring. The human Sabbath which was thereupon given to Israel is represented as the marriage ring itself of the covenant people, because in the Scriptures it is called a sign of the covenant between God and his people and serves to teach that he had consecrated the latter to himself. The violation of the Sabbath was at all times regarded as the most definite evidence of the breaking of the covenant. The greatest reformatory prophets, Isaiah, Jeremiah and Ezekiel regard the salvation of Israel as impossible without the sanctification of the Sabbath, and as in olden times, so to-day the desecration of the Sabbath if not the result is the source of idolatry, perfect atheism, and the deification of sensual pleasures. Man needs, though he stand ever so high, his weekly period of rest, devoted not alone to rest but also to devotion, in order not to become blunted in his daily vocation, not to forget his loftier destiny. This evil has, at present, far-reaching dimensions, and it will if unchecked sooner or later destroy all moral, fundamental principles in the individual life, as well as in the family and in society.

Great is the ignorance of our people in regard to their peerless history and world-nourishing treasures of mind, just as great is the rude presumption to deride the highest questions of humanity, with which the greatest minds of all nations have busied themselves with the profoundest reverence. Little polish and a full purse make now famous philosophers, ready to challenge the wisdom of centuries; at the same time theories are advanced that man is nothing but an animal. These theories are spread abroad by the public press, and are devoured with eagerness, especially by immature youth. There are thousands of Jews who will have nothing in common with congregations, and not a small number hurries every Sunday to those places where atheistical poison is offered to them in alluring cups. Can you still doubt what the end will be when the great number of the members of our congregations are continually refraining from regular attendance at divine service? Must you not admit that parents themselves are sacrificing their children to the all-consuming Moloch—are denying them a communion with God, and are making for them a hell on earth notwithstanding all their vast worldly possessions? "Change the Sabbath to Sunday," many exclaim, "and everything is safe." But, alas! the patient must needs die by this innovation. Once, at a rabbinical convention at Breslau, I heard the following remark: "The Sabbath could certainly be buried on Friday evening, but in vain would we look for its resurrection on Sunday." This is the true state of affairs. Such resurrection would require the abilities of Elias, who was able to revive the dead child by his divine fire; but such fire, however, does not exist in the present generation, and least among those who clamor for this change, who are desirous of bringing about such a rent between old and new Israel. Such a change of the bridal ring would appear to countless Jews who are longing for it only as a renouncement of the God of Israel and a union with Christianity, and so the faithless bride would also quench the last spark of the fire of love. This we can, should and must do in order to arrest the evil, viz.: introduce a monthly Sunday divine service of a non-Sabbatarian character. Such a measure can not, justly, be attacked from any point of view and will at the same time bring great blessing. Truly, we live in very earnest times. Unmistakable signs are not wanting to prove to us that we are steering toward the kingdom of the Messiah; but there also rise up before us the unwished-for struggles which precede it, struggles between truth and falsehood, which, far worse than the old heathenism, will desecrate everything and uproot the ideas of right and morals. Then it is for us above all to assist the old bearers of truth for our God in narrow phalanx like firm walls, and especially to array ourselves against the traitors in our midst. Then, it is for us to consecrate and sanctify our Sabbaths and holidays to God to protect our families from the great plague; also to give the masses instruction on week days, and not to speak of unattainable sacrifices, of sacrifices which our rich people spend so willingly for their splendid palaces, when the great question is the support of the foundation of Judaism. Congregations that remain deaf to these pressing demands merit destruction and God will select other instruments in their places; for Israel, which has for centuries wandered in such a wonderful and woful manner, can bear no lie; its halo of splendor, which it wore for so many centuries, bowed down, and yet borne so proudly as a martyr's crown, can not fall from its head. It will come forth from all these struggles victorious and triumphant, its splendor only enhanced by the combat, so that all nations shall admire its beauty and journey toward its light. Amen.

www.ingramcontent.com/pod-product-compliance
Lightning Source LLC
Chambersburg PA
CBHW031733230426
43669CB00007B/335